# MOM
## GOD'S GOT THIS

Karen,
God's grace is always sufficient!
2 Cor. 12:9
Karen Norton

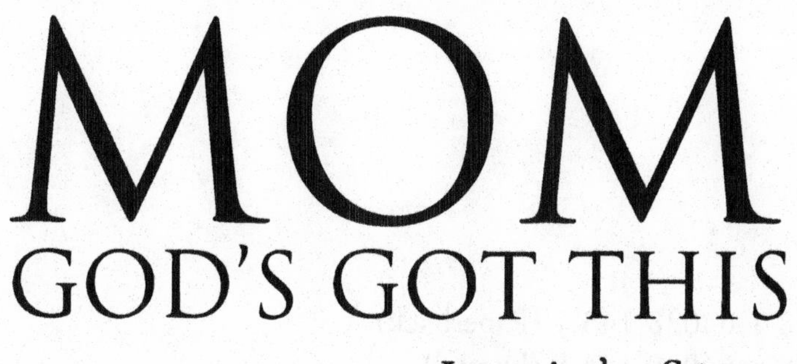

# MOM
## GOD'S GOT THIS

*Jamie's Story*

KAREN F. NORTON

ISBN 978-1-64028-143-1 (Paperback)
ISBN 978-1-64028-144-8 (Digital)


Second Edition


Christian Faith Publishing, Inc.
296 Chestnut Street
Meadville, PA 16335
www.christianfaithpublishing.com



Cover picture of Jamie Norton, 2002
Author photo by Samantha Miller Photography, Lufkin, Texas

Printed in the United States of America

I dedicate…

*Mom, God's Got This*
to my beautiful grandchildren
Sage, Graham, Caleb, and Karen Vi (Viola Mei)
Indeed, you are our glory and joy.
1 Thes. 2:20
But from everlasting to everlasting
the Lord's love is with those who fear him,
and his righteousness with their children's children.
Ps. 103:17

# Contents

# Preface

I invite you to step into the very private heart of a mother and her daughter. This is Jamie's story, and it must be told for several reasons. First and foremost, her life's story will bring praise and glory to God. Secondly, it will encourage others to follow God's call wherever He leads, no matter the cost. Jamie did. Finally, it's the story of a mother's heart as I walked with my daughter from life to life everlasting and the ensuing roller coaster journey from grief to joy. I hope you will see clearly these three glistening threads. Her story has changed my life forever. I trust it will impact you as well.

I have journaled since our daughters, Jamie and Janet, were toddlers, so basically I have their entire lives in a journal. Furthermore, since Jamie's initial diagnosis of breast cancer in spring of 2011, I have written daily and extensively about this journey. Jamie must have acquired this pastime from me, because she left behind many journals, some extremely personal and some of her many God-adventures. She wrote of faith and doubt, sin and obedience, victories and struggles. Jamie was not a perfect child, but then there are no perfect children or perfect parents for that matter on this earth. What a freeing relief that realization is! There is and always will be only one perfect Father and one perfect Son. I have not walked this journey flawlessly; I'm still learning and growing every day.

In addition to the many journals, she must have saved almost every card and letter she ever received during childhood through high school, college, and beyond. She saved many writing assignments throughout her school years, hard copies of personal e-mails, numerous pictures and mementos, and over the years, put everything in boxes and placed them in our attic. A year after she passed, I began lowering those boxes and gradually read every word, all shimmering glimpses into her delicate soul. How she valued words, and friends, and very special friends, and family! I'm sure she read every note several times before gently packing them away.

I learned a lot about our Jamie from those boxes—her tender heart, her crushes, her dreams, and her disappointments. Many were reminders and much was new information. I gently held and read every tattered and faded elementary English writing assignment and smiled at every piece of French horn music from high school. I spent many hours reading hundreds of letters and cards—birthday, Christmas, graduation, anniversary, marriage and baby congratulations, you name it; she saved it! I laughed and cried. So many precious treasures. So bittersweet. To top it all off, I discovered her own personal history that she wrote in 2004.

You will read many direct quotes from these prized possessions and journals. This is real life, and much of it is written in real time. Where there's a date, you will know it comes directly out of mine or Jamie's journals or letters.

One of the difficulties I encountered was discerning which of her life's snapshots were actually relevant to her story or just special to me as her mother. And finally, many scriptures from God's Holy Word enveloped within these pages tell Jamie's story, compelling us to search our own hearts. So keep your Bible close, because you may want to look up Scriptures referred to in the text.

> Finally, brethren, whatever things are true, whatever
> things are noble, whatever things are just, whatever things
> are pure, whatever things are lovely, whatever things

> are of good report, if there is any virtue and if there is anything praiseworthy—meditate on these things.
>
> —Phil. 4:8 (NKJV)

What a beautiful description of the characteristics of our Lord and Savior Jesus Christ and the Holy Bible! Notice that "whatever things are true" is mentioned first. After all, Jesus is the way, the truth, and the life (Jn. 14:6). My intention was to think *and write* about such things. What follows is a true account of the events of Jamie's life and death. Truth is not always pretty, but true nonetheless. I envision *noble* as taking the high road; it's the fulcrum on the seesaw between *true* and *just*. I must balance truth and justice in a noble way.

Now zoom out with me and envision another seesaw. Whatever things are *true, noble, and just* are one end of the seesaw while those things which are of *good report, virtuous, and praiseworthy* are the opposite end. Both ends are balanced on the fulcrum of *pure and lovely*. Christ-likeness and balance are my goals. In other words, Philippians 4:8 has served as my filter in writing Jamie's story. Other benchmark scriptures in this process are Philippians 4:4–7, 13, 19 and Micah 6:8. In summation, I have endeavored to write the truth in the right way, pleasing to God and honoring to Jamie.

As you will discover, *Mom, God's Got This* is an extremely personal look into a young woman's life and death and the days and months following, much of it written while on my knees through countless tears. To do otherwise would be flagrant disobedience to God's clear directive.

Therefore, I submit this tribute in honor of Jamie, *Mom, God's Got This*, to you the reader and to the Lord to use for His glory however He so chooses. Some names of people and places have been changed or omitted. So much more could have been written. Nothing is fabricated here; it wasn't necessary. Her life's story is captivating enough.

> Enter his gates with thanksgiving and his courts with praise; give thanks to him and praise his name.
>
> —Ps. 100:4

Karen F. Norton
May 2016

# Prologue

"His grace was sufficient for me."

—Jamie

I stood outside and looked at this large beautiful house with many windows for a long time. Only one window was open. At just the right moment, my Father told me to enter through that open window and begin exploring each room. "The time is now," He said. "And it's best if you stay inside until you're done. Remain focused and devote your full attention. You may look out of the window occasionally, but it's now time to complete what you started."

So I entered this fascinating place. I discovered each unique room fully and superbly furnished. I touched everything—the furniture, the accessories, and so many exquisite one-of-a-kind works of art that made me smile in awe and wonder. I picked up each piece, looked at it from every angle, and put it down again. However, there were a few pieces that made me question. "Why is this here? Where did it come from? I don't like this piece. It doesn't belong here" (2 Tim. 2:20). Nevertheless, I inhaled each new experience and slowly, ever so slowly, progressed through each room.

I did it! I worked my way through every nook and cranny and emerged from that open window, but I was not alone in there. Jesus Christ walked beside me. I will never forget this house, and I will never be the same.

# Chapter 1

## *Heaven's Hints*

The year 1963 in Colmesneil, Texas

I opened the door and walked into the old white A-frame house that was once a café. After all, this was my Mamaw and Papaw Howell's house; I could walk in anytime without knocking. My mother had put a few coins in my nine-year-old hands to give to Mamaw; it was change left over from a purchase at the store. As I opened the door, I heard a familiar sound. She was praying—again. But this was different. I could not barge in and interrupt this holy moment. I walked slowly through the living room, rounding the curve leading into the small kitchen. There she was at the kitchen sink, completely oblivious to my presence, praying, crying, washing dishes, praying in words I did not understand, her solid white hair in a loose ball at the back of her head.

I froze between the half walls, shelves on my right and left. Small green dishes lined those shelves, free gifts retrieved from packages of oatmeal. I have one to this day on proud display in my dining room hutch; it reminds me of her every time I look at it. I glanced into the back bedroom to my right, looking at the watermark clouds on the ceiling. How many times had I looked up at that ceiling from the bed below, imagination rampant?

China. She was praying for China, tears falling into the dishwater, interceding for China. Why? I didn't understand. The closest encounter I ever had with China was when my little brother, Ricky, was four years old and he ran into the house yelling and crying that Rock, our big yellow dog, was digging a hole in the yard all the way to China! So I just knew China was directly on the other side of the earth from Texas. Tears filled my eyes; I didn't understand that either. China must be a very special place to God for my Mamaw to pray and cry so much over it. I quietly put the change on the counter to my left, backed up, and walked out the front door, wiping my eyes.

Fast forward to December 31, 1975, Huntsville, Texas

It was two thirty in the afternoon and I had just arrived home from work. My water broke. Gene and I were about to have our first baby—two weeks early! I was deliriously happy; he was scared to death. Our bags were already packed and ready to go. You know how it is with your first baby; you're over-prepared. We jumped in the car and headed for Dr. Jones' office just to make sure. Well, I was sure, and the watery trail I left behind proved it! He sent us to the hospital. We just might have the New Year's baby! There's always a picture of the first baby of the year in the newspaper.

It was not to be. This baby liked 1975. And so it was, at 8:33 p.m., Jamie Renee Norton greeted the world. I missed it; I was asleep at the time. I tried so hard to have this baby naturally and was doing quite well until just before she was born. I couldn't stand the pain any longer, so the doctor put the mask over my face, and I went to sleep. However, I woke up about eleven, and Gene told me we had a baby girl. Jamie immediately got on her daddy's good side with her early birth, because he could now count her as a tax deduction for 1975! In came the tall slender nurse carrying a tiny pink bundle. I could hear firecrackers outside, someone ringing in the New Year a little early. She put the six-pound, eleven-ounce soft bundle in my arms. I uncovered her face, her little lips pursed, ready to nurse. I noticed her skin was a little yellowish (slightly jaundiced) and her squinty eyes. "She looks like a little China baby!" Those were the first words out of my mouth when I looked at the beautiful daughter God had given us. As she nursed, the fireworks exploded outside our hospital window, ushering in 1976.

Our beloved pastor, Joe Barnes, dedicated our precious baby girl to the Lord on a Sunday morning, her eleventh day of life. Gene and I, awed by the responsibility God had given us, dedicated our lives to raising Jamie for God. We did our best.

# CHAPTER 2

## *No Ordinary Child*

Truly I tell you, anyone who will not receive the kingdom of God like a little child will never enter it.

—Mk. 10:15

I was focused and intentional. "Lord, I want to remember this moment forever. Burn it into my memory." Jamie was about two years old—running and giggling freely in the big backyard as our beagle puppy, Sparticus Manchester (Sparky), nipped at her heels. That chuckle was her signature laugh which she never outgrew, outrageously contagious. God answered that prayer. I still see those moments so clearly in my mind's eye (Lk. 2:19).

She did not start out running well. In fact, she had trouble learning to walk because of severely bowed legs and pigeon toes. She would trip herself. Gene and I took her to a doctor who prescribed a brace to be worn at night and special shoes for the daytime. After four months of that nightly brace, Jamie's legs were straight, and she could walk with no problem. Another prayer answered. God has done that a lot for us over the years.

I will never forget the time we went for a checkup a few months later. Jamie and I were in the midst of those fun potty training days. While in the filled-to-capacity waiting room, Jamie needed to go. I took her to the restroom. Upon our return to Gene and the crowd, she proudly announced for all to hear, "Daddy, Mommy teeteed too!" She was so proud; I was embarrassed, but everyone else clapped and cheered!

The day we brought baby sister, Janet, home from the hospital, we also brought baby doll, Maggie, home to Jamie. Now Mommy and Jamie each had a new baby. I never detected an ounce of jealousy from twenty-month-old Jamie. Whenever Mommy rocked Janet in her big rocking chair, Jamie rocked Maggie in her little rocking chair. Speaking of Maggie, I found her in the attic, saved among Jamie's childhood keepsakes—a little rough around the edges but still loveable. Attic heat and age are not kind to a doll's hair.

Jamie loved her sister so very much. Before Janet was born, Jamie would entertain herself for hours playing with her toys in her room or playing with the Tupperware all over Mommy's kitchen floor. Janet never had to entertain herself; she had Jamie.

Jamie's love affair with books and reading began at a very early age. As a toddler, she carried her books with her everywhere, along with pencils, crayons, paper, and weeble people, stuffed in a purse or whatever else she could find in her toy box. She loved to write on paper and walls! Her first sentence at age eighteen and a half months was, "I got you." We had many children's books and Bible story books (her favorite). "Read the book, Daddy." At twenty-one and a half months, Jamie knew what she wanted. We read stories every day. She quickly memorized many books and would pretend reading the stories to me. Another one of her favorite things as a two-year-old was *Mr. Rogers' Neighborhood* on TV where she would sit enthralled until he said good-bye.

My father passed away suddenly from a massive heart attack shortly before Jamie's second birthday. She missed her Pawpaw and talked often of him living in heaven with Jesus. "Jamie, where is Pawpaw?" With a smile and uplifted eyes and arms, she would say, "Way high in heaven!" She knew.

I remember Christmas 1978 very well. I was into making ceramics as a hobby, and I created many colorful tree ornaments for my two little girls. The tree was beautiful with brightly colored Santas, gingerbread houses, angels, stars, toys, anything and everything Christmas, and on the back of each one, the year '78. Jamie, not quite three years old, was curious and enchanted by all the lights. One day I heard a loud crash coming from the living room. I ran to the door to find the tree on the floor and Jamie nowhere in sight. She was under the tree—giggling—broken ornaments strewn everywhere! I lifted the tree off her; she was unscathed. I collected the ornament fragments, now more precious than ever because of this memory. Yes, I hung many of those ornaments every year thereafter. We always had a nostalgic tree, overflowing with childhood treasures, very beautiful to this mother. I stopped hanging those ornaments in 2012; it was too painful. Maybe this year.

The first memory verse she learned in Ms. Peggy's class at church was Matthew 5:16. At age three and a half, she astounded the fourth grade Sunday school class I taught by quoting perfectly the Lord's Prayer and Psalm 23. If my three year old could do it, they could too! She read so well by age four that we had her tested at the local university where she scored at second grade level. That was not a surprise to us. However, distinguishing right from left and walking on a straight line proved a bit more challenging for her.

I worked part-time for Pastor Joe Barnes at Huntsville First Assembly of God for two years while our girls were preschoolers. Some days, I took them to a babysitter while I worked a few hours. I made three dollars an hour and paid my sitter two dollars an hour. Some days I took them to the church office with me and tried to work. I said *tried.* At times I could take work home and type letters whenever possible.

~

November 20, 1980—I thank God for developing an attitude of prayer in my children. They want to pray about their needs, and God answers their prayers!

~

November 22, 1980—I have felt for some time that God wants me to study for the ministry. Today, I received my first course from Berean. Lord, help me! You know I have two babies! Last year, I started spending early morning hours (5:00–7:00) in prayer and Bible study. This will be a good time to work on these ministry courses each day.

It happened today with no coaxing from me. Jamie and I were kneeling beside her bed saying our bedtime prayers. "Mommy, be quiet. I want to pray. Dear Jesus, please forgive me of all my sins and come live in my heart. I love you, Jesus. Amen." Wow! Could I believe my ears? Did my four-year-old just get saved? We talked about it. She convinced me. She understood exactly what she was doing.

And she never turned away from her Savior.

~

December 8, 1980—I thank the Lord for what He is doing in the lives of our children. I caught Janet kneeling down beside Jamie by the loveseat praying for her. Janet is my prayer warrior! Jamie continues to amaze me with the knowledge she has of Jesus and His Word.

~

December 17, 1980—My alarm went off at the usual time of 5:00 a.m. I went soundly back to sleep when I was awakened at 5:03. I had the strange sensation of a hand gently shaking my leg.

No children were in my room. The thought immediately came to me that I had been awakened by an angel. Yes, Lord. I will get up and spend this time with you!

~

December 18, 1980—Janet woke with a swollen eye (looked like a sty). I went to get some medicine. She said, "Mommy, just pray!" So Jamie and I laid hands on her and prayed, and almost immediately her eye was well (ten minutes). PTL!

# Chapter 3

## *Elementary*

I will give thanks to you, Lord, with all my heart; I will tell of all your wonderful deeds.

—Ps. 9:1

Our family moved to Lufkin in Deep East Texas in March of 1982. We quickly settled in. Six-year-old Jamie started kindergarten at Trout Elementary with Mrs. Brooks as her teacher. Four-year-old Janet started playschool at the Chambers Park rock house. Both of our daughters loved their new schools and friends. First Assembly of God in Lufkin became our church home and has remained so throughout the years. What a great town and church in which to raise our daughters!

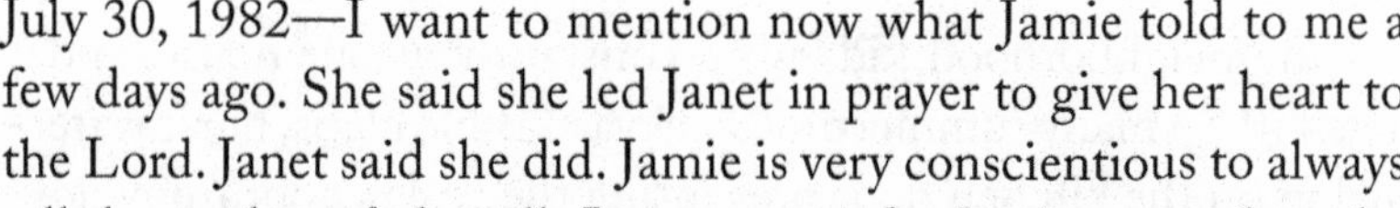

July 30, 1982—I want to mention now what Jamie told to me a few days ago. She said she led Janet in prayer to give her heart to the Lord. Janet said she did. Jamie is very conscientious to always tell the truth, and she tells Janet to pray for forgiveness when she knows Janet is fibbing about something!

I remember Jamie telling me she prayed with a little boy to accept Jesus while having lunch in the cafeteria in first grade. Thus began her quest for souls! She constantly invited classmates all through her school years to church, and she saw many give their hearts to Jesus.

~

August 16, 1982—Yesterday was a special day for Jamie. The Lord truly blessed her and made Himself real to her. She kept saying that it was a special day, the services were good, she felt His presence, and that she was so happy. Thank you, God. Jamie has read her Bible story books through several times and loves and knows the Word of God. She wants to be baptized in water.

In looking through the many photo albums and school-days books, remembering with smiles and soft tears, caressing each picture, and reading every word of childhood lettering, I found a picture of Pastor Bob Lewis baptizing our Jamie in water on September 5, 1982. So sweet.

In first grade, Jamie complained of a stomach ache several times when I picked her up from school. I finally realized the culprit was Jamie! She would not go to the restroom all day for fear she would miss something in class. She finally understood it was not a good thing to hold one's self all day.

The elementary years flew by me! Where did they go? It seems I remember so much more from preschool, junior high, and high school. Why is that? Perhaps the reason is "more changes" in those years. The elementary years were smooth sailing for the most part. Please allow me to continue my journey down memory lane.

The neighborhood kids were constantly at our house, and I loved it! So many summertime backyard Bible clubs, burst watermelon on the kitchen floor preventing the fridge door from closing (Janet thought she could carry it), taking friends to Sunday school, Vacation Bible School, and all girl sleepovers. You haven't lived until you have a house full of squealing, laughing, hungry, wide-awake until the early morning hours, let's play one more game, make one more craft, trying on each other's clothes, fussing, crying, primping, just one more story—girls!

Gene and I are so blessed to have had two little girls! Have I mentioned that Gene is the best father in the world? I'm convinced that God created him especially to raise two precious daughters. They loved their daddy. I have always believed that the second most important relationship in a family after that of the husband and wife is that between father and daughter. Gene perfectly embodies unconditional love, affection, discipline, forgiveness, a godly example, devotion, and a giving, protective heart. No wonder Jamie and Janet always said they would marry a man just like their daddy.

~

October 5, 1982—God blessed Jamie Sunday night during a tremendous service! On the way home, she said she had a vision of heaven. She described the tree of life, the twenty-four elders, the golden candlesticks and the river. PTL!

I started working part-time in the church office on September 19, 1983, and so began my thirty-year career at Lufkin First Assembly.

~

January 16, 1984

> Dear Mr. and Mrs. Norton,
>
> Well, we are now in about the middle of the school year (second grade), and I just wanted to let you know how much I enjoy having Jamie in my class! Not only is Jamie an excellent student, she is also a very sweet and caring young girl. She is such a pleasure to have in my class.
>
> I know you must be very proud of her also.
>
> Sincerely,
>
> Mrs. Hicks

I opened the refrigerator freezer door the other day and noticed that familiar crumpled foil-wrapped frozen brick, and the memory came rushing into my brain. It's funny how that happens. I could see my two little girls, hungry on a hot summer day, looking for something to eat. Where was I? I don't know. They spied the foil in the freezer and were delighted to see cake! They got a sharp knife and proceeded to slice off a piece, which was no easy task, considering it had been in the freezer since our wedding day—June 9, 1972. Yes, it was the top tier of our wedding cake. Disappointed at the tasteless frozen chalk, they threw the piece away and quickly squeezed the foil back around the relic. They later confessed to their crime. It was okay. It is still okay as it sits today in my freezer, forty-four years young, minus one piece.

February 15, 1984—Jamie was baptized in the Holy Spirit last night (Tuesday, Valentine's Day) at the altar during this wonderful Don Brankel revival! She stammered and spoke in tongues for an hour after we got home and while brushing her teeth and in bed trying to go to sleep! That was one night I didn't tell her to be quiet and go to sleep! Thank you, Lord.

November 18, 1984—The Lord refilled Jamie with His Holy Spirit at the altar tonight. She worshiped the Lord in tongues for almost an hour! Praise the Lord!

Jamie began competing in Junior Bible Quiz while in third grade. Her love for the Bible, her ability to memorize, and her naturally competitive nature created a winning combination, enabling her team to win first place. I often said she knew more of the Bible by age six than I did when I was twenty years old. Her favorite Bible story books were *The Bible in Pictures for Little Eyes*

(1978) by Kenneth N. Taylor and *Egermeier's Bible Story Book* (1969) by Elsie Egermeier, which she read all the way through several times by first grade.

January 3, 1985—Gene and I have started reading the Living Bible this year. Jamie is reading the King James. She said one of her favorite people in the Bible is Queen Esther and how much she looks forward to meeting her in heaven one day. Queen Esther always did the right thing and left the consequences to God. God honored her because she spoke the truth in the face of great loss.

Spelling was a favorite subject and so began competitive spelling in fourth grade. Jamie worked hard, and she was good at it. I worked right along with her, recording words on tape for her to use when I did not have the time to personally recite "eleemosynary." Jamie won Angelina County's first individual speller in fifth grade, advancing to compete in the East Texas Bee in Houston on April 1, 1987. She placed sixth out of fifty-two spellers, eliminated by the word *whorl*. Where did that word come from?

> April 18, 1987—Dear Easter Bunny/Parents,
>
> I love you so much! Not only do you give me eggs and candy every year, but as good parents, you clothe me and feed me every day. But above all, you let me go to church and worship God. Thank you for everything. I love you!
>
> Love,
> Jamie Norton

She also took piano lessons, enjoyed collecting stamps from all over the world, accumulated a vast array of business cards, and acquired numerous books on Princess Diana. Jamie never enjoyed participating in sports; she would much rather use her brain. She completed the Missionette program at church and was crowned a Star on December 4, 1988, at the age of twelve. She worked hard at everything she attempted.

Mrs. Steed (fifth grade) was one of her favorite teachers. She always went the extra mile with her students and proved that with Jamie on the day Jamie started throwing up in class. When she could not reach me on the phone, she drove Jamie home. She even cleaned our hallway floor as Jamie continued being sick all over the place. Truly a saint!

> "My Life Line" written by Jamie Norton on August 27, 1992
>
> Brandon Elementary school teachers have long ago chosen and forgotten their teacher of the year. She and the other candidates have melted from our memories like snow in the early spring.
>
> One teacher from 1987 whom I will never forget is Mrs. Steed. She was not teacher of the year, but she deserved and still deserves that coveted title.
>
> Mrs. Steed, who was barely taller than her students, had the patience and the love of a mother. Her skin, the color of homemade vanilla ice cream sprinkled with dots of brown sugar encased a heart the size of the ocean. Mrs. Steed's eyes were peaceful and still like the eye of a hurricane.
>
> Mrs. Steed was pious, a quality lacking in many teachers. Every day, she, not caring what the Supreme Court ruled, led us in prayer before our noon meal.
>
> When we, her adoring students, needed encouragement, Mrs. Steed was always there. Like a mommy kissing a booboo, she gave us kisses on our cheeks whenever we needed them.
>
> Because she coached the spelling bee team, Mrs. Steed stayed after school to practice with me and others daily. The affluent speller helped us spell words like *pseudosyllogism*

and *supercentrifuge.* To begin a practice she would say, "Are you ready, sweetheart?" Ready? I was ready to walk to the moon for Mrs. Steed.

One day after school, Mrs. Steed was practicing with some choir students who were preparing for a musical. As I waited for her to practice with me, my stomach began to churn. I started to feel as if someone was stirring my insides like a cook stirs batter. I feebly walked to Mrs. Steed and said, "I'm sick. I can't stay after school." With concern in her eyes, she answered, "I'll take you home." While Mrs. Steed hurriedly finished the musical practice, I went to the restroom and saw my lunch for the second time.

"Jamie," said a voice that contained the love of a mother, the dutiful concern of a teacher, and the kindness of an angel. Of course, the voice belonged to Mrs. Steed. She was there for me when no other human was. That was a big deal to a sick little fifth grader.

After an uneventful drive, Mrs. Steed and I arrived at my vacant home. Although I had a house key, no one was there to care for me. No, someone was there—Mrs. Steed.

Upon entering the house, I looked at the phone. It stared back at me menacingly as if it knew I wouldn't be able to reach anyone. It was right, for my mom was not at work. Suddenly, knowing I had to get to a bathroom quickly, I dropped the phone and ran. Not being as swift as Achilles, I threw up in the hall. I also made a mess in the bathroom that resembled the aftermath of a nuclear explosion.

When it was all over, Mrs. Steed did not just sit down and act concerned. She had me sit down, and she cleaned up after me. This was so important because although she was not at school on the payroll, she sacrificed herself for me. She looked like an angel.

When Mom drove up, she warmly thanked Mrs. Steed. The angel with the vanilla ice cream skin, halo glowing, said, "It was nothing," kissed me on the cheek, and drove away.

> I am now in the eleventh grade. I don't think of fifth grade often, but when I do, my mind and heart always remember Mrs. Steed.

Once Mrs. Steed gave her class a writing assignment in which each student was to write what they wanted engraved on their tombstone. "Here lies Miss Jamie Renee Norton, age 92, a missionary to China all her life, leading many people to Jesus Christ." Jamie found that piece of paper many years later as she was looking through some things in the attic. We had both forgotten that assignment but were completely amazed at God's working in her young heart. It was then I remembered going to the school and confronting Mrs. Steed with the assignment that I felt was inappropriate for fifth graders. She started to cry. That was Mrs. Steed—compassionate and tender-hearted.

Years later, while Jamie lived in Northern Asia, I had to give her the news of Mrs. Steed's untimely passing. It was a sad day for Jamie. But now—today—I'm sure they are enjoying each other's company in heaven, laughing about those days in fifth grade.

I'm thankful for the many excellent teachers our girls had growing up in thirteen years of public schools. Mrs. Steed and Mrs. Allen spent many spelling bee hours with Jamie and had a profound influence in her life, establishing in her the importance of a healthy education, planting seeds in her little girl heart. How does one combine ministry and education into something pleasing, life and destiny-changing in students? And so it began to grow in Jamie's heart.

# Chapter 4

## *Path of Purity*

How can a young person stay on the path of purity? By living according to your word.

—Ps. 119:9

January 17, 1989—From a hand-written note found in one of Jamie's photo albums:

Father, each day you show me
Usually in a different way
How much you love me
As you did today.

You helped me on my tests,
You always do,
Even in life's tests
You always pull through.

You're more than a friend,
You're my precious Savior.
You're always the same,
That's why to you this is for.

I love you.
Jamie

Lawrence recruited Jamie for Teen Bible Quiz while she was in sixth grade. One had to be in seventh grade before one could compete in quizzing. He groomed her for competition because he could see her potential. Jamie enjoyed studying, especially the Bible. Memorization was easy for her. She loved TBQ through junior high and high school and did very well. Lawrence meant business when it came to his TBQ team. He intended to win every event. The team knew if they did not practice up to his standard, they would be running laps around the church. He claimed running would pump blood to the brain! He said God didn't intend for their heads to be lamp shades! So run they did. Many times Jamie would come home red faced and in tears. I would get so upset with Mr. LP! However, Lawrence was one of Jamie's most favorite people in the entire world. He challenged, motivated, and impacted her life like few others. He remained a lifelong friend and much like a second father. Thank you, Lawrence.

I always loved playing the board game of Bible Trivia, but no one enjoyed playing with me because I would win (ninety-eight percent of the time). Except Jamie. She was my one true challenge in our circle of family and friends when it came to Bible Trivia. We enjoyed playing each other because we were pretty evenly matched, although neither one of us relished losing; but we did always seem to learn something, which was an added bonus.

Little girls grow up, and at times it's not easy. From the very first menstrual cycle, Jamie experienced extreme pain the first day or two every month—pain so excruciating, she often could not stand but could only crawl on the floor. Nothing seemed to bring much relief. The doctor said she had endometriosis, a condition for which she sought help and healing all her life.

Once in junior high school, while standing outside during physical education class, someone threw a hard ball at Jamie that hit her on the top right breast. She never saw it coming and never saw who threw it. Suddenly she was in pain that brought burning tears to her eyes. Still hurting that night, she showed me where the ball made contact. A large, hard red lump marked the spot that was painful to the touch. In a few days, the knot was gone, but I never forgot that incident.

Jamie first realized the call of God on her life at age thirteen. She walked into the living room and sat down beside me on the sofa. She was crying. "Momma, I think God has called me to preach. I had a dream and I saw a sea of people with black hair. There were so many people crowded together, and they don't know who Jesus is." We prayed and cried together.

Not long after God called Jamie, Satan began his assault on her mind and heart (her greatest God-given assets). It became difficult for her to concentrate in prayer. Her thoughts raced. She fought hard to gain control over this, but it always resurfaced. One major struggle in her thought life was the doubts she wrestled with concerning her salvation. Was she truly saved? As her mother, I tried to understand the torment she was experiencing. I always believed and told her that Satan was lying to her and trying to derail her life and God's call on her life. We prayed for hours many times over the years until she would feel some relief and could drift off to sleep.

Only many years later, after marriage and preparing for the mission field, did a doctor diagnose her problem—a mild form of OCD—but enough to cause havoc in her thought life. Satan could never gain control of her mind and heart, but that fact never stopped him from trying. Her knowledge of God and His Word and her heart of love and compassion for those who don't know Jesus continued to grow stronger within. She struggled, but God protected her brain and heart until the very end. "Whose weakness was turned to strength" (Heb. 11:34).

Once in seventh grade, she saw a girl who wore jellies to school in freezing weather and was at the nurse's office because her toes were frozen together. The next day, Jamie took socks and shoes to the girl at school. She also gave her new coat away. As an older teen, she cut off her beautiful long, thick wavy hair and donated it to Locks of Love.

~

September 1989—It is not uncommon for Jamie to invite friends to church who then get saved and filled with the spirit.

~

June 9, 1990—Jamie and Janet and their love for God are some of my most precious blessings. This past week, I coordinated Vacation Bible School for the Spanish Assembly in town, and Jamie and Janet helped me so much.

~

From Jamie's collection in which she received a big red check mark from her teacher in the middle of the page:

September 28, 1990—If I Could Be a Color

If I could be any color, I would be pink. Not black, not blue, not red but pink. Pink is the color of a little bright-eyed girl's cheeks. Babies are born with pinkish skin. When the sun sets, at times a beautiful pink can be seen in the sky. Pink is the color of wonderful strawberry ice cream. It is also the color of some pretty flowers.

The abovementioned things bring joy and are associated with happy times. Other colors at times do this, but pink has a sense of innocence to it—light pink, that is. It is the color little girls wear and decorate their rooms with. It is the color of a girl's childhood. It is the color mommies everywhere dress their little precious baby girls in. Words cannot describe everything pink means to me, but one thing is for sure: it is a special color.

~

Oh, the beauty of having teenage daughters! There was never a dull moment. Like the time Janet wanted to borrow one of Jamie's shirts. This was not out of the ordinary because Janet constantly borrowed Jamie's clothes; and always out to make a fast buck, Jamie would charge her for that privilege. Janet also borrowed money from her sister occasionally for which Jamie charged her interest. This particular shirt was not anything special, according to Janet, but Jamie said, "No." In a cranky mood, Janet slapped her sister across the face. Immediately, Janet realized the peril she just stepped into. "Please don't tell Mom! Please don't tell Mom!" Jamie just smiled at Janet, closed her bedroom door, and never did tattle on Janet. Later they discussed that interchange, Janet apologized, and Jamie told her she loved her. She kept her promise and never told me.

"It makes me so sad to think that I slapped her beautiful face over a shirt that she wouldn't let me wear."—Janet

April 10, 1992—Jamie broke up with Joshua on March 11 because she wanted to date. On March 12, Kerry asked her out, and she has seen him every weekend. She is going to the prom with him tomorrow night.

Gene and I created our "infamous list of fifty questions" (it seemed like fifty to the young men) which we would ask each young man who wanted to date our daughters. Kerry was the first to experience this pain. Janet was in her bedroom listening and cringing and promising herself she would never date! But we wanted to know these young men. "Tell us about yourself and your family. Where do you live? Have you ever received a speeding ticket? Have you ever had a car accident? Ever been arrested? Where do you go to church? Do you have a personal relationship with Jesus Christ? What kind of grades do you make in school? Have you ever drunk alcohol, smoked, or taken drugs? What do you plan to do when you graduate? What are you interested in besides our daughter? And oh, by the way, if you are five minutes past curfew, we will come looking for you."

Much to her dismay, I insisted Jamie wear a dress for her very first car date with Kerry. Jamie and Janet tried to convince me that wearing a dress was not a good idea. Who knew that Kerry would show up in shorts and a T-shirt and would take her to Taco Bell? The girls never let me live that one down. It seemed a good idea at the time.

Jamie loved playing the French horn in band and she practiced relentlessly. Do you understand how deafening a French horn can be inside the four walls of a house? Finally, one day I had about all I could stand. "Jamie, please go outside and practice for a while." We lived in a small neighborhood in the country with big yards and plenty of room.

She thought it was a great idea. She could practice her marching at the same time by marching around and around the house.

Well, that didn't last long! Soon a neighbor walked outside and told her to go back in the house! She was mortified!

August 21, 1992—The Final Challenge by Jamie Norton

It was a big disappointment. I had practiced my music very hard to retain first chair. All year long, Jeff and I had challenged each other for the first chair French horn position. In each of these challenges, the challenger always won, dethroning the first chair player. I earnestly wanted to break this cycle that had been created.

Finally, my chance came. Jeff challenged me for what would be the last time. I, determined to win, practiced very hard; I was ready.

When the day of the challenge came, I tried not to get nervous. Regardless of my efforts, however, I made a mistake in the scale that I usually played perfectly. I also messed up on the piece of music. This was devastating, for never before had I performed so poorly in a challenge.

Mr. Ward, who judged the competition, took forever to post the results of our challenge. Assuming that I had lost due to my flawed performance, I traded my first chair part to Jeff for the second chair music without even waiting to see who won. I began to accept being "second chair." I was still disappointed however.

Finally, Mr. Ward posted the results. Afraid to see the evidence of my "defeat," I peeked slowly at the announcement. I had won! Elated, I took my first-chair music from Jeff. The cycle had been broken and Jeff would never challenge me again.

"To be on time is to be late. To be early is to be on time."—Mr. Ward

June 5, 1992—Jamie is still dating Kerry. We had a long talk with both of them before the high school band Disney World trip about abstinence and no compromising situations. He just graduated and goes into the air force in September. Jamie has two jobs this summer: Chick-Fil-A and Lerner's. Janet has a job too—babysitting three girls, ages six, eight, and ten, from nine to five Tuesday to Thursday. They paid for their own camp, which is next week.

For most of our lives, Gene and I have lived nickel to nickel. I learned to sew in high school and made most of my clothes for many years. I saved a ton of money by sewing clothes for the girls from birth through most of their school years. The last dress I made was a prom dress for Jamie's junior prom. Sweet Janet wore many hand-me-down clothes until she was big enough to say, "Enough is enough! I want to buy my clothes now!" In reading through my journals, I noticed many prayer requests centered around enough money to pay the bills. We made a commitment to God to tithe and give offerings in the second year of our marriage and have endeavored to keep that commitment throughout the years. Somehow, someway, God has always met our needs. Most of the time I cannot explain how He does it; He just does it. God is faithful to His Word. Regardless, I often worried how in the world we were going to make it. Then when He met the need, I wondered why I ever doubted. God is a good God. "But if we have food and clothing, we will be content with that" (1 Tim. 6:8).

Once when money was tight, I threw an evening paper route; it was April and May of 1993. The girls detested me picking them up from school with all those newspapers in the backseat. They knew before we went home, they would have to go with me to throw newspapers. They would lie down in the floor of the car so no one would see them. And all of the stopping and starting made them car sick. On top of that, I think I almost ruined their love for Taco Bell burritos, because often we would pick up something to eat before going home, and their stomachs weren't ready for that.

May 17, 1993—We took Jamie to Dr. Franklin at Texas Woman's Hospital in Houston. She will be on medicine for three months and then return. He believes she has endometriosis.

October 10, 1993—Kerry and Jamie broke up.

January 1, 1994—Kerry was at our church's watch-night service last night.

April 6, 1994—Jamie broke up with Kerry after dating him for two years. She also quit Lerner's last week after working there for almost two years.

It was during Jamie's senior year in high school ('93–'94) and Janet's sophomore year that I made the tough decision not to renew my ministerial license. Yes, I had been a credentialed minister since 1984 and by this time, I was having more opportunities to speak in churches and women's events all the while working full time at the church. However, God was dealing with my heart about spending even more time in prayer for our daughters. This was a critical time in their lives—the teenage and college years. Life was challenging and major life decisions would be made soon. I needed to spend more time with them, focus more on them, and pray more, so something had to drop. I don't regret it.

I began waking even earlier to pray and read the Bible, a discipline I have continued throughout the years. "In the morning, Lord, you hear my voice; in the morning I lay my requests before you and wait expectantly" (Ps. 5:3). I love spending those early morning hours (4:00–7:00 a.m.) on my knees in the living room with a hot cup of tea in prayer, Bible study, journaling, listening to God, and allowing Him to direct my day. I guard that time; it is precious to me. Eight years later in 2002, I renewed my credentials, went back to college, graduated, and was ordained in 2006. God has been good to me.

May 27, 1994—Tonight is Jamie's graduation at the Expo Center. She is graduating with honors and third in her class. We are very proud of her. She enrolled in Angelina College last night for the first summer session and will take sociology and history. She has received more than enough scholarships to completely pay for her first year at Stephen F. Austin State University. Gene and I gave her a jar of money we have saved all year—$227.32.

# CHAPTER 5

## *College Chronicles*

Study to shew thyself approved unto God, a workman that needeth not to be ashamed, rightly dividing the word of truth.

—2 Tim. 2:15 (KJV)

January 10, 1995—Gene and I took Jamie to see Dr. Franklin again yesterday. He scheduled her for a laparoscopy on March 13. She is not any better. We are still trusting God for Jamie's healing.

March 4, 1995—Jamie and I went to college days at another campus on Thursday and Friday. She went with an open mind and spirit. I went with a prayer that she would know God's will. We attended different classes and seminars. Before we left for home, Jamie paid her application and dorm fee! She will attend there beginning this fall! She said sitting in on Dr. Amy's American literature class and attending chapel helped her decide. Now, our prayer is that God will provide the finances. Thank you, Jesus.

March 16, 1995—Jamie had a laparoscopy at the Women's Hospital on Tuesday and is doing great. God has really answered our prayer. She does have endometriosis, but Dr. Franklin said it was a mild case. He lasered patches from an ovary, the bladder, around the bowel, and in the pelvic area. He also lasered nerves that should help alleviate some of the pain. She is taking three shots of lupron, one a month that will shut down the ovaries. These shots cost $400 each. She will also be on the pill. He doesn't want her to have more than two or three periods for one year. She is a little sore and is moving slowly, but she is doing great. Praise the Lord!

May 22, 1995—Jamie finished this semester at SFA with a 4.0. She was awarded two small scholarships to her new school. She starts to work tomorrow at Clark's for the summer. We are so thankful to the Lord for all He has done.

June 20, 1995—Jamie received another scholarship for $1,800.

September 14, 1995—She has met a guy who seems very interested in her. They are going to the Fort Worth Zoo on Saturday with another couple.

Jamie's journals:

In the beginning, I was not looking for guys. I planned to go through the semester focused on my studies, the Lord, and friends. About the second day (August 18) at my new school, however, a tall and handsome young man walked into my life. Susanna introduced me to him, but he didn't even give me the time of day. Within the next two weeks, I wrote home about a guy who seemed to be sensitive. I began to notice this man of God from afar. Darling, on September 2, 1995, you brought our worlds closer together. (Actually, the Lord did.) That night I came back to the dorm from work to find you watching a movie in the lobby. I sat down and watched the end of it. I believe the movie was *The Secret of NIMH.* When I told you I had never seen it before, you suggested that I watch the whole movie. I slyly suggested that I didn't want to watch it by myself. I believe you got the hint because you offered to watch it with me!

Then you asked me out on a date for the next Saturday! I was glad, but I didn't want to seem too happy. A week later, on September 16, you drove me and two of our friends to the Fort Worth Zoo. It was so fun! You were disappointed that they didn't have apes though!

I'll never forget our first date with just the two of us. On September 29, I wore my roommate's dress to Red Lobster with you! You knew it was my favorite. I got my usual popcorn shrimp and baked potato. Afterward, you suggested that we go to a movie, so we went to *The Big Green.*

On October 20, we officially became a couple. What you mean to me: Darling, I don't tell you how great you are to me as often as you tell me sweet things. But my heart has found a heart to care for; my hand has found another to hold; my voice has found ears to listen. You are a gift from the Lord to me. The Lord led us together. When I am with you I feel safe.

January 4, 1996—We enjoyed his visit. Gene picked him up on Friday and he stayed until Monday when Gene and Jamie took him back to DeSoto. He stayed in the evangelist quarters at the church. Jamie had a great twentieth birthday on Sunday. We all went to the watch-night service too. Gene and I are impressed with her boyfriend. He has a genuine love for and commitment to the Lord. He loves all people, is very sensitive to the Holy Spirit, and he and Jamie really like each other.

~

May 14, 1996—His card to Jamie:

Hi Beautiful. How is my rose? I really miss you a lot! Honey, I'm sorry for not calling you on Monday. You are very special and I'm learning now just how special you are because I miss you so much. Thanks, Jamie, for knocking me right off my feet! I never dreamed that would happen to me this last year. You don't put on an act but you're transparent. I love you more today than yesterday.

~

May 27, 1996—Jamie is in DeSoto this weekend. He broke up with her last week. She called last night, and they are back together.

~

June 8, 1996—They broke up again, this time for good.

~

July 4, 1996—Dear Jamie: Thanks for calling last night. It was great talking to you again. Jamie, you need to allow God to be your security; a boyfriend can't, a friend can't, a position can't—only God can. I'm thankful God has given me a best friend like you. I want you to know you can date other guys at school. It won't hurt me. You need to get to know a lot of people and make friends with a lot of guys. I will no longer discuss the way I felt when I found out there was another guy because I have forgiven you for that, even for calling me him by mistake. I know we are not perfect and things happen sometimes, and I have forgiven you. Please forgive me for any of the ways I've hurt you. Jamie, I pray that you will allow me to be your best friend. If you really care for me, you will.

~

July 11, 1996—Jamie went to Dallas last weekend and saw him. They are "just friends" again.

~

July 21, 1996—Dear Jamie: Hi. How are you? I'm sure that you are getting ready for your big trip to Europe where you will have the time of your life. Make every moment count because that sure will be a trip of a lifetime. There are some things I need to let you know. First, we are no longer a couple; and secondly, I am not going to get back together with you this year. This year I want to be a friend to you and I pray that you will let me.

~

August 19, 1996—Jamie and Janet are attending the same college this year. It is Janet's first year and Jamie's third year of college. Jamie is a resident assistant in one of the dorms.

~

September 16, 1996—He told Jamie that he is not going to get back together with her. He believes God wants him to give her completely away, to let go of something that's dear to him. Her heart is broken.

~

September 17, 1996—His letter to Jamie:

> Dear Jamie: I wrote the following in the journal you gave me last night: Tonight was very hard for me because I had to tell Jamie that I'm not getting back together with her indefinitely. I told her this because I believe God wanted me to give her completely away, to let go of something

> that's dear to me. I also want to be honest and straight forward with her and not lead her on, giving her hope that just maybe we would get back together. This has been very difficult for me, but I will not question God when He tells me I must let go of the thing I love (Jamie). I must obey Him and let go of her. Lord, you have given me peace about this. I am still torn inside, but I trust you and will not question what you want me to do. I do believe that sometimes when we let go of what we love and give it to you, God, you give it back to us in your time!

October 16, 1996—Jamie has been struggling spiritually lately. The enemy tries to beat her down with discouragement, tiredness, and depression. She really is very tired. Being an RA is a twenty-four-hours-a-day and seven days-a-week ministry. We prayed. I am trusting God to supernaturally lift her up.

November 11, 1996—His letter to Jamie:

> Hi beautiful. You are a very special young lady. I'm thankful God allowed our paths to cross more than a year ago. You have been a tremendous encouragement to me this whole semester. Your gorgeous smile always brightens my day, and the fact that I can cry and get some of my feelings out with you means so much to me. God is creating something more beautiful in you every day, the Jamie that I love and the Jamie that's dear to me.

November 25, 1996—His mother passed away from breast cancer on November 19. God is using Jamie to help him with his grief.

Christmas card from him to her:

> Dear Jamie: Thank you for being my best friend and really being there for me this whole semester. I can't express in words how much your caring, sensitive and sweet spirit has lifted my spirits this semester when I really needed it. I don't really know what to say because I've hurt you so badly. I am trying to say I'm very thankful to God for you. Please forgive me. Please drive carefully and give your parents a hug for me.

December 27, 1996—He broke off with Jamie again after his mother died. He doesn't want any relationships right now. She was very hurt. Jamie had a perfect 4.0 this semester.

He was a prolific letter and card writer who crammed every available space with his attractive script. His hundreds of correspondence declared his thankfulness for and admiration of Jamie and eventually his love for her. Apparently, she cherished these countless notes of affection and love and their habitually repeated words.

# CHAPTER 6

## *Turmoil*

I thank my God every time I remember you.

—Phil. 1:3

January 21, 1997—Jamie and he spent the weekend with us. They are back together. He apologized to Gene and me for hurting Jamie. He still doesn't understand why he said what he said and did what he did. He was in so much pain and grief when his mother died, and it is still very painful for him.

February 4, 1997—Jamie called last night and told us she went to the school counselor. She has for a long time struggled with her salvation, ever since seventh grade when God first called her into the ministry. Satan lies to her because she does have such a strong call on her life. She felt better after talking to the counselor and will continue to see her. It has gotten to the point that it is always on her mind, and it is causing depression. But Satan is already defeated. She will conquer this through Jesus Christ. She is so precious. She said she really loves her classes, and everything else is going well. They are attending church together at Oak Cliff and love it.

February 16, 1997—Letter from him to Jamie: To my lovely Jamie, You know what? You're beautiful! Wow! And I'm falling for you!

February 26, 1997—Jamie, my sweetheart. You look so pretty today—your hair, your gorgeous eyes, and your beautiful smile. I really am falling for you bad! Jamie, you are precious to me and you become more precious with each passing day.

March 7, 1997—Dear Jamie: I want you to know I'm praying especially for you now because I know that you are totally crushed and hurt inside. Please know I did not do this on purpose. You may think I'm a jerk, but right now in my life I have to be honest with myself before you, friends, and most of all God. I know that you really love me to let me obey the Lord and do what He told me.

March 22, 1997—Dear Jamie: I just wanted to say thank you for listening to me and being there with me when I needed to cry. I was really missing Mom, more than usual. It meant a lot to me that you would be willing to do that, when this whole time has been much harder for you. Your whole attitude has been incredible; it has shocked me! You have shown a lot of strength and maturity. You are truly a beautiful young lady.

April 8, 1997—Jamie is doing well in school as always. They have called it quits again. He needs more time to get over the death of his mother.

April 14, 1997—Dear Jamie: I know you're hurting. God wants to do something so special in your life. I had to realize that I was saying to God, "Hey, God, I want Jamie and I want you to approve of her." Instead, I should have said, "God, have your way." He reminded me by saying, "What have I called you to do?" I said, "Go to Africa." It felt like He took a two by four and wacked me upside the head!

April 19, 1997—Jamie received two scholarships totaling $1,250. Thank you, Jesus. She is having a hard time getting over him. Lord, help her.

April 29, 1997—Jamie called last night to tell us she was elected RA of the year by her peers. This is a very high honor. A resident assistant is an associate dorm pastor. He received the male RA of the year.

Spring 1997—Dear Uncle Gene and Aunt Karen: I want to express my thanks to you for the love you have shown me during this hard time. I can't really say in words how much you both have touched and impacted and blessed my life. It is an honor to have a friend like Jamie. I feel I don't deserve the privilege of dating someone as special as her. I want to honor what you said, Uncle Gene, about not hurting her again. The thing I love about Jamie the most is her heart after God and her sweet spirit. I try my best to treat her like a young lady should be treated—with respect. Thanks for the great meal and thanks for the love you've shown me. I can feel His presence in your home and that is awesome. I love you guys. Uncle Gene, I understand why you were upset with me. Please forgive me. I didn't intentionally try to hurt Jamie. I wasn't myself and I regret what I did. Thank you for making me still feel loved. I look up to and respect you. Thanks for forgiving me. I love you. Aunt Karen, it was a special treat to have you make a meal just as good as my mom would before she had cancer. Thanks so much. You're more special to me now because I have a new appreciation for mothers. I love you.

April 30, 1997—Jamie's journal: God has shown me His love so much that I want to show the nations His love. In His presence, I am free. Today the Lord assured me to be strong and take courage, to not fear or be dismayed, for He will walk before me. And His love will show me the way (in my mind battles).

May 15, 1997—This is the first full day of my summer. Oh Lord, change me this summer. Restore your desires into my heart. Give me a new love for you this summer. Restore in me a love for the lost. Change me. I ask you to do whatever necessary this summer to change me. By August eighth, I want to be closer to you than ever before. This is my summer prayer: to have total faith in you, to love you totally and to be revived. I humbly pray for these things. Thank you for holding on to me this year. Thank you for changing me this summer. Thank you for your presence in my life. PS: Restore to me a soft heart. "Ye shall seek me and ye shall find me when ye shall seek me with all your heart. I will be found of you," declares the Lord.

May 26, 1997—Jesus has given me a new strength. Yesterday and today, when the mind battles came, I chased the devil away, quoting Scripture. I have a new dedication to follow Jesus. I think about other countries a lot. It isn't fair that in America, we have so many chances (though I praise God for mine), but some people die without ever hearing the name of Jesus. I want to be a missionary, but I don't know if I am called. Mom told me that I have a missionary's heart, but there are many areas of missions. I want what God wants. I pray that my motives for missions will be pure. I need to know God's will. "Jesus, help me to stand! In the prophecy Sunday night, you said that you use weak vessels. Okay, but help me stand. I love you." PS: My feelings for him are lowering. I am not going to worry. "God, just do your will in my life."

June 6, 1997—"Oh Lord, I am twenty-one and a half, and I don't want to be single all of my life. Mom was married and had a baby by the time she was my age! I don't want to be single forever. I will though, if you want me to. I will because I love you. Lord Jesus, please don't forget my desire for a husband. If it's in your will, bring him to me. Lord, I would really like to have an engagement ring soon. Have your way!"

June 27, 1997—Romans 15:20–21 came alive to me today! Paul's goal and desire was to preach to those who had never heard too! That is my goal! "Do it, Lord Jesus!"

It has always been my ambition to preach the gospel where Christ was not known, so that I would not be building on someone else's foundation. Rather, as it is written: "Those who were not told about him will see, and those who have not heard will understand" (Rom. 15:20–21).

July 4, 1997—"Oh Jesus, today you reminded me of my need for tenacity, that bulldog-like 'hanging on to you' that will not give up. Make me like Jacob who did not let go of you until you blessed him. Make me like Joshua who stayed in your tabernacle long after Moses left. Make me like it says in Hebrews—one who does not shrink back and is destroyed. Make me like Paul who put aside hindrances and what was behind him and pressed forward. And make me like you who resolutely set your face to Jerusalem though you knew death awaited you there. Make me tenacious."

~

July 6, 1997—My three role models: Mom and her love, sweetness, and serving heart; Dr. Amy and her loving teaching; Mrs. Lund and her missionary heart.

~

July 9, 1997—"Oh God, please build your character in me. It will be a slow, hard process, but do it. As a seed grows, let me fall to the ground and die, so I can live. Break me so I can grow. I believe you. Show me what I need to get out of my life to be totally yours. Lord, give me more of you. Thank you for this hunger. Fill it and then give me more hunger for you. I love you. I want to know you more!"

~

November 18, 1997—Jamie is strongly considering graduate school at the University of Texas in Arlington, possibly a fellowship where she can teach freshman English while working on her master's.

~

How, then, can they call on the one they have not believed in? And how can they believe in the one of whom they have not heard? And how can they hear without someone preaching to them? And how can anyone preach unless they are sent? As it is written: "How beautiful are the feet of those who bring good news!" (Rom. 10:14–15)

# Chapter 7

## *Poignant Recollections*

I will remember the deeds of the Lord; yes, I will remember your miracles of long ago.

—Ps. 77:11

From Jamie's journals: Fall Semester, 1997

September 2, 1997—This bed I'm lying on has been a refuge, a place to cry secretly several times. It seems that a lot of unnecessary tears have fallen on my pillow over boys. But there is another deeper issue that I have cried about for many years now.

I surrendered to God's call to the ministry at the age of thirteen, lying in a bed in my teenage home. Not long after that, I began to struggle with my thought life.

God has helped me very much through the years, but sometimes I still have a hard time. Since last November, however, I have struggled with doubt. I don't feel comfortable discussing this with my classmates because I am a resident assistant and an example to girls. I have also committed my life to Christ to be in the ministry.

But how do I know that I know that I know that the Bible is true? As I have grappled with these questions, my faith has gotten smaller and smaller. I am still hanging on, but I pray that God will do something to settle this issue in my heart.

I have been called to the ministry. I would go anywhere for Jesus, but I want to be totally sure of all this. It is as if two people are arguing inside of me. One person really wants to spread the gospel, but the other is asking, "What if you go to Africa and spend twenty years preaching something that is not true?" I know God will get me through this. I honestly want to do His will. I honestly want to make it through this. Once I know that I know that I know that I know what I believe, I will be able to tackle other things for God.

~

September 3, 1997—My Hiding Place.

Most of the time, I pray when no one else is around. In the dorm it is hard to do this. I am an RA, so I am interrupted a lot during the day. I have found two places in town to pray undisturbed.

One place is at Getzendaner Park. I love its beautiful trees and swings. I just feel away from everything when I drive around its big circle, park my car away from everyone else, roll down my window and pray. Sometimes I even swing as I pray. It relaxes me. I can go to the park worried about something and drive away knowing that God has heard my prayer.

The other place I go to pray is actually in my dorm room. I lock my door and crawl under my bed, pulling the comforter over the edge of my bed so no one can see me. When people knock on my door, I ignore them. Praying under the bed is for those serious times when I need to be free from distraction. It is hard to be sidetracked lying on the floor under a bed with no room to move around!

Back home my place of prayer is the chapel at our church. I can go there when no one else is there because my mom has keys to the building. I carry my Bible, journal, and a pen, dim the lights, and pray. I enjoy walking up and down the aisles as I pray. Many times as I pray, my mind wanders to those sacred times when God touched me in that very room. I was baptized in that place—in water and in the Holy Spirit. I have felt peace there. I have felt freedom there. I have seen a crippled person walk away from the altar area healed. I have even seen Jericho marches in that holy place. There is something about praying in a chapel. It just feels like God's house. I feel closer to God sometimes in that place. God is everywhere. He can hear my whispered cry as I walk to class just as well as He can hear my shout of praise in a chapel service with a thousand other people, but there is something special about one's special place.

~

September 4, 1997—My Best Friend

God gives us friends to share fun times with and to be ourselves with. But He gives us best friends to lean on in the hard times, to bear our soul unafraid of their reactions.

I use the term "best friend" all the time. I guess I have about four or five really "best friends." But really when I think about it, I have one very best friend other than my family and my God. Her name is Lana Lovetta Ingle.

Lana and I met each other in the ninth grade by accident. The pastor's daughter at my church went to school with Lana and invited her to our youth group. Lana and I were not very close until we both liked the same guy! Stephen was so handsome, but he was interested in Lana, not me!

What did I do? I tried to get them together, so I could have an excuse to talk to him. Whenever Lana and I got together, all we talked about was him and other boys!

Our friendship remained rather superficial until around the eleventh grade. In high school, students really draw the line between living for God or the world. Lana and I had both stepped onto God's side years before.

We found out that we could confide in each other about how our English teacher made us feel by slamming our Christian principles every week. We could encourage each other when he directly offended us in front of the whole class.

Somehow Lana understood me. Sure, we had other Christian friends, but we had a special bond, a kinship. She was non-Pentecostal and I am an Assembly of God stickler, but we had something special, something sacred.

College came and we both met wonderful men. However, Lana's home and family began to fall apart. When Lana's college boyfriend decided that perhaps he didn't want to marry her after all, it was almost too much for Lana.

Through these things, we prayed together and I tried to encourage her. Lana would call me on the phone so frustrated and confused, but she knew I would listen.

The beautiful thing about our friendship is that I wasn't always the helper and Lana the "helpee." Things went both ways.

Lana listened several times to my stories of men breaking my heart. She has listened to me talk about having to take a stand for my convictions and encouraged me, even though she did not agree 100 percent with me.

I am an RA. This position limits my true friends considerably. I am there for the girls, kind of a mother figure who will listen to all of their problems but rarely share my deepest concerns with them. Even my fellow RAs look up to me more than I would like, putting a wall between me and them. I love the ladies on my hall and my fellow RAs, but I miss having someone on my level that I can really be myself with.

Besides my parents, the only person I have found to fill this need is Lana. I thank God for Lana. There's one more thing. Even when we are apart, we do not have to write letters between colleges, but we know things are okay between us. We are both so busy that we don't have time to correspond much, but because Lana and I are sister-friends, we don't let empty mailboxes come between us. Praise God who knows exactly what each of us needs in a friend!

~

September 6, 1997—"And they lived happily ever after." From the time we are born, we are raised to believe an illusion.

A handsome prince meets a beautiful lady, pledges his love to her, marries her, and they live in a castle surrounded by riches—happily ever after. They never suffer from loneliness, depression, or trouble. They never divorce. And they never die.

Little girls sit in amazement as they listen, with childish wonder, to stories about lovely princesses. They love to look at pictures of enchanted castles far away. They dress up as fair ladies going to the ball where they meet their Prince Charming.

Then they grow up. Suddenly they are going to proms where their goal is still to look like a princess. At their weddings, they are princesses!

Somewhere along the way, girls and boys begin to follow the lives of real-life royals. The Windsors in England give them a glimpse of the other world, the actuality of a fairytale.

The whole world watched Prince Charles marry Lady Diana Spencer. For the next sixteen years, they were obsessed with Diana, the people's princess. She lived before them every mother's fairytale and every little girl's dream.

We watched her suffer from anorexia and depression. Slowly the illusion began to crack as the world watched Diana's marriage dissolve. Diana didn't give up, however. She still had the smile, beauty, and grace of a fairytale princess.

The crystal illusion shattered when she died. I have had a hard time believing that she is dead. Princesses live forever. Right? They are immortal and always beautiful. Right? Wrong.

On the day Diana's Mercedes crashed into a Parisian wall, my childhood fantasy died. As I watched her funeral in the wee hours of that Saturday morning, I realized that the same lady who had ridden a horse-drawn golden carriage to St. Paul's Cathedral on her wedding day was now being carried to a nearby cathedral in a box.

There is such a sense of loss in my heart today, not for Diana as much as for a dream that is over—no, shattered. The world grew up on the day our beautiful princess died.

~

September 7, 1997—Ring by Spring or Your Money Back!

Bridal College—I mean Bible College—is a fine institution where a young lady can come to get a bachelor of arts, a bachelor of science, or simply, a bachelor. Most students would not admit to coming here just to find the perfect spouse, but many do have this desire somewhere down in their hearts.

What better place, realistically, is there to find a Christian spouse, called to the ministry, than at Bible College? As each semester progresses, couples begin to pair up, two by two, as if they're headed to Noah's ark. Sometimes the rest of us feel as if the ark is leaving us in the cold rain, as was the legendary unicorn.

I want to tell my fellow unicorns not to give up. The best place to find a mate is not Bible College; it is wherever God has your mate waiting for you! I have attended this school three years now, and it looks like I won't be walking across the stage with a diploma in my right hand and a diamond ring on my left. But that's okay, because all of the eligible bachelors in the world, believe it or not, do not live in these dorms!

I'll just wait on God to bring me the right person. Only God knows who is best for me and only time will tell how long I will have to wait. He just might come walking around my corner tonight.

~

September 9, 1997—I was disappointed today. People can say the most awful, harmful words without realizing the damage they cause.

A girl named Kendra, who lives on my hall, came into my room discussing her bad attitude. She admitted to me that she was not looking forward to this week of spiritual saturation. After she explained her feelings, this freshman told me that she hadn't heard one good thing about spiritual saturation weeks of old. She said all the returning students stated the week would wear you out. She had never heard of anyone receiving a touch from God.

I know God moves in spiritual saturation week, and I am very disappointed at those "mature" students who helped discourage my freshman from receiving from God. Freshmen see us as role models, and if we are too lukewarm to receive anything from God, we should keep our mouths shut rather than quench someone else's fire. Three other freshmen on my hall told me in the first week of school how excited they were about what God was doing in their lives. Then they said that some returning students had told them that their fire would burn out sooner or later!

I warned my girls to guard their passion for God. We older students need their zest for worship. We need to remember why we are here and seek what we have lost.

I wish we would guard our tongues better. We never know whose faith we may destroy with our cynicism. God have mercy on us.

These are apathetic students crushing freshmen's dreams. As returning students, we should be model vessels of what God can do in four years of dedication to Him, not empty, hard stone jars that are unfit for service. I pray these old brittle vessels will throw themselves into God's fire again to be melted into new creations that He can pour His living water into. God forbid that we leave this campus any other way.

September 10, 1997

Once upon a time, there was a fair maiden named Jocelyn who left home to live in a far away land with strangers. The strangers were kind to her and took her into their fold.

One day, a handsome prince saw the lady. He thought, *I would give all of my wealth to meet her.* Day after day, he noticed Jocelyn, and he began to talk to her ladies-in-waiting about her.

"What is Jocelyn really like?" he would ask. "What must I do to win her heart?" And the ladies-in-waiting would chatter endlessly to the prince, telling him this and that.

The prince decided to write Jocelyn a poem. You see, he had grown to love her so much that he had to tell her.

He had his servant boy leave it by her window with a single white rose. Jocelyn blushed with an innocent joy as she read his confession of love. At the end of the poem, the prince had written, *If you could ever love me, meet me at sunrise by the fair hickory tree.*

Jocelyn knew she loved the prince. He was so sensitive and charming, so compassionate and sincere. But she was new to this land and knew not the way to the fair hickory tree.

At sunrise, the prince rode his majestic horse to the old hickory tree. He carried in his hand a white rose. He waited as the sun rose to the top of the sky, but she never came. The prince watered the ground with his tears, left the dying rose and returned to his castle.

The fair maiden had searched all day for the fair hickory tree, but her search was in vain. She fell asleep, wondering if she would ever hear from her prince again.

At sunrise the next morning, the sound of a man's voice rose up to her window and awakened her. Her love was serenading her with a beautiful song. When he finished, he threw a white rose onto her window and left. Attached to the rose was a note. *If you could ever love me, meet me at sunrise by the fair hickory tree.*

All day long, Jocelyn and her ladies looked for the hickory tree, but they found none. When the prince rode to the tree the next morning carrying a white rose, she was not there. The rose began to wilt as the sun rose in the sky. The prince again watered the ground with his tears and returned, alone, to his castle.

That night, a foreign land declared war on his father's kingdom, and the prince had to leave with all his servants to fight. He passed the fair lady's window mournfully, knowing he was leaving his heart with Jocelyn. He could not leave without climbing into her window and laying a beautiful white rose beside her head on her pillow. She looked so beautiful in the moonlight, and he stole away, watering her pillow with his tears.

At sunrise, Jocelyn awoke to the sweet smell of the rose lying on her moist pillow. Her servants ran into her room to tell her that her prince had left for war. Jocelyn wept for her prince. He did not know that she loved him. Perhaps she would never see him again.

Seven days later, a page boy saw Jocelyn in her garden and handed her a white rose with a note. Her prince missed her dearly, it said, but the war looked like it would never end. At the end, he had written, *If you could ever love me, one day meet me at the fair hickory tree.*

Jocelyn still did not know where the fair hickory tree was, but she had an idea.

Seven years passed before Jocelyn heard from her prince. She thought about his handsome smile and his loving eyes every night and wondered if she would ever see him again. She had done her part, but had kept it a secret. If only he would come back, the prince would know she loved him now.

After seven years, the two warring kings called a truce, and the warriors returned home. The prince rode as fast as he could back to his land and to Jocelyn. He arrived at her castle gate at sunrise and stopped his horse in amazement at what he saw. All around Jocelyn's castle were young hickory trees. In the middle was a white rose bush, bursting with blooms, and his love standing there, looking as young and innocent as the night he left for battle.

They wept as their eyes met. The prince picked up his rose, embraced her, and basked in the shade of the hickory forest all day long. The End.

September 16, 1997—Him

There is a small plaque on my mother's bedroom wall which reads, *Some people walk into our lives and leave. Others come into our lives, stay a while and leave footprints on our hearts.* He is that kind of friend to me.

We dated each other a long time. The more we got to know each other, the more special we became to one another. Our love grew and grew until we each decided we wanted to spend our lives together in Africa reaching the lost. He and I both prayed, "Lord, if it is your will, I want to marry her/him."

I guess God had a different plan. One day I will understand why we had to separate, but for now I am content just to know that I was once close to his heart.

He loved me for who I was to God. He gave me such unconditional love that I could be comfortable around him even without makeup. When we ate breakfast together and I, a non-morning person, was in a bad mood, he was patient with me, even though he had to listen to my grumbling. He showed me genuine care and concern, and was always willing to listen to my secret struggles, without condemning me. He told me his secrets.

He had the ability to see things in my life. He would say I was patient, sensitive, and unselfish even though I couldn't see those qualities in myself. Over the past year, the Lord has been developing these fruit in my life, and he saw them all along! Once he told me that I was like a butterfly about to come out of my cocoon, spread my wings, and fly. Lately I have started to "fly," and I think of him every time I see a butterfly.

Obviously, I write this as someone very biased. You may wonder if I have been blinded to his faults by his charm and my love for him. I don't think so.

I admit that he has broken my heart more than once. He once called me his "rose," and several times he has crushed my petals, one by one. His mother's death was hard on him, and he did things to his "Southern Belle's" heart that he normally would not have done. Sometimes people have criticized him for hurting me. They have had the audacity to talk harshly about him in my presence.

I will always thank God for bringing him into my life long enough to place his footprints there.

His East Texas Rose

September 22, 1997—My Adventure

This weekend I went where no resident assistant has gone before. I did the unthinkable, the unheard of. I loaded up twelve girls from my hall and took them home with me.

I had girls of all kinds: quiet girls and crazy girls, church girls and questionable girls, young freshmen, and a couple of seasoned seniors, girls from Colorado, Texas, Alabama, Oklahoma, Arizona, Utah, and Ohio! All in my house, all weekend.

My brave parents welcomed the girls to our home in the piney woods of East Texas, and then fled next door to my grandmother's house!

On Sunday morning, people at our church were amazed that Mr. and Mrs. Norton, a calm respectable couple, would open the doors of their home to all those girls! We just laughed at their amazement and told them how much fun everyone was having.

Mom and I had decided that she would fix a big meal for everyone on Friday, and we would cook out on Saturday. Mom worked so hard cooking and preparing and cleaning for thirteen women. After this weekend, I have a deeper appreciation for her.

The slumber party was a success. Girls told me they were able to spend time with girls they hadn't known before. We went to the lake on Saturday, and they were able to relax. Some swam, some hiked, and some studied.

On Friday night, we prayed together, and I gave a short devotion about God's strength during hard times. It seemed like it was from the Lord!

The weekend was a success! It was exactly what we all needed.

~

September 24, 1997—He Took My Pain Away

On the outside, I may look like a person who hasn't seen hard times. I smile so much and act so sugary that surely I must have had it easy. Don't let a mask trick you.

I have known pain. I know what it is like to lie in a room and feel alone and rejected. I know the feelings of one who has been tossed aside, because I have been thrown away.

When you have been loved, even cherished by a man of God and are then discarded, it does something to your sense of self-worth. You have stood with him during black times and have defended him when others just didn't understand. You have set aside your desires and needs to fulfill his. You have breathed him into your every dream until his dreams are yours, and then he deserts you.

Your dreams are shattered. You no longer understand where you belong. Suddenly there is no person to fulfill your needs. Who will stand by you when you need someone?

A preacher once said, "Blessed be the night, for it reveals the stars." As he preached that message on November 19, 1996, I didn't realize that the sun was about to set in my life. On that day, a missionary to Africa of no particular fame, passed away. I was dating her son, and something in him died that day too.

He began to treat me differently, holding his precious jewel at a distance. When he told me we would never be a couple again, I was torn between a desire to help him and a desire to hold him. I wanted both, but it couldn't be.

During the midnight following November 19, he crushed my heart several times. I felt so downcast, unloved, and rejected that even the stars didn't seem to shine.

I began to just softly say, "Help," over and over to the Lord. Lying on the floor surrounded by the broken pieces of my dreams, my heart, and my self-esteem, all I could utter was, "Help me, help, please help me," over and over.

God heard. The next ten months were not easy. I lived for his love and approval. If he smiled at me, I was happy. If he smiled at another woman, I bled inside.

I loved him. My heart broke over and over.

I began to even wonder if I should trust God again. After all, He had sent me to him, and I got burned. A dim hope hung in there that God could still be trusted. I kept sending prayers up to Him, and He carefully collected my tears in a bottle, as He promises in His Word. A dull pain, a numb feeling was lodged in my heart.

Today, I realized the pain was gone. It has been gone for at least a week. God has intervened and has slowly put my heart back together. His stars were shining during my night all along. Now I know that He will always be there during my nights.

October 7, 1997—He was the most wonderful guy I have ever met. If he hurt me, who else could I trust? When I became his girlfriend, my heart was surrounded by walls left from another painful relationship. He slowly helped me break those walls down, and I showed him my naked heart. Then he stomped it.

I don't want to be hurt again. I don't want to show any guy my real heart again. I am scared to trust someone again. His deserting me has been like my father deserting me (though my dad has never done that). When he left, he took my sense of security and self-worth. He left and my dreams shattered.

I want to let go of him and to move on with life. I have been thinking about relationships and about the past. I went to the park yesterday to settle the problem in my mind. I tried to let go of him. It takes time.

"Dear Lord, I want to move on. I don't want to mistrust men. Just because one has hurt me does not mean the next guy will. You are the mender of hearts. Do what you need to do in me. I love you, Lord."

~

October 30, 1997—To my husband on our wedding night

As I write you this letter, I may not even know you personally, but I look forward to our times together as man and wife. I want to tell you that I have kept myself pure for you. Somehow, the Lord has helped me save myself for tonight, and I am ready to give you all of me.

The Lord has brought us together for "such a time as this." I have shed rivers of salty tears over many boyfriends (one in particular). I have wondered when I would ever fall in love, when "my time" would come. Sometimes the loneliness made me feel such hurt, and I wondered if I would be single forever. Now I know the Lord was saving me for you.

Like girls often do at Bible College, I made a list of the qualities I wanted in a husband, and God has fulfilled my every wish in you. You are the only person in this world who fits exactly with me. Surely, I am "flesh of your flesh and bone of your bone."

Some of the qualities I love about you are your prayer life, your faith, and your compassion. I wanted a husband who would be a true priest in our home, and I know you will be. Your childlike faith catches me by surprise sometimes, and your compassion for others reminds me of our Savior.

As your wife, I promise to stand by your side and build you up rather than tear you down. You will always be able to depend on me to stick things out with you, no matter what pressure you are under. I will be there to take care of you when you are sick and to play with you when you just want to have fun.

All I ask of you is that you have an unquenchable faithfulness to our Lord and to me. Tonight is only the beginning of our new adventure together. I love you.

~

November 4, 1997—"Home is where the heart is." That old cliché just doesn't describe my home well enough for me. My home is my haven. Everyone needs a haven, a place they can retreat to when life gives them an unmerciful blow. That is what my home is to me.

As a college student, I never know what problems I will face. These years away from home have led me through struggles I never expected to face. For some reason, a college student's problems happen at night a lot. During those wee hours of the morning, I can feel so alone and homesick. My problems magnify when I realize there is no one (except the Lord, of course) here to help me.

Hesitating to wake my parents up with the telephone's ring, I remember their words, "You can call us anytime." So I do. They are never irritated with me for waking them up. They listen to me as I cry over the phone, pouring out my broken heart to them. We always pray before hanging up, and they always offer advice, assuring me that things will work out.

I do not know what my college life would be like without a haven. I had this haven growing up but did not cherish it until I moved away.

One day I will provide a safe haven for my daughter. I want her to feel like she can run to me no matter what storms come her way. And I have a good pattern to follow. Praise the Lord!

~

November 4, 1997—Determination

I hate quitting. Quitting never gets you anywhere. If you passionately start something and set a goal you think is important, you should follow through with it. If the Lord calls you to do a job, you lose the "right" to give up whenever you want. Tasks that He commands you to do are His business, and you should faithfully work at them until He tells you differently.

How many people come to this university, positive that God has called them, and have left after a semester or two? Sure, sometimes the Lord tells students to attend school for a short time, but others just give up when it gets rough. When they have money problems, they go home. When classes get hard, they give up. When problems arise at home, they run back.

Just because we have problems while doing what the Lord has called us to do does not mean we should give up. Sometimes those problems arise just because we are in His will. When difficulties come our way, we should look to Jesus rather than the circumstances. The One who walks beside us can help us and teach us how to persevere if we will give Him a chance.

I have wanted to leave this university more than once over the years, but just knowing that the Lord has called me here has kept me here. I hope the students here will learn how to stick with things now before they really get tough.

~

November 4, 1997—Love

We throw around the word *love* all the time, as if it were a minor thing. I "love" Chinese food. "I just love rollerblading," and even, "I love you."

Loving someone is not a small, insignificant act. When you love a person, you cannot turn on or turn off your love like it is a water faucet. You either love a person or you do not.

I realize that there are several types of love; some are more intense than others. The one I want to write about is the genuine, everlasting romantic love between a man and woman.

When two people are "in love," they care about each other over anyone else of the opposite sex. They long to be together, both in public and in private. They love each other even through sickness, mood swings, and bad hair days. They commit to loving each other forever, regardless of feelings that come and go. True love puts the other person first, even when it hurts or is uncomfortable. Love always seeks the other's good.

Unfortunately, love must be vulnerable. If I love someone, I must lay down my life and comfort zones, risking hurt. I have to trust my lover, hoping he will remain loyal to me. When love is for real, this gamble is worth it! "Love is of God."

November 24, 1997—Whoa! Yesterday the Lord got my attention. I was doing my daily devotions, reading Psalm 106. The passage describes Israel's continual rebellion toward the Lord after times of His blessings. One verse says that Israel cried out to God for something that was against His will. He gave them just what they asked for along with a disease. At the bottom of my Full Life Study Bible was a mini-sermon about the danger of going after things that contradict God's will. I had underlined everything that it said.

Then I looked in the left margin. I was stunned as I saw his name and August 1996 scrawled here! In August, before he and I had ever gotten back together from a breakup, before the pain *really* started, before *everything* God had warned me—to seek His will instead of my own. If I had only listened and remembered...

Last year I cried a waterfall of tears, and my heart crumbled into pieces over and over again, as he pulled me to him, then pushed me away, pulled me to him, then pushed me away. I lay in bed hopeless, *my* dreams shattered. A few times I even became angry at the Lord.

I asked God, "How could You let me get hurt?" The Lord understood my frustration, but He knew that He was not to blame. I had been warned back in August, but had gone my own way. Now I certainly do not want anything in my life that contradicts or is even God's "permissive" will. I have learned my lesson.

The Lord has been looking out for me all along. His way really is the best way, but oh, what a price I paid to learn this lesson.

~

December 1, 1997—"Dear Lord, show me how to die to myself and truly love You and others. Let agape love, that life-giving, never-ending love, grow in me."

~

December 2, 1997—My Legacy

Yesterday, Sister Debbie had Heather and I read statements to the other RAs about the RA position. I shared with them how I want to be remembered when I am just a memory next semester.

I want the girls to remember me as a woman who loves God. When they think of me, I hope they will be encouraged to pray and walk righteously. I have tried to be a good example in these areas. I hope some of it will rub off on others.

I hope my fellow RAs have seen in me a deep respect and love for my dorm pastor. She deserves 100 percent loyalty, and I have hopefully modeled that to them.

My heart's desire is that the sixty-plus girls I have had under my care for the past year and a half will remember that I loved them. I tried to serve them before myself, and I hope they learned something from my deeds. In watching me, maybe some of them learned more about what being a minister means.

Last night, person after person honored me by saying what I meant to them. I don't think I deserve a lot of what was said. I am not happy with many of my actions as an RA. I want more than anything else for the Lord to be pleased with me. This has been a labor of love for Him and His ladies. I hope He is pleased.

I have prayed that every girl who has been under my care will carry a "mark" on her. If any of them ever start to turn from the Lord, I pray that the Lord will deal strongly with them. The most wonderful gift I could ever give the Lord would be sixty-plus souls in heaven. Maybe one day I will be able to say as Jesus said, "I have not lost any of those you gave me."

# CHAPTER 8

## *1998–1999*

February 4, 1998—Jamie is checking into the master's program at the University of Texas in Arlington. She found out yesterday that fellowships are available (TAs) in linguistics. She can get a master's in linguistics while teaching foreign students English.

Dear Jamie: I want to tell you how much I appreciate you. I remember you from the first time I came to this campus last summer. We stopped unexpectedly, and you were the one who showed us around. It's ironic that you would be my RA! My mom said it was easier to leave me here knowing I was being taken care of. I thank you for all the advice you've given and for the love you've shown me. I really feel you get to know individuals, not just the girls on your floor. You know and care for each one of us. I've been told by many people that no one will be able to replace Jamie Norton, and I agree. You've impacted my life a lot this semester. I've grown to love this school so much. At times, I struggled with homesickness and other things, but God is bigger and God is greater than those things. He's taught me some hard lessons, but I know it's all to make me stronger. I've made some mistakes, but God was there to show me when I went wrong. I've changed so much in the past four months. God has become so much more to me. He always was, but it's become deeper, so much deeper. This is a special place and I thank God for it every day.

Jamie, I'm praying for you as you move on to a new part of your learning here. My prayer is that God will show you where He wants you and that you will be so filled by His love. Trust Him and you'll be all right. I will miss you. God bless you in all you do. I love you. Kate

May 8, 1998—Thank you card from Jamie on the day of her college graduation:

> Dear Mom and Dad: Today is a big day for me. I want to tell you both that I could not have done this without you as my parents. Thank you for raising me in a godly home full of love and always believing in me which has given me confidence all my life. I thank God for you. Love always, Jamie.

May 8, 1998—Jamie, I know this isn't the best of stationery, but I hope it will do. I want you to know how much I love you and respect you. I told you tonight that I could have never asked for a more wonderful sister, and it is true! I know we haven't always agreed on everything, and sometimes we got on each other's nerves, but throughout the entire time, I have looked up to you as my role model. I have seen in you for the past twenty years a love for the Lord and others that I have always desired—a loving heart that only you could have—and the sweetest spirit of anyone I have ever known. And for all that I say, "Thank you." Thank you for being there for me, typing my papers, playing with me when we were small, letting me wreck your car (and not killing me), but most of all thank you for being my very best friend in the whole wide world. Jamie, I am so proud of you—you summa cum laude graduate! I am so excited to see what God has for you. I know that it is *huge*! I love you Sis. Janet.

~

May 14, 1998—Jamie graduated summa cum laude with a bachelor of science in secondary education with emphasis in English. She is home for the summer and will work at Gene Lee's office and teach English to two Japanese foreign exchange students for ten weeks.

~

July 18, 1998—Jamie has been dating Greg a couple of weeks now. "It's different this time!" Anyway, she is cooking him breakfast this morning.

~

August 12, 1998—Jamie and Janet flew with Uncle Glynn to New York City Saturday morning. They are spending five nights. Monday they took the Amtrak to Washington, DC. I know they are having a wonderful time.

The best part of the entire trip—the one thing they remembered and talked about the most over the years—was the plane trip home. Janet tells it better than anyone:

After Jamie graduated from college, our Uncle Glynn took us on a really fun trip to New York City. We had a great time and stayed in the fanciest hotel and ate the fanciest food (which wasn't all that tasty to two young women who grew up in East Texas). He bought each of us a ring from Tiffany's—beautiful gold bands engraved with Roman numerals.

On the flight back home and following a layover, we boarded a tiny plane with about twenty-four passengers. As we walked onto the plane, there was a young lady already on board about nineteen years old who had obviously never flown before. She was freaking out and asking everyone on the plane, "Are we going to die? Are we going to die? Have you ever flown before? 'Cause you're still living so tell me you've flown before!"

Everything was going great until about thirty minutes into the flight when we hit a bunch of turbulence. The plane literally rocked! All the window covers slammed down with a loud noise! Flight attendants fell over in the aisle! The drink in my cup flew straight up out of the cup, over my head, and landed in Uncle Glynn's lap, who was sitting directly behind us.

Everyone was screaming hysterically except for me because I was laughing my head off at Jamie! She was sitting next to me, praying and crying out to God, speaking in tongues, and saying crazy things! "Mom and Dad will never know that it's us when the plane crashes because they won't recognize our bodies because of these rings on our fingers!"

"Jamie, shut up! You're not making any sense!" I yelled while laughing uncontrollably. She was punching me and praying at the same time, and I could not stop laughing. I had tears streaming down my face, terrified because I really thought we were going to die. But she was talking such nonsense trying to make me stop laughing that all I could do was laugh. I was pretty sure I was going to die laughing!

A man sitting on the other side of the aisle started laughing at me, and absolutely every other passenger on the plane started screaming at us to shut up! It was impossible! I could not stop laughing at my hysterical sister who was punching, slapping, praying, and kicking my butt all at the same time!

Meanwhile, this young woman who was flying for the first time was screaming profanities at all of us because we all lied to her that flying was a cinch and that we would all be safe. "You all lied to me and you're all going to hell because you lied to me! We're all gonna die!"

Jamie began screaming prayers over all the passengers for cursing because she really thought we were all about to meet Jesus!

When everything settled down and we landed, the pilot walked back to us and apologized to everyone for the rough ride. He asked the little six-year-old boy on the front row what he thought about the flight. "I'm just glad I was praying to Jesus!" We all were.

~

August 17, 1998—The girls packed on Saturday and we moved them back to school on Sunday. Jamie is in an apartment with Nathalie.

~

October 26, 1998—Jamie broke up with Greg. They are still friends, but the relationship was going nowhere. Jamie is okay with it.

~

February 22, 1999—Dear Jamie: Hey, what's up? There's a lot going on here. I'm really having the time of my life. I'm doing great—really ready to come home, but doing great. It's funny to sit around and think about all the things I used to take for granted like hair and sleeping until seven. The biggest thing though is church. Spiritually, I'm doing great. I think it took putting me in this kind of a situation to realize how faithful God has always been to me. My Bible and prayer time have been great. It's like for the first time, I know that no matter where I'm at or what I'm doing, He is always with me.

Jamie, I have always looked up to you a whole lot. I know you probably think this is goofy, but I kind of think of you as a big sister, even though I'm bigger. Ha! Anyway, I guess I'm trying to say that I really appreciate all the support and prayer (Bible Quiz coaching) you've given me through the years. I really do owe a lot of who I am spiritually to you. I've sort of always wanted to tell you that, but it's pretty hard to do in person. So, I took the easy way out and wrote it in a letter. That doesn't mean I mean it any less though.

I think the best thing about being here is all the marching. I'd forgotten how much I really loved it. It's a little different but mostly the same. I think I'll be a band junkie for the rest of my life. Well, I gotta go for now. Write again soon. Love in Him, JR.

March 28, 1999—This afternoon I was feeling really bad—still battling with unbelief. I was to the point of thinking perhaps the church wouldn't want to send me to Northern Asia, and maybe I had failed God so much that I shouldn't go. Then tonight at church, Dr. D spoke and gave the altar call for people who needed strength, perhaps even who felt like they were so weak that they might be about to slip away from God. I went up for a touch from God, for faith, strength, and revival. God spoke to my heart and said that I am exactly where I need to be and that His hand is on my life! After all my failures, joy filled my heart once again! After service, I walked up to Dr. Amy and told her of my desire to teach in Northern Asia. She said that she sees me as being a good teacher there. She said that I am precious to the Lord and to her.

May 28, 1999—The Lord really touched me today. This morning I awakened at three thirty. I am scared to write my thoughts for fear that someone might read them. But what happened must be written down regardless of the cost. The last few days, ever since the Lord touched me on Sunday, I have continued to doubt Him and have sinned in my mind. I called out to the Lord many times, but my thoughts were getting worse. When

I woke up, I sinned again in my mind. Without writing details, I felt that perhaps I had blasphemed beyond forgiveness. I was so upset. I got my Bible and went to the living room and tried to pray. It was so hard and I wondered if I had crossed the line. I kept trying though and finally I could pray. I asked the Lord to forgive me again, and then the Lord spoke to me so clearly. He said, "Not by might nor by power, but by my Spirit, says the Lord Almighty" (Zech 4:6).

It just hit me! I knew God was still there, and I had the assurance that we would get through this thing together. Peace. I felt such mercy and grace. I really began to see, for one of the first times in my life, God's forgiveness and my sinfulness and undeserving of His grace. It really is amazing! I am starting to see myself in a different light. I am so grateful for God's mercy this morning. I will arise and go forth in the name of the Lord of Hosts, for He has conquered every foe through His mighty name.

> How long must I wrestle with my thoughts and day after day have sorrow in my heart? How long will my enemy triumph over me? But I trust in your unfailing love; my heart rejoices in your salvation. I will sing the Lord's praise, for he has been good to me.
>
> —Ps 13:2, 5–6

July 17, 1999—Jamie has been offered a full time staff teaching position for the next school year at UTA! She plans to finish her last year of graduate school too and graduate in May.

September 17, 1999—"Help me, Jesus. Help me, Jesus. Help me, Jesus. Help me Holy Spirit. You have been my shield in the past. You have been my refuge. I have called to you, and you have answered.

Come make yourself more real to me than you ever have before. I believe in You Jesus. I trust in you, Jesus. I wait on you, Jesus."

~

September 19, 1999—The Lord says, "Trust me. I care more about your spiritual walk than you do."

~

November 13, 1999—Well, now I am twenty-three years, ten months, and thirteen days old and still single. It is time for me to write my mission statement: My purpose is to glorify God (Father, Son, and Holy Spirit) in all that I say, think, pray, and do. I will impact the world for eternity by opening my eyes to the harvest, praying for the lost daily, and reaching out to the unsaved and unchurched. God has called me to Asia, so I will go to Asia, leaving my future husband here, if that is necessary. Oh, how He loves you and me!

~

November 22, 1999—Today was one of the best days of my life. It ended by me and one of my best friends, Josh, talking on the phone and him rededicating his life to the Lord! I am so thankful that Alvin asked me about Josh's soul, and God gave me the opportunity, desire, and boldness to be straight with Josh. Today, God told me to give thanks continually.

~

November 24, 1999—Jamie was informed this week that she could be leaving for Northern Asia as early as July if all goes well. Dr. H wants her on his team and he's working to get the paper work expedited. Jamie says she has peace and that all the puzzle pieces from her whole life are falling into place for this moment. God's will be done.

# Chapter 9

## *An Oasis*

> How beautiful on the mountains are the feet of those who bring good news, who proclaim peace, who bring good tidings, who proclaim salvation, who say to Zion "Your God reigns!"
>
> —Isa. 52:7

Jamie's life was an oasis. "That person is like a tree planted by streams of water, which yields its fruit in season" (Ps. 1:3). An oasis in a vast, hot, dry desert is a natural (God) phenomenon. God in His great love and mercy distributes oases around the globe where they are most needed. Through the centuries, the oasis has been critically important on trade routes for nomadic tribes. When nations went to war against each other in the area, whoever controlled the oasis had a definite advantage. An oasis could mean the difference between life and death.

An oasis is a place of water and vegetation. So where does the vegetation around an oasis come from? When migrating birds stop by an oasis, they pass along seeds from their droppings which grow at the water's edge. Seed tucked away in the gut of a bird can travel thousands of miles and produce life without the bird ever realizing it. The bird just does what comes naturally. The One who forms the seed watches over it. Likewise, migrating birds also pick up seeds from around the oasis and carry them many miles over land and sea where they are planted and produce life.

So it is with us and God's Word. God forms the seed, watches over it, and we farm it. The farmer sows the seed which is the Word of God (Mk. 4:14). This is a powerful combination: God's love and God's Word. Jamie was filled with both, so she did what came naturally to her and went to those who had neither. The seeds she planted and watered produced fruit, bearing more seed, which has since been carried to other dry and barren places, planted, and continue to produce fruit unto salvation. May it be so with each of us who call ourselves Christian.

January 2, 2000—Today I went to pick out cakes with Janet. For two hours, we talked about the wedding stuff. I came home and cried. I am really hurting. I want to get married more than anyone knows. I have cried and prayed a lot these holidays, but my family doesn't know. I am embarrassed that I hurt and I am embarrassed to admit my desire for a husband, but it hurts so much. I feel like I deserve a wedding and a husband. I would be a loyal wife. I want to love someone and to be loved. I don't understand why I have to go overseas without a husband. I hope one day this will make sense to me. A lot of girls have been called to mission fields, but they got married instead. I have obeyed. Where is my reward? This is an awful way to feel. I can't tell anyone this. They would think it is a sinful thought, and no one in my whole family would understand, and those stupid people on TV or radio that write books about being single—what do they know? A lot of them got married before the age of twenty-four. I am going to obey God though. I hope He isn't making a mistake. I know He isn't. His ways are perfect.

January 3, 2000—Tonight, I was hurting so much for a husband. I talked to my parents about it. They understood and really listened to me. Then they prayed with me. I really felt peace. It meant a lot to me that they cared and listened and prayed with me. Dad told me to remember one thing. He is forty-eight years old, and God has never failed him or anyone in the Bible. We fail Him, but He never fails us. He told me to remember that. It comforted me. Thank you, Jesus, and thank you, Mom and Dad!

January 4, 2000—Gene and I prayed again with Jamie last night concerning her loneliness and her desire for a husband. It is very hard for her to watch Janet so happy and planning her wedding. She is following God's call on her life no matter what, and she believes she will marry someday. But it is very hard for her now. "Dear God, please take away the pain in Jamie's heart. It is too big for her. Help her to totally trust you today and whenever that battle rages within her. Give her your peace today, that peace that comes from above. Thank you."

January 16, 2000—Jamie called yesterday and she has been preapproved for missions. She will leave in mid-July.

January 17, 2000—Last night I had a dream from the devil. I was in a foreign land on the mission field. Someone gave me a gift that was cursed. I knew it was cursed, but I ignored it. Then, a Satanist walked through the streets screaming at people and quoting Revelation 3:20, twisting it, so that people would come to him. In the dream, I realized what he was doing. I went straight up to him, asked him who he was and rebuked him. I woke myself up quoting the Scripture to him out loud, "No weapon formed against me shall prosper." As my voice woke me up, I lay in bed and recognized the attack that had happened. I began to quote Scripture aloud and proclaim, "Jesus Christ is Lord." I held my Bible in my hand and rebuked the demon.

After about five minutes, I called my parents. It was 6:00 a.m., but I knew my mom would be up praying. Mom and Dad answered the phone and began praying, quoting Scripture and rebuking Satan with me. I explained to them how I felt like God was preparing me for the future, and how He is changing me and growing me, because in the dream I went straight to the opposition to get rid of it for Jesus, rather than waiting for it to come to me. Mom and I talked a while and I told her I felt a little scared. She reminded me that we do not go on our feelings but on our knowledge of Jesus Christ and on His Word. We hung up the phone.

I read some Scripture and went back to sleep. I didn't tell her that later on that day, I got really scared. I began to think, "Well, I really don't like battling demonic forces, and I don't want to have to deal with open satanic opposition." I began to pray and ask God to show me a glimpse of His power that would help me to trust Him.

Later that night, I was reading in Deuteronomy. In the first seven chapters, God reminds the Israelites why their parents were unable to go into the promised land but instead had to wander in the wilderness for forty years. He reminds them that the reason their parents were punished in the desert is because they had let fear persuade them not to trust in God, even though they had seen His miracles in the past. I was getting more and more encouraged, and then I read Deuteronomy 7:17–26. It was exactly what I needed. It assured me that God will go with me. I don't need to be terrified of what is before me, whether visible or invisible. Instead, I must remember what He has done for me in the past.

When I arrive to my new home across the ocean, I must not allow any false religions to survive. I must not compromise the gospel. Their false religions and symbols, no matter how sincere and well-meaning, are detestable to God and are the results of their forefathers rejecting Him. God will be with me. He has called me to these people "for such a time as this" (Es. 4:14), and I must not let evil supernatural forces scare me or make me tremble. "You, dear children, are from God and have overcome them, because the one who is in you is greater than the one who is in the world" (1 Jn. 4:4).

January 17, 2000—It is early now. Jamie just called. She was awakened by a demonic dream. We prayed. God is victorious and Satan is defeated. She has six months before she leaves for Northern Asia. God is preparing her. Satan tries to plant fear and discouragement. God turns that around and teaches her from it. "Dear God, fully equip Jamie for what you've called her to do."

January 26, 2000—Tonight, I went to church where Dr. H spoke. Mom and Dad came, and Dr. H introduced me to the congregation. He asked the church people to pray for me over the next two years. After he spoke, he had the whole church come and lay hands on me and pray. Dr. and Sister G prayed for me. Dr. G placed his hands on my cheeks and prayed over and over for grace to do the work. That is what I need more than anything. He also prayed that every day I would know Jesus is with me. After he prayed for me, he took both of my hands, which were clenched, and he said, "Relax. Untighten those hands. Relax." He assured me that God will be with me and will take care of me. What a humbling experience. God is good.

March 27, 2000—Last night was Jamie's commissioning service at church. Janet and Jeremy came for it. Jamie spoke about ten minutes and Pastor Todd commissioned her for missionary service. Our family stood with her. An offering was received. Rob gave a tongue and interpretation. God confirmed the call on her life. He said He would be with her, not to fear; He loved her and the people in her country. The presence of God was powerful! Pastor even broke down right before the tongue went forth. Praise the Lord! The message from the Lord also said that He has raised her up for such a time as this. Everyone was moved by this service. Dan Norman was the guest speaker; he gave the offering received for him to Jamie.

March 28, 2000—The offering that came in for Jamie last night was $7,744.43! Praise the Lord! She needed to raise $6,500 up front and $400 in monthly support. Several people took monthly pledge forms.

April 8, 2000—The church rounded up Jamie's offering to $8,000. God is so good.

LFA was Jamie's biggest financial supporter by far for the twelve years she served in missions. Many individuals from our church and community supported her in prayers and finances faithfully during that time. Many knew her since she was six years old when we first moved to Lufkin, and they watched her grow up. Our family has always been actively involved in the church. God used these precious brothers and sisters in Christ to reach the uttermost through Jamie. Gene and I will always be grateful to the Lord and to our church family.

~

April 13, 2000—from Jamie's journal

Our battle is against spiritual forces of wickedness in high places. Above all, take up the sword of the Spirit which is a tested weapon as were David's stones. This Islamic stronghold may be coming in like a flood, but the battle belongs to the Lord. "Have I not commanded you? Be strong and courageous. Do not be afraid; do not be discouraged, for the Lord your God will be with you wherever you go" (Jos. 1:9).

~

May 22, 2000—from a note written in the margin of Jamie's Bible

Nathalie reminded me of Psalm 20:1–5 today, my last day in our apartment together. As I leave, I have such an overwhelming sense of satisfaction and peace. I am pleased with what God has done in and through me to date, and have an amazing sense of being in His will. Last night at church, God showed me that these next two years are a gift from Him that not everyone receives—a gift to really seek Him and who He is and what He has called me to do. It is better to go single because I can focus on Him and receive blessing and knowledge directly from Him and not from a husband or anyone else.

> May the Lord answer you when you are in distress; may the name of the God of Jacob protect you. May he send you help from the sanctuary and grant you support from Zion. May he remember all your sacrifices and accept your burnt offerings. May he give you the desire of your heart and make all your plans succeed. May we shout for

joy over your victory and lift up our banners in the name of our God. May the Lord grant all your requests.

—Ps. 20:1–5

June 9, 2000 (night before Janet's wedding)—Jamie, out of every sister in the whole wide world, God gave me you—the most precious sister on the face of this planet! Over the years, I've learned so much from you. You are the exact big sister any girl would want to look up to! Thank you for being so great.

I know I've not always been a bundle of joy. I slapped you across the face in your room one day, for crying out loud! I am sorry for that, by the way! But, of course, you didn't hurt me back. You didn't even tell on me. I'm telling you—you have always been so amazing! Thank you for all of your help with the wedding. My personal shower was awesome. Please know that I am so grateful to you for that. I will miss you so much while you're away. I love you. Janet

July 6, 2000—The night of the fourth, Jamie felt God's presence in a powerful way in her room. Last night, Gene wakened me from a dream that grieved and tormented me. He prayed, and at the very moment he spoke to Satan and commanded him to go, Satan left—like wind out of my bones. God ministered to me and I went back to sleep. "For our struggle is not against flesh and blood, but against the rulers, against the authorities, against the powers of this dark world and against the spiritual forces of evil in the heavenly realms" (Eph. 6:12). This is such an emotional week for me. Jamie and I will have another very busy day today. She is doing great.

~

July 10, 2000—A blessed Lord's Day yesterday! Everyone in our church family is so supportive of Jamie. God is using His people to bless her spiritually and financially. And God is helping Gene and me too. Today, we will finish packing. Jamie is praying that God will give her seven in her new city to win to the Lord and disciple. We will miss her so much.

"When you can see the invisible, you can do the impossible." This is only one of many notes written in the margins of Jamie's Bible. "For we live by faith, not by sight" (2 Cor. 5:7).

~

July 12, 2000—Jamie left today from Dallas/Fort Worth Airport to Osaka, then to Bangkok, then to Chang Mai. Everything went well at the ticket counter. Janet, Jeremy, the Yancey family, Josh, fellow teacher Tanya, and student Yoko were all there to see her off.

~

July 30, 2000—Jamie called yesterday morning from her new home (first time). She sounded fine. She is teaching over ninety students for three weeks and loves it. It's very hot and there is no air-condition. She sweats all the time.

For those first two years overseas, Jamie felt as if she were dropped on another planet, basically alone, not knowing the culture or language and not able to eat the food. Thus, the reason I mailed a package to her every week or every other week. More often than not, the postage cost more than the actual contents. She entered this two-year adventure with only two suitcases, and her neighbors called her a rich American! Lucky for her, God created her to instinctively care more about other people than for personal belongings. She always held loosely the things of this world.

~

September 10, 2000—We talked to Jamie yesterday. She has had a difficult week. She ate some carp that made her sick for three days. She has a bad cold and is very homesick. Men have been working in her apartment and have made a mess. And Sundays are the worst day of the week for her because she misses the "community meetings" so much. "God touch her, love on her, encourage her, and show her the silver lining. I can't hug her, but you can. Thank you, Jesus."

~

September 15, 2000—Around 8:00 p.m. last night I felt restless in my spirit and felt the need to pray for Jamie. The word *threatened* loomed in my mind, so I prayed. When Gene came home, we prayed together. I felt the Lord intervene. (I later found out from Jamie by phone that at that exact time, although she was fourteen hours ahead of our time, she experienced a very threatening situation. She knew why God prompted me to pray at that moment. Although she could not discuss the details, since her phone is bugged as are her apartment walls, we were both very grateful to our Father.)

~

September 24, 2000—We received a letter from Jamie yesterday. She is adjusting and doing well. She loves where she is and what she is doing. She loves her students at the small university in the mountains where she is teaching English. God has really blessed her and given her favor. She is receiving our packages.

~

October 9, 2000—Barbara told me something interesting last night after church. About three weeks ago, she was in the store buying groceries. She saw one of Jamie's prayer cards on the floor. She picked it up. She said something came all over her and she could not finish her shopping. She went home and prayed for Jamie interceding in the spirit. I thank God that He called Barbara to pray for Jamie, and that she was obedient to do so. PTL!

~

October 16, 2000—Gary and Sandi bought Jamie two warm jogging suits and two pairs of socks that I will send to her. God has blessed so much in meeting Jamie's needs. It will soon be very cold there, and with no guarantee of heat in her apartment or classrooms, I am sending lots of thermal underwear and warm clothes that she can layer. She said her students often wear seven layers of clothes, rags, and anything else they can find just to stay warm.

~

November 7, 2000—Jamie called yesterday. She had a dream. God spoke to her: "Any sacrifice is worth it."

# Chapter 10

## *Her Adventure Begins*

From Jamie's Overseas Journals:

July 13, 2000—It is good to finally be out of Texas. I have been planning to go to my new country since November 1999. There is no turning back now. I have followed my dream, and I know I will live the rest of my life following the Giver of the dream.

~

July 20, 2000—Thailand has been a great experience, but now I am excited to be on a plane to my new home. Three years and four months ago (March of 1997) this dream began. I am so excited. I'm here! Last night when I finally went to bed, I thought about my life and each step of the way, how I got drawn to this land. I remembered something I had forgotten. In the 5th or 6th grade, we had author day, and we dressed up like an author and told people about them. I had read "Jacob Have I Loved" or something by that author. I remember dressing up like her in one of my teacher's kimonos. Very interesting. Last night I read the story about the widow's mite. Jesus approved of her for giving everything she had. That is what I am doing here. I am away from family, a good job, my car, my friends and food and cleanliness for the sake of the dream. Why am I here? I am out of my comfort zone. I can't even order a bowl of rice, and crossing the street is scary. Most buildings don't have a/c, so it is very hot. I guess I will get used to it. The streets smell like manure. I don't know how I can get used to that. This is all for a dream. I know I am supposed to be here, even though I am not happy with my present circumstances. All for the gospel!

~

July 22, 2000—This is where the rubber meets the road. Yikes! Do I really, really believe in my dream? Yes. Do I really, really have my priorities straight? Is the dream as important to me as I have acted all these years? It is strange how altar call after altar call, you sing things like, "I surrender all," and "I'll go where you want me to go, Dear Lord," but when the rubber meets the road, can you really follow through? I will pray that I can become focused on the ultimate goal and never lose sight of it.

~

July 29, 2000—I have really enjoyed my classes. I have a 7:30, 8:30, and 9:30 a.m. class. No a/c, only one chalkboard, four ceiling fans that work sometimes. Windows stay open for air, but unfortunately construction is going on so there are loud noises coming through the windows! Sweat! Each morning I drink two bottles of water while I teach. Actually, it is kind of exotic to teach with no a/c in a third world country. It just feels neat!

I have decided, after today, that every culture has a different definition of the simple word *fun.* More later.

A friend of the university took me to a restaurant that had a picture of a hamburger on the wall. I got excited, but on closer inspection, I decided that was not beef. Definitely false advertising to an American! I still don't know what the mystery meat inside was. I contented myself with a tortilla look-alike that appeared to have pizza like spices inside and some bread and sweets. First of all, it was not a tortilla, and second of all, it wasn't pizza-like. I just hope it wasn't dog.

Last night, I had an amazing dream. Around 4:00 a.m. this morning, which would be around 2:00 p.m. Saturday afternoon, July 29, in Texas, I dreamed that I was at our home in Lufkin with several people from LFA. They started praying that God would raise up the sleeping giant, the church, in my country. I started praying in my sleep, and I awoke feeling the spiritual reality of the dream. It wasn't just a dream; it was from God. I lay there and prayed. I don't know if people were praying for me then, but it reminded me of the great army of people back home praying for me and my new country. It also pointed out to me that God wants to raise up the church here to the next level of strength and power and witness. He wants to build His church in this land so that the gates of hell cannot prevail against it! PTL!

August 1, 2000—Sunday was a cool day. Actually, Sundays are the days I feel the most homesick, because I miss church. Sunday is just a regular day here.

Quite by accident, my friend and I discovered an underground church nearby. It was very exciting, but we didn't want to know its exact location, and we knew we could never go there, being foreigners. I can't put into words how I felt Sunday night. Here I am, far from my home in Texas, and Jesus is alive and well in this dark land. The church is alive and well. In fact, it was well known about in the community. Government can't stomp it out.

August 2, 2000—The curriculum I am supposed to teach is pathetic. Whoever put this together has no concept of English as a Second Language (ESL). I will ask Mom to send me some of my books from home. Now that I have released that venom,

I feel better. I guess I don't want to be labeled as someone who can't teach ESL. I have a lot of improving to do, but I want these teachers/students to see excellence in my preparation, lectures, comments, knowledge, teaching techniques, and demeanor. I want this to reflect Christ and my expertise, and I want the students and the university to get their money's worth through my teaching.

I want a bean burrito. My mouth is watering; I can almost taste it! I was in the middle of a conversation with a friend about one of her friends, when a picture of a bean burrito flashed through my head with no warning. Not just any bean burrito, a bean burrito from Taco Bell with a fluffy soft tortilla and no onions but with sour cream. Two bean burritos with no onions and sour cream. And a large, crushed-ice glass filled to the rim with a fountain drink Dr. Pepper. It has been twenty-two days since I have had Mexican food and twenty-one since I had a Dr. Pepper. It takes, according to some who know, twenty-one days to break a habit. Well, why is my mouth watering like Pavlov's dog at just the thought of a bean burrito? Yikes, it is going to be a long two years!

A thought: I am changing. I have been here three weeks, and I see changes in me already. First, I am growing spiritually. When thoughts come into my head, I am using spiritual weapons better to combat them. Truths I have listened to for years in church, chapel, and at home are finally being put to use. How much easier it is to fight spiritual battles with God's weapons rather than my own! No duh! Secondly, I am becoming a more thankful person. Instead of dwelling on discomforts and things I miss sometimes, I thank God for the great things I had in America. I am more thankful now, for example, for little things like a washing machine, twenty-four-hour hot water, air conditioners in buildings, *toilets*, toilet paper, forks, enchiladas, clean water, Dr. Pepper, bean burritos, fruit you can eat without peeling, Chips Ahoy, and peanut butter. Not to mention a good waitress who understands English and who knows that French fries are not supposed to have sugar on them.

Dear Mom and Dad, of course I am thankful for ya'll and Janet and Jeremy too. But I have always been thankful to God for you! I love you!

Third, I am becoming less wasteful. I now try to use only one or two squares of toilet paper at a time. I used to take a whole wad. Now I turn off the shower while I wash my body and hair. I used to keep the water running the whole time. I try to fill up every possible space in postcards and letters. I used to not care if I used two or three pages. People change in a country where toilet paper is a precious commodity, clean water is scarce, and students write on paper so thin you can see through it. Don't get me wrong. These people are happy with what they have. They don't complain about their limited resources. It's all they've ever known. They are kind and generous with what they have. It is the rich American in me that must die.

August 14, 2000—Traffic here is worse than a roller coaster. No wonder traffic accidents are the number one cause of death for foreigners overseas. Those solid lines in the middle of the street are suggestions. One-way streets can be two-way. There is always room for one more car in a lane built for two cars, or one more pedestrian, or one more bicycle, or one more mule and cart, or one more moped, or one more bicycle cart carrying bottles of gasoline. You may even see a cow walking down the sidewalk. The city has 6 million people, but you still may see a cow. Very strange. Not many dogs though, especially around restaurants! Ha!

To cross the street here as a pedestrian the rule is, "Don't look before you cross." If you make eye contact with a driver, he knows you see him, so it is your fault if he hits you. If you don't see him, it is his responsibility not to hit you. Something about that doesn't make sense to the American mind, but it works around here.

I love you and Daddy so much. It is weird being so far away. Dr. G's words, "The closest distance between you and anywhere in the world is on your knees," has become clearer to me. I don't think my love for my family can possibly grow any more. This first month here has been great. Liz from Great Britain and I will take the night train to my new home next week. No great miracles to report. I do feel that my faith is growing. I'm not feeling my niche yet and still unsure exactly why I'm here. But I just take one day at a time, like you always used to tell me to do, and ask God to use me however He desires. I'm not here for my purposes and dreams or to have great stories to impress people with; I'm just here to be obedient. And we will see what happens. I love you!

August 18, 2000—I will live in a part of the world where 100 million people have never heard the story of Jesus Christ. I am hungry to know Him intimately. I have left the comfort of home, family, mentors, and friends—people who love me and stood so faithfully near me.

August 22, 2000—I arrived in my new city yesterday. The mountains surrounding the campus are beautiful. As I rode from the train to the university, I was suddenly reminded of the words, "Shout, for the Lord has given you the city" (Jos. 6:16). It was an amazing moment, and I will stand on that promise.

August 24, 2000—Before I arrived here, I prayed for joy. I have so much joy here! Not overwhelming happiness, just an inner joy that makes inconveniences seem not so bad. It is a quiet peace which helps me keep moving forward. I guess it comes from doing and being in God's will. I love it here. It is now 9:00 p.m., and the power has been off since 2:00 p.m. (happens a lot). I am sitting here with three candles to write these words. Thankfully, the stove is gas, so I am boiling water (It is my specialty, you know!) I decided to seize the moment and make hot chocolate. Mom packed some in my suitcase.

August 25, 2000—My walk from my home to classroom/office is a brisk fifteen minutes one way. But it is quite different than a fifteen-minute walk at UTA or other universities. I start by walking down a rocky brick slope for quite a while. Then I walk on a concrete street, dodging wet spots and manure trucks (someone has to haul it). Then I smile at children and get stared at a lot. Then I keep on walking and end up back on a dirt path. I go through a brick archway that has little rooms in it. I pass a lot of cave houses and shacks and apartments and class buildings and a couple of gardens, and get stared at a little more; then I am there.

September 3, 2000—Another extremely packed bus ride today! By the time I got to my stop, I was thinking about the old commercial, "Aren't you glad you use Dial? Don't you wish everybody did?" Actually, in this city you are more likely to wish everyone used Listerine, but that is a thought for another day.

September 5, 2000—Yesterday, I killed five spiders and a centipede. Today I killed another centipede. Both times I feel like God caused me to see them so I could kill them. But I am a little scared and freaked out. I have holes everywhere in my apartment.

I called Dad. He and Mom will mail some canned foam to me so I can seal all the holes. I hope I receive that package. Of the last seven letters Mom and Dad have mailed, I received the last two. The post office is working at a 2/7 ratio of success. Unacceptable in the twenty-first century! Better get used to it.

September 6, 2000—I am terrified of all the bugs and mice. Again, I better get used to it. Today I took up my students' journals and read them. They can write about anything they want. Evidently there is a mouse problem in the dorm. One night three mice ran around the room, even jumping on beds, terrifying my students. (Eight people share a tiny dorm room here.) The girls were afraid to go to sleep, so they stayed awake as long as possible until they couldn't fight it off anymore. Then at least one of them had nightmares, because she wrote about it in her journal. Here I am in a two-bedroom apartment (however primitive by American standards) all by myself, making more money in one month than some people in this city make in a year, and I am fretting over a harmless centipede and spiders that actually kill other bugs! I need to get my act together and stop being a spoiled American.

September 11, 2000—Today and yesterday were good days. I went to the legal church with three students to help translate for me. The really cool thing that happened was that the sermon was for me, but I understood less than anyone else in the room. The text was Matthew 6, about not worrying over clothes or food because God will take care of you. The night before I had been earnestly praying for some warm clothes to arrive from back home soon, and my food was getting very low, but I can't get around town yet. It is very scary without a car, a sense of direction and a handle of the language. So I prayed about it. When the lady preached the text, it reminded me that God will meet these needs. Then we had free lunch supplied by the church!

Today after my class, I wanted to go get some fruit. Near my apartment is an open air market. I had been there once with Liz and remembered it being loud and scary and me not being able to communicate. I made myself go alone today. I was terrified as I walked toward the market area. People stared at me, of course. I went to an apple cart and showed him two fingers, but he didn't understand, so I just started picking up apples. I handed them to him and he put them in a bag and set it on a really old-fashioned thing and told me the price, but I didn't understand him. I ended up buying five apples and just handing him two kwi (0.25). I stood there and he didn't yell at me for more or give me change, so I said thanks and walked away, hoping he wouldn't yell at me for more money. Next I bought two potatoes. It's so scary not being able to understand them. They tell you the price and you just have to hand them money, not knowing how much it really is. Eggs were next. I bought six. Eggs don't have to be refrigerated. In fact, they don't have to be in cartons. The man just had them piled in his cart, sitting in the sun, near the whole chickens for sale. I paid two kwi for them. Then I left, thanking God that nobody laughed or yelled at me, although I was probably ripped off by at least one of them.

Saturday, a lot of the senior male students had to move off campus to a new building, a fifteen-minute walk away in order to make room for the newly arriving freshmen. The condition of these dorms is horrible. No water. The boys live on the fifth floor. To get cold water only, they have to go outside and carry up clean water. In one room, thirty-six guys live there together, with no doorknob on their door, so all their stuff is vulnerable. These are difficult living conditions.

~

September 18, 2000—This morning, I was jolted awake with these words, "Jamie, what do you want to do after here?" I realized I don't care where I go next, what I do next, or who I do it with, just so I can be close to Him. After all, He asked me to go to the end of the world, out in the sticks, away from my family, friends, language, community, and food, and I am happy. He has proven to me that as long as I am with Him, what I do and where I go is of no consequence. He will lead me wherever, but what He really wants is to draw me closer to Him. The place isn't as important as His closeness to me. I can survive and thrive as long as He goes with me. "And surely I am with you always, to the very end of the age" (Mt. 28:20).

Actually, this city is becoming my comfort zone. I love living in this apartment alone. I love my students. I love teaching. I love having a humble office. I like learning the language and the culture, and I'm learning to like all the noodles and the food. The living conditions are doable. The staring hasn't killed me yet, and the insects are generally friendly. I love it here. It is my second home.

September 21, 2000—Happy birthday to my beautiful sister! All day long I have thought about her. I hope her first birthday as a married woman is her best yet!

Tuesday was an interesting day. I was studying a book in the garden with two students when all of a sudden my hair started blowing and papers rustled. People began running for shelter. I looked in the distance and saw a dust cloud blowing. I tried to shield my eyes from the dust because I wanted to watch everything. We sat there and watched people run for cover when it dawned on me—if the natives were taking cover, so should I! I learned later that this was a minor dust storm. The more powerful ones are in the spring.

Wednesday was amazing. Last week in European Culture Class, I asked for four volunteers who would like to act out a skit in class this week. Mary, Noah, Lacy, and Joe (I give my students American names) volunteered, so I gave them their roles: Eve, God, the snake, and Adam. They came to my office on Friday, and I explained the significance of the story to them, complete with the first promise of a Savior found in Genesis chapter 3. The students and I planned for about an hour. They were very interested in showing the emotions of the characters. They asked for my input, but they insisted on planning the skit themselves, which impressed me.

On Wednesday, they put on a first-rate production that was the best interpretation of the fall I have ever seen. I sat in the audience and was amazed at the beauty of their presentation. They started with the creation of man. Noah (God) interpreted it so beautifully. Soft instrumental music played in the background, and Noah squatted on the stage, scooped some imaginary dirt in his hand, and beautifully and lovingly made motions as if he were making a clay sculpture. The expression on his face was of genuine love and concern for his creation. He gently formed the head and body, even putting eyes where they should be. He did this so tenderly to the music, as if he were performing in a human video at nationals. Then he took his imaginary man behind the podium, bent to where no one could see him, and then stood up, holding the hand of Adam (Joe). God and Adam walked hand in hand on the stage. The students interrupted the scene with clapping when Adam appeared. They thought it was very creative. The creation of man portrayed there—a God so loving, carefully forming each part of the man, and walking with him hand in hand—is so different from what these students have been taught all their lives in school—that man is just a glob of tissue that just appeared, a little bit more than a monkey. What a contrast! I hope they noticed it.

After the creation, Adam named all the animals. One by one, the "horse," "bird,"…ran/flew across the stage. The girls did a wonderful job of acting like animals. I had offered to let them use some small animal figurines that I have, but they insisted on acting out the parts themselves! It was really funny, and the audience obviously agreed with me.

Then came woman. Adam lay down on the large podium, sleeping. God, to beautiful music, gently took a rib and began to shape it with his hands. He shaped and shaped, lovingly forming every curve with eyes so intently focused on His creation. Then he reached down behind the podium and out came Eve. She looked at Adam, sleeping so peacefully, and loved him. Then she laid her head at his side. It was so tender and innocent. Adam awoke, saw Eve, and was quite surprised, but he loved her. They walked through the garden together, to beautifully romantic music. Eve had the grace of a ballerina. She beautifully danced around the stage to show her happiness, and Adam, dumbstruck with love, followed her, dancing with his Eve. I will never forget them doing ballet together across the stage.

Then, tragically, Adam left the scene, and in came the snake. Eve stood at the tree, and the snake, with a wicked laugh, tempted her, telling her eating the fruit would make her as wise as God. She contemplated the decision, thinking out loud, and the suspense grew. Would she eat the apple? Finally, she ate it. The snake left, laughing quietly at her triumph. Adam came back. When he saw the partly eaten apple, his face fell with disappointment. "Eve, what have you done? Now you will die." "No," she said. "I ate the apple, and I am not die! I am not die! I am alive!" She convinced Adam to eat one too, so he too could be as smart as God. Adam ate the apple, and it was as if lightning struck, because terrible music suddenly blared from the player. He looked up from the juicy apple, and his eyes met Eve's. Their eyes got big, and they ran from shame to opposite ends of the stage, embarrassed because they were naked.

Then came God. "Adam, Adam, where are you?" Adam finally came out, his coat tied around his waist like a loincloth (over his pants of course). Eve came out, her sweater tied around her waist. The audience roared with laughter. God called the snake and ordered her on her belly. As he spoke, the snake cringed in terror and hate in God's presence; then she slinked away. God pronounced punishment on Adam and Eve and then said, "Get out." And the story was finished. The students and I loved it! It almost moved me to tears. They showed the account so well—God, the loving creator and holy friend, Adam and Eve in love and perfect peace and joy in the garden, and the wicked serpent, bent on destroying mankind. Wow! If only I had a video camera!

September 25, 2000—Sunday was church again. It was raining and I was very tired, not wanting to go. It is really a sacrifice to go when you don't understand it, but it is important for several reasons. First, students always want to come translate. Secondly, it shows the students that church is my priority, which is a foreign concept in their minds. I left the apartment at 8:20 and arrived at the church at 9:15. Buses aren't exactly famous for their speed. I had to sit in the back, the only available seats. At one point, I guess the driver decided to make up for lost time, so he sped up, which made my ride uncomfortably bumpy. Then, he hit a pothole, and I flew into the air. The jolt back to earth really hurt my back. So going to church became even more of a sacrifice.

Today, I received my application to apply for an absentee voting ballot that Mom sent. I have to mail it back immediately, but alas! That means I must go to the post office. I won't have any classes in the morning, so I have to go then when my students have classes. In other words, I will have to go alone. I am afraid. A friend made me a map with Chinese characters in case I get lost, so I can just point to them, but I am scared. What if I get lost? What if people stare at me until I just melt away into the ground and die? It is bad going to town with one foreigner friend, but at least people can stare at either one. But going alone? I will have their complete attention—100 percent of it. I am nervous, but I must go to become independent. I have been here five weeks, and I must be brave. May God help me, but if I don't return ever again, and if this is my last journal entry, just know it was the staring that killed me!

~

September 26, 2000—"I live on the third floor of the caves, so if you have time, please come to my cave." These words were said to me by an old professor as we parted after walking together on the sidewalk. I had just returned from a successful and painless trek to town. He is a fellow teacher in the department, and when he saw me, he began to walk with me, as we were going the same direction. I couldn't resist writing down his words in my journal. This is the only place in the world someone would invite you to his cave!

The generosity of the people here is striking. On Sunday, the preacher spoke from Matthew 25 about helping those in need. She said that they should give to the poor because in doing so, they are giving to Jesus. I looked around the room and saw people, peasants wearing the same clothes they wear every Sunday, and very old shoes. Looking at their wrinkled, worn faces and yellow stained teeth, I thought, *These people are in need. They are poor.* Yet, the preacher is encouraging them to give to others. Sometimes the poor are like the widow with the mite; they are the most generous of anyone.

It is obvious that I survived my trek to the post office. I got off the bus where I was supposed to and began to walk to the post office. I was afraid, because I had to walk by about fifty idle men standing on the corner. They stand there hoping someone will come and hire them, just like in the parable in Matthew 20. That many men standing around was intimidating, so I just looked straight ahead, ignoring the stares, and mustered a "don't mess with me" look. (I learned it in Dallas.) No one did mess with me! (Maybe it wasn't my look, but my angel walking beside me.) I followed my map, crossing intersections where it is acceptable to stop at green lights and go on red. I misunderstood the map a little, but I backtracked and made it to the post office, where I successfully got postage for my American letters and postcards. I can't explain the feeling of accomplishment I had as I slid the letters in the mail slot. Thank You, God!

~

October 11, 2000—I received letter #7 and package #11 from Mom and Dad today. I am so amazed by their generosity. Very few parents, even good parents in the family, would help me as much as they are. I am wearing the warm long underwear right now, and they feel so good. They even sent caulk to seal holes in my apartment walls!

The good news is they're numb; the bad news is they're many. The last few days, flies have been pouring into my apartment. Right now it is sixty-four degrees in my room, warmer than outside, but still cold. The flies swarm in to be warm, and I can swat all day and kill many of them. Their joints must be frozen together. Mine sure are!

~

October 21, 2000—My students ask me so many questions about what I believe. I can answer their questions, but cannot openly proselytize. Many questions come following my culture class. Yesterday, I told my seventy-five students about John 3:16; it was in their textbook. I also got to tell them all about my best Friend. The book talked about Him, but not about His resurrection, only

His death. Hmmm. I completed the account to the students. I intended to let them get out of class early, but they started asking questions in front of the whole class to clarify their understanding. I tried to be wise. One question in particular: If God loved the world, why did He send His Son and not Himself? I gave an answer that Brother Steve told me in children's church when I was about eight years old. "Fathers love their sons more than themselves, so it was a bigger sacrifice to send His Son."

October 24, 2000—Well, my grade three students did very poorly on a writing assignment. I had warned them not to misspell words or make grammatical errors, but they must have not taken me seriously. Yesterday, I gave their bad grades to them along with a lecture, in which I let them know I was angry at their carelessness and lack of diligence. I found out today that they complained to the dean of the department about me! But he said I was doing good to be strict with them! Hee Hee!

November 11, 2000—On Saturday, I went mountain climbing with three guys and three girls. We walked up the slope behind the school, carrying a picnic feast with us. We passed several tombs and graves along the way. One of the senior guys assured me that I need not fear the ghosts, even though we were walking by several graves, because the sun was shining. Many here believe that spirits of the dead stay on earth as ghosts. We kept walking. We stopped on a flat area on the second highest peak. They wanted to go further, but their American teacher was tired. We spread newspapers on the ground and sat, admiring the view. Before us were many hills covered with dirt. Hills and valleys were all around us. Some hills were cut into terraces for potato farming. In the distance, I could see a small village in a valley. It was beautiful. No trees, though, because the people have destroyed the environment trying to survive without thinking about the future. Everyone started taking out their food to share—cats' ears (chips shaped as ears, very crispy, and luckily not really feline), roasted dried small round beans, jello (they don't eat it cold here), oranges, pears, apples, very spicy homemade crackers, chestnuts, and my American chocolate contribution. The chocolate was a hit but not to one guy. He took a Reese's peanut butter cup in his hand and said, "American chocolate" to himself as if he was excited to try the real deal. But when he put it in his mouth, his face betrayed his taste buds. He jumped up, ran to the edge of the hill, and spat it out. Dad, is that a sin to spit out a Reese's? It should be!

After we ate, it happened. The leader of our group (Yes, we had a leader today; these people are really into leaders) suggested someone sing a song. They seem to always do this at their parties. Different ones sang in their native language and in English. Then they asked me to sing. Telling them you can't sing does no good, so I sang "Santa Claus Is Coming to Town." Then one of them asked me to sing a religious Christmas song, so I sang "Joy to the World."

November 12, 2000—Today I've been here four months, and I haven't seen my mom or dad in 122 days. A week ago I saw something that touched me. A man was driving his cart down the school's road, letting an old woman holding a large plastic bag have a ride in the cart. The woman's face was haggard and worn. Her clothes had had many wears, and her shoes were in shreds. As I walked by the cart, Coke in hand, suddenly the woman yelled at the driver. She jumped out of the cart, ran down the road and onto the soccer field where she picked up a small piece of plastic to sell. She is one of several elderly ladies who creep around the campus, looking in trash cans barehanded, and taking out the plastic and cardboard. In her mind, she found a prize on the soccer field, for every piece of plastic was important to her. I watched the old lady briskly walk back to the man and his cart. I looked at the almost empty bottle in my hand, poured it out on the ground, and ran to her with my bottle. She thanked me. Today, I read in Luke's gospel about Lazarus and the rich man. Lazarus lived at the rich man's gate, and all he asked for was the rich man's scraps. Looking around me, I have Lazarus everywhere. I must open my eyes, see Lazarus and give, for I am the rich man here.

On Tuesday, November 5, we had our first snow, and it wasn't melting the instant it touched the ground like in East Texas. The snow was sticking and turning everything white. A few friends and I decided to have a little fun. We went to an area between the dining hall and dormitories. Innocent students unaware were walking around the corner of the dorm, soup bowls in hand, headed for suppertime. Waiting on the other side of the corner were me and my friends with a fair supply of snowballs. We began hitting students, one by one, some we knew and many we didn't. Some ran and squealed. Others stopped, scooped up some snow, and hit us. This lasted about thirty minutes. Many students were surprised that the foreigner was hitting them. Our biggest mistake of the fight was hitting a few little boys. They banded together like an army, made snowballs, and ran toward me, all at once, screaming and laughing. They had really good aim. When the fight was over, I walked home and looked in the mirror. I was covered with snowflakes. My hair was caked with snow. I was a real live snow-woman! As a result of our snow fight on Tuesday, for the next few days I couldn't walk safely across campus without having to dodge snowballs. Everyone remembered being hit by the foreigner, so I was an easy identifiable target for revenge for the remainder of the snow days. However, I can hold my own.

~

December 12, 2000—You know you're here when you see kids playing ping-pong at night by the light of candles sitting on the ping-pong table. You know you're here when you're wearing two pairs of long johns (tops and bottoms), a shirt, a turtleneck, a sweatshirt, an overcoat, two pairs of gloves, a scarf, jeans, two pairs of socks, and snow boots, and you're still cold. You know you're here when one person's (me) Christmas card list wipes out the stamp supply at the main post office of three hundred thousand people.

Today, Mom's e-mail said she wanted to let me know my friend, Zepha, has moved to a new address, 317 Niah. Mom is very creative! She has this talking and writing in code thing down! "The Lord your God is with you, the Mighty Warrior who saves. He will take great delight in you; in his love he will no longer rebuke you, but will rejoice over you with singing" (Zeph. 3:17).

~

December 21, 2000—Once a band nerd, always a band nerd! Last night, as I was walking to my apartment, I heard the familiar strains of "Edelweiss" from *The Sound of Music* filling the winter air. As I walked along, I realized that the music was coming from several instruments, if in fact, you can call it music. The discordant notes reminded me of my days in the Junior High East band—and even worse—the Dunbar Intermediate band. I cringed as I listened to their notes clashing together as I am sure their director was also doing. But as I cringed, I felt so warm inside. The acrimonious tune was actually music to my ears. I traced the sounds to their source where I saw several people sitting in a row blowing horns. I stopped and listened, straining to see in the second floor window, although it was far away, and cherishing every note. To have a French horn again, to play in an orchestra to make music like days gone by—this is my desire.

December 24, 2000—All day, no power, no heat, and no water. A student wanted to take me to dinner for Christmas, but the tiny restaurant had no electricity, only red candles. Much to my chagrin, she ordered mushroom noodles. When the waiter brought them to us, I saw those little meatballs floating that I call "dog-food-flavored mystery meat." We had nothing to drink because they couldn't heat the water without electricity. No water for my mystery meat. My student, thinking the mystery meat is the best part of the noodles, put one of her meatballs into my bowl with her chopsticks. (I haven't used a fork in over five months now). This is a very cultural thing to do when you host someone for dinner. Oh my. I ate, thinking, *Jesus, this is for you,* as I chewed. Somehow I survived, almost vomiting as I walked home. It was a stretch, but it meant so much to me that she wanted to treat me to Christmas dinner. It made it finally feel a little like Christmas, even though Mom never serves mystery meat. She prefers turkey or ham.

Christmas Day, 2000—It finally happened today. After all the many near misses in little red taxis, the collision was a surprise. I just knew it would be another close call, but not this time. The big blue truck hit the taxi on my side, hurting my shoulder. I got out of the taxi and walked away. It could have been a lot worse. A bruise and whiplash. I will survive.

# CHAPTER 11

## *2001*

Our Journals:

January 21, 2001—Jamie called and asked us to pray for her as she is smuggling Bibles in boxes of clothes.

~

January 22, 2001—While in another city today, I went to the store to get some food for the next two weeks. I got my food, put it into a broken basket and went to the checkout line. I couldn't get to the register because people kept cutting in front of me! In America, cutting in front of someone is rude, but it's called survival here. At one point, I literally had my basket on the counter next to the register, and ladies walked in front of me and put their food on the counter. Then their friends passed stuff to them from behind me. I stood there and glared at one of the ladies, but I didn't know how to argue, and I'm too kind to push someone out of the way. It was terrible. I waited forever for a taxi or bus too. Even an old man cut in front of me when I was waiting for the taxi. All I could think of during this traumatizing time was how much I hate it here! I'm the politest person in this city! Of course, God instilled in me the heart of a finisher—not a quitter. I finally returned home.

I asked God why He sent me here. I'm so imperfect. There I was, hating everyone around me in a place that He called me to, a place that yesterday I was ready to take by storm. Then I realized that God sends imperfect people who are willing, because He gets glory through us. "That is why, for Christ's sake, I delight in weaknesses, in insults, in hardships, in persecutions, in difficulties. For when I am weak, then I am strong" (2 Cor. 12:10). And I'll try, by God's grace, to love these pushy people tomorrow.

January 27, 2001—Today, I went downtown and walked to the Internet café. A little boy walked up to me and asked me for money. I said no. He grabbed my leg and kept asking for money. I kept on walking, but he kept walking with me, touching me, asking for money. Finally he gave up and went away. I almost never give money to beggars because they do it all the time instead of working. And often a parent teaches their child to beg and puts them on the streets for that purpose. I have learned the hard way that when I do break down and give something, I am quickly inundated with multiple beggars. It is a horrible social problem, but giving pocket change won't help it.

January 31, 2001—(written in the margin of Jamie's Bible by Psalm 25)

This Psalm is exactly what I need today, the day I found out he is engaged. Thank you, Jesus!

February 2, 2001—Two days ago, I was told he is engaged. It really caused me a lot of pain. But that night I read my Bible and prayed about it. I decided that I wasn't going to let what he does dictate my feelings or actions. I am going to use these two years to the best of my ability to know God more and to see this city changed. I feel so much grace right now. A year ago, or six months ago, I would have been depressed. But God has strengthened me and prepared me for this and other challenges. Within about ten minutes of the time I found out about him, my Aunt Ollie died. I am happy for her. She has wanted to be in heaven for so long. I also take her death as a symbol for him. He is dead to me now, just as Aunt Ollie is dead to this world.

February 13, 2001—A discussion I had with a friend reminds me again how difficult it is to accept a religion viewed as "foreign." Though she is actively seeking, though she has had several genuine Christian friends encouraging her, and though she has found an answer to satisfy her, she still hesitates to embrace Christianity because it would mean, to her, letting go of her parents and a part of her culture. She has so many things in her favor, so much more than most of my students, yet she hasn't crossed the line. What am I trying to do? This job is too hard for human strength alone. I need guidance, wisdom, and anointing to reach these students. If I can reach them, He can pull them across the barricades of doubt and hesitation.

February 14, 2001—Valentine's Day. It's a special day. Today marks seventeen years since I was first baptized in the Holy Spirit! That eight-year-old girl speaking in tongues as she brushed her teeth had no clue that seventeen years later she would be on the other side of the world! Amazing!

Today, Lawrence called me at 9:00 a.m. to wish me a Happy Valentine's Day. He's such a good friend, more like a second dad. I also got a Valentine card from Mawmaw and Janet and a letter from Nat and Heather. Dad called to tell me he loves me. I was so happy. He put a package in the mail for me, but it hasn't arrived yet. It will get here! He always gives me chocolate on Valentine's Day. The fact that all these precious people remembered me today is so special to me. That's what this day is all about!

I guess I should briefly record my feelings about him. I recently found out that he isn't dating anyone anymore. He told me that via e-mail and encouraged me to call him or e-mail him. I have decided not to think about him much while I am here, not to lose my focus over him. I feel very strongly that I am in the right place at the right time, so why should I waste time worrying about someone on the other side of the pond? I have decided this and am sticking to it. Maybe he will be in my future—maybe not—but it's no concern of mine at this moment.

I ate fish head the other day but not the brains or eyes. Sorry, but I'm learning my limitations. I also ate two-foot-long noodles and lotus root (the root of a lily pad). Actually lotus root is becoming one of my favorite "veggies" here, if you can call it that. Two days later, I was puking—morning, noon, and night—food poisoning. No more fish head for me! That does it! I don't need that lesson twice!

February 12, 2001—I received an e-mail from Jamie yesterday. He had e-mailed her and said that his girlfriend had broken up with him. "Dear God, please guard Jamie's heart; don't let her be hurt again."

February 15, 2001—As my friends from high school know, if a person gives me a word, I can tell them instantly how many letters are in it. Of course, no one here knows about this talent. Last night, when I was talking to one of my students, she told me she had a special ability. If you give her a Chinese word, she can tell you how many strokes of the pen it takes to make the word! It is the same as my talent, only since these words have no letters, she knows the number of strokes! I was so shocked that I found someone on the other side of the world with my same "unique" talent.

~

February 21, 2001—I have been so sick for one week now. I called Mom and she put me on the church prayer chain.

Something really cool happened. I have been trying to hear Pastor Todd's tapes, but I couldn't get my tape player to work. I tried one more time yesterday, praying that it would come on, and it did. He was saying that it doesn't matter in what circumstance we find ourselves, we can have joy and God is always with us. Then the tape faded out and would not say anything else. I took that as a miracle, a special message from God to me. I went to bed knowing that as I slept, many people were praying for me. I slept better than I had the last six days.

I had a dream. In my dream, I was walking down the road, and five men, knowing I was a preacher, tried to kidnap me. Suddenly, a giant brown bear sprang from the woods, scared them away, and I woke up, safe and sound. Immediately I knew the dream had a meaning: God will always protect me. For over a week now, the Holy Spirit has been telling me, "When the enemy shall come in like a flood, the Spirit of the Lord shall lift up a standard against him" (Isa. 59:19, KJV).

The dream also reminds me of something Dr. H told me years ago. "Often when someone has a big call on their life, the enemy comes against them strongly to keep them from that call." Since before I got sick, I have felt like I am being tested big time, like I am going through the furnace, facing trials and temptations. The sickness is only part of it, but I can see God moving and helping me through it all for the better. This isn't a setback in the new semester. God can use it all in His plan for my good and His glory in this city.

February 22, 2001—My first class today was pathetic. They were so pathetically unresponsive. I told them they were a bunch of bumps on a log. I wrote it on the board without explaining it. Maybe they will figure it out sooner or later. Or maybe they just don't care about my class.

What they do care about is the Band 4 test of English, a nationwide exam that is worth more than their four-year diploma in English. If they don't pass the test, they say they won't get a good job. So they choose to spend hours with their nose in a book about English instead of *using* English.

I think they think my class isn't about the test, so why bother? I take that personally. They better start caring and respecting my class, or they will not pass, even if I have to fail every single one of them. One student told me that after the May 9th exam, he will practice his English conversation. He's dreaming. If he doesn't work in my class until then, he will fail so hard that he will never catch up. They ain't seen nothin' yet!

I hated blow-off classes and teachers that I couldn't respect in high school and college. I refuse to let my class be a blow-off one. It's time for some good old-fashioned pop tests to get their attention.

March 4, 2001—I have learned that the father of one of my students is a pastor in another city and has been giving Bibles to his son to give to other students. In fact, this student wrote the entire Bible by hand twice when he was younger for his father. Bibles don't grow on trees around here. "Listen, my dear brothers and sisters: Has not God chosen those who are poor in the eyes of the world to be rich in faith and to inherit the kingdom he promised those who love him?" (Jas. 2:5).

~

March 11, 2001—I ate pig stomach today without flinching. Okay, I only ate one piece, but it was with a great poker face. I wish I had it on video.

Mom, when you come here and go to church with me, be sure you sit in the middle of a bench. As I have said before, everything here is a group effort. That includes standing and sitting on benches. If the person at one end of the bench gets up whenever she wants, the person at the other end has an embarrassing fall. So the two people on the ends coordinate their movements. I learned this the hard way, of course.

~

March 11, 2001—Jamie is doing well. She recently led one of her students to the Lord. One seventh of her goal!

~

March 20, 2001—On Sunday afternoon, we went to town with students to eat. There are always a lot of people standing around selling things like tomatoes, fruit, shoe insoles, and paper grasshoppers. All of a sudden, the ladies with their baskets started hurrying away down the sidewalk to a new location. The tax man was coming! Every once in a while, a man comes to collect taxes from the vendors. But they see him coming and flee to another street before he finds them. It's very amusing.

One of my students bought a grasshopper for me made of bamboo paper. I don't know what I'll do with it, but it is the thought that counts. While I waited for her to bargain for the grasshopper, I was surrounded by three little children beggars carrying bowls which they put in front of me. It was pitiful. I was eating the most expensive kind of ice cream in the city (from Britain), so I couldn't refuse them. It was very sad. Today in town, I saw a crippled girl who wanted money. She had no shoes, and her toes were warped and her feet turned in. I heard that some parents actually break their child's feet so they can beg for them. That is macabre.

Yesterday, when I prayed for God to send more workers here, I felt like maybe I should stay here in the future, longer than these two years. I can't shake the feeling. I'm not certain. I will listen more and wait for confirmation. I have only told Mom and Dad. I know it will be harder to say yes next time, because I no longer have an idealistic view of this nation. I will understand the sacrifice more when I say yes. But if I am called, then yes, I will answer.

March 25, 2001—Today, I went with four students to a restaurant where we had an excellent meal for US$10.00. The manager was so happy to see a foreigner there that she asked for permission to take an action shot of me eating her food. Tomorrow, I'll probably be on buses advertising her food. I can just see a big picture of me plastered on the side of a double-decker bus. The price of being a celebrity!

April 9, 2001—So, Mom, please take money out of my account and start sending me one English book a month, and mail it to "Renee." They can fit in an envelope. If you send one a month, beginning now, it will be great. Make it the Good News Version. Please try to bring two in your suitcase and carry-on bag as well. If you are uncomfortable, bring one. Please! Just continue this until I get home next summer. Please start as soon as possible.

This is worth spending my personal money for. There is nothing better to spend it on.

April 11, 2001—I do want to say one more thing. About three weeks ago, I was praying for more workers to come here. I felt like God's answer may have been, "You." I am not sure, but I am praying about it. I know if He wants me to stay, He will make it clear to me. Before, I came here out of obedience alone. Not because of a love for this nation or its people did I agree to go, but because I heard him say, "Go." Now, my prayer is, "Let me stay. They need workers. Please let me stay here." We will see what His answer is.

April 26, 2001—Something exciting happened Tuesday in my conversation class. I had each student blindly choose an English cultural quotation and explain it to the class in a short speech. Lilly chose "Love Conquers All." Her speech was about how in the past she never said she was sorry. She was fiercely independent, but this semester she has a friend whom she knows loves her. She follows her friend and he gives her strength, so now she can love others and admit when she is wrong. "I cannot tell you my friend's name. It is a secret." But I put two and two together, although no one else in the room probably did. I watched her giving her speech, trying to hold back her emotion as if she were close to crying. It reminded me more of testimony time than a speech in a Communist country's classroom. I still hope to talk with her soon, but I have a feeling she has crossed over!

May 1, 2001—I think Sissy has become a Christian. Terri has really talked to her a lot lately. Some of her friends have asked her, "Why are you so happy now?" She told them, "Because I have God in my heart." And she is trying to help her friend. In fact, she let her friend borrow her Bible. I wanted to chat with her this week, but the opportunity for privacy never availed itself. It sounds to me like she has made the decision. How exciting! Prayer works miracles.

And I'm seeing students pray for their friends and family and share their faith with others. God is putting His heart for the lost in these students. This is the way it should be, everyone operating in their sphere of influence, and young Christians sowing, watering, and harvesting. They can have much more impact on their friends than foreigners. The snowball effect is coming! I now know of eleven people on campus who are Christian (three of which God allowed me to plant seed into their lives, water, and harvest). It's a small percentage on this campus of about four thousand students. There's more to come!

May 22, 2001—Monday morning at 1:00, I was awakened by a storm. Wide awake, I began to pray for Jamie. I woke Gene up and we prayed for Jamie, that God would surround her as with a shield. She called me at the church this morning and she was sick from something she ate. I asked her what she was doing at 2:00 p.m. on her Monday. She said she was involved in a struggle; she knew exactly why I had prayed for a shield.

June 3, 2001—You never know what you'll see here. I have seen more men and children using the bathroom on the side of the street than I care to remember. Yes, having bathrooms "anywhere you want" is certainly convenient, but I get tired of seeing their convenience so vividly! Yesterday I saw a woman stop on the nice steps to a store, waiting for her little boy to relieve himself on the steps as a hundred people walked by. At least that was better than the little boy at the school squatting, pants down in the dirt doing you know what. But as he did it, he played in the dirt right next to him with his hands. And only here will you see what I saw today, a taxi pulled over on the side of the road, empty. For some strange reason, I looked for the driver, of course seeing him (back toward the road) taking a pit stop. It reminded me of the story a friend told us about asking a lady where the "comfort room" (that's what they call it in Thailand) was. "Anywhere you please," she said politely. This is why I never wear sandals.

A couple of friends visited my campus and had a chat with several students. One of them asked the students if they had questions for him. Bill said he had a comment. He believes that all religions worship the same God. Buddhists, Muslims, and Christians all worship the same God and all will be saved. My friend thanked him for his opinion. Then he talked about travelling to Beijing and needing to be on the right road to get there, that all roads don't end up at the same place. Bill and the others listened intently.

That night my friends trained to another city. I was sad to tell them bye. They are such wonderful and funny people. Just before I told them bye, they each hugged me, and he told me he was proud of me and that I am doing a good job. Those words meant more to me than a million dollars. I will treasure them always. I can't imagine how it will be when Jesus says, "Well done, good and faithful servant." Those words will last me for eternity.

June 5, 2001—A phenomenon has occurred. In a land of few smiles (compared to Texas), people, especially children, are smiling at me as they pass. Yes, people still stare, but others smile at me very deliberately, recognizing me. It is mostly children, but not just children I have given candy to. They just see me and smile so big and say, "Hello!" They have always done this, but now they do it with a look of familiarity and friendship in their eyes. Even one of the old ladies who collects bottles for recycling saw me from a second floor balcony. I nodded and smiled at her, and she smiled back. The lady I buy Cokes and water from gave me free ice cream yesterday. These may sound unimportant, but it has taken living here nine and a half months for this to happen. It is as if they are seeing me as one of them.

The coolest thing happened yesterday in town. I was walking down a claustrophobic's nightmare corridor, passing people closely. All of a sudden, I saw an old lady who looked at me as she came toward me. I nodded politely to her, although I don't know her. She stopped in her tracks. And suddenly made the sign of the cross, Catholic style, and bowed her head and closed her hands, a symbol of prayer. I was so excited! I nodded my head, tried to make the sign of the cross, and I walked by. On a busy street, in a narrow corridor, in the middle of a city of three hundred thousand people, two Christians had met unexpectedly and felt the love for each other only found in the Body of Christ. Though we didn't know each other, the bond was real. In fact, age, culture, race, and social status didn't keep us apart because of Jesus's love. My theory is that she attends the Catholic Church, which is near our legal, government-regulated church. She has probably seen me walking to church on Sundays, so she knew I am her sister in Christ Jesus. Really, really cool!

~

June 6, 2001—Did I tell you I discovered a new American wannabe restaurant with pictures of hamburgers and French fries on the walls? They looked so delicious that I went inside and ordered. The owner was so excited to see a foreigner in his restaurant that he came and sat down beside me and asked to take pictures of me eating in his restaurant, and the food would be free! Free is a good thing! So I ate (fair, but not American), and I posed for his pictures. Well, I went back there today. Sure enough, there were three framed pictures of me with the restaurant staff. One picture is right above a picture of Tweety Bird! I have arrived! I can't wait to bring Mom here so she can get a picture of me in front of my picture! I'm famous!

Friday was Children's Day, so we had an open mike party at the English café, where anyone could offer entertainment as long as it was in English. For my second time here, I performed that oldie but goodie, "I'm a Little Teapot," with all the motions to go with it (my personal childhood favorite). When the crowd begged for more, I chose to sing, "There was a farmer had a dog, and Bingo was his name-o, B-I-N-G-O, B-I-N-G-O, B-I-N-G-O, and Bingo was his name-o." The school obviously doesn't pay me for my entertaining abilities!

June 12, 2001—I received an e-mail from Jamie yesterday. He has been e-mailing her; he wants to renew their relationship after four and a half years of heartache for Jamie. "Dear God, please don't allow Jamie to be hurt again."

June 18, 2001—Terri is having a difficult time. Her parents and school officials do not know she is a Christian. She is under so much pressure to join the party. When someone joins the party, they must sign a paper that says they will never become a Christian. She doesn't want to join. She risks so much if she tells them the truth. I am praying for her and others who face this same challenge.

June 20, 2001—He came to our home yesterday at 4:15 and stayed until 9:30. (Janet was home so she heard all this too.) He shared his heart and intentions regarding Jamie. He asked for our forgiveness. It has taken four and a half years, but he said he finally feels emotionally healthy after his mother's death. He wants to renew his relationship/friendship with Jamie. He answered "yes" when Gene asked him if he loves Jamie. He said he will never hurt her again.

~

June 25, 2001—Terri told her father that she is a Christian. At first he wasn't upset, but the more he thought about it and after school officials talked to him, he forbade her to be a Christian or to attend church. He knows that my friend and I have influenced her and threatened to run us out of the city. Much prayer is needed.

~

July 2, 2001—Yesterday, I was invited to another wedding. They had a big feast. Basically that is all there is to getting married—no vows, no officiate, just food and a party. Chicken gizzards aren't too bad, and donkey meat is especially good.

Today, I climbed a hill with one of my students. He wanted to talk about his future, possibly of being a pastor and how to know what God's will is. I got really sick about halfway up the hill, possibly because of what I ate last night and not eating anything this morning. So he goes back down the hill to get a bottle of water for me. The mountain was beautiful. It got hot, but it was worth it.

Afterward we had brunch at the school dining hall. He assumed I would want "American fast food." He bought, so I decided it was the right time to try an "American" hamburger. I knew the Ronald McDonald signs hanging on the walls were sick jokes, but I hoped they wouldn't be too sick. When I got my hamburger, I, as always, opened my bun to take off the lettuce. This turned out to be a big mistake, because opening my bun gave me a good look at the "beef" inside. It was two black, one centimeter thick, non-ground pieces of meat. I immediately asked for ketchup. The lady said they don't put ketchup on burgers, and I said, "America does!" And if any hamburger ever needed ketchup, it was this one! In fact, I used two packets on the burger. Heinz can cover a multitude of sins!

# CHAPTER 12

## *My Adventure*

My journal from my trip to Jamie's city, July 5–19, 2001:

Jamie met me at the airport. She was beautiful! The first thing I noticed was a thinner Jamie. I should have expected such, considering how much she has been sick from the food this first year. She is adjusting, however. I wonder what it will do to me. We boarded another plane.

We toured the Terra Cotta Warriors. Jamie endeavored to educate me as much as possible in ten days in the rich surrounding history and culture. No wonder she loves this place!

The taxi rides are an experience in themselves! "Oh, that was a close call!" "That wasn't a close call, Mom." "That was a close call." "That was not a close call." I say one inch from hitting another car, bus, taxi, bicycle, three-wheel thing, or person is close. Better than any roller coaster I've ever ridden!

We had to take an overnight train to Jamie's city. When we finally arrived at her apartment and walked inside, she gave me the not-so-grand tour. I became overwhelmed at the sight and started crying. I couldn't believe my daughter had lived in these conditions for the past year. I had never experienced such extreme poverty in all my life. She could not understand my tears. She told me she had cleaned and prepared so much for my visit. (This was the only time I cried. I think that's a pretty good record.) I was relieved to learn that she will be moving soon to a new and more updated apartment on campus. She highly suspects that a more sophisticated bug will be planted there.

Jamie explained the reason for so much dirt in the air, on the furniture, and in my ears. Over the years, the peasants have cut down all the trees to use as fuel. When the wind blows over the mountains, which is most of the time, it lifts the dirt and carries it everywhere. She has helped others in planting trees on the mountainsides to try to reforest and alleviate this problem. She can't open her windows or doors because of the dirt, flies, and rats. There is garbage everywhere on the streets.

People stare at us everywhere we go, but I never feel threatened. They're just curious. I met many of her students outside and inside the English department. They are so friendly. I can tell they love Jamie very much, and she loves them. I feel like a real celebrity here! Those who know Jamie are excited to meet her mother. They just never see foreigners here. She is building beautiful relationships. That must be done first. Sometimes it takes years and the love and efforts of others before someone actually comes to know the love of the Savior. Jamie is a big piece in the puzzle of many of her students' lives. She has fallen in love with this city and its people.

Jamie took me on my first bus ride in her city. What fun pushing our way through people and taking our lives in our hands while crossing streets! I held tightly to Jamie's arm. She was not going to lose me here! And Jamie's definition of a crowded bus is not the same as my definition of a crowded bus. I call having my nose in someone's armpit crowded. Jamie was sure we could have gotten ten more people on that bus. People often crawl through the windows to exit the bus! I love it! Every moment is a new adventure for me.

Whenever Jamie and I talk and pray together, we must do so in hushed tones, because she said her walls have ears. We speak quietly in code to each other. Even walking on the street, we are careful to speak (pray) softly with eyes open so as not to attract attention. I learned that it is always better to ere on the side of caution. She knows she cannot openly share her faith, but she can answer questions. And if a student asks enough questions, they may learn enough to make the biggest decision of their lives.

By the way, our American idea of university is not the same one in this city. It is a good day when the copy machine works here!

July 11, 2001—What a beautiful day! We met some of her students at seven this morning and went hill climbing behind the school. It is so beautiful there. There are tombs scattered everywhere and vegetable gardens wherever there is a little flat piece of land. The people in the area grow their own vegetables. One of Jamie's students introduced us to some of his friends who live in a cave house. They were very kind to let me film their home. Cave homes are holes dug into the mountain side many years ago. They cook outside near their door. There is a community toilet nearby. They must bring their water in buckets from town. This home was very neat with only one bed and personal items. We were told later that we were being followed by officers who asked some of the students why I was filming. They explained who I was and said it was for my personal use. I soon learned of the high possibility that we were being followed everywhere.

July 12, 2001—I went to the school's PE field at six thirty this morning to run. It has been several days since I ran. Many students were already playing basketball and volleyball. Others were running and walking around the field, older people as well. I ran ten times around the field (about two and a half miles) with some of Jamie's students. They were surprised and thought I may be getting tired. It felt good to run again. I went back to Jamie's apartment and stood under the shower (a big bucket I fill up with water first before taking out the plug). Next I sweep the water (yes, with a broom) into a hole in the floor. I forgot to mention that Jamie is blessed to have a Western toilet instead of a squatty potty (hole in the floor). Thank You, Jesus!

July 14, 2001—Her city I have seen this week is very poor, dirty, loud, and hardworking. Everything is much slower here, everything except the taxis and buses. They drive all over the street and blow their horns constantly. What will I see as I walk the streets this morning? Lots of children playing, babies with split pants (now I understand why shoes come off the second you step into someone's home), men hammering big rocks into little rocks, stares, people squatting (that's how they relax), men all in a circle brushing their teeth while squatting (dental hygiene leaves a lot to be desired here), and people setting up to sell their vegetables and other things for the day. Jamie and I have lunch and dinner appointments today, but I have my doubts if I can make it. I have the feeling Montezuma's revenge is finally catching up with me. Jamie says that is very common. I brought an arsenal of medicine. She says it won't help. That's encouraging!

July 15, 2001—Jamie says there are 800 million peasants here. This is the real Northern Asia, not what is commonly portrayed on television. I woke early this morning, thanking God for allowing me to come here. Today is my last day in Jamie's city. I will miss these people. I am asking God to never let me forget this week. I want to always remember these kind and warmhearted people and always remember to pray for the students I have had the privilege to meet.

We caught a bus that took us to the train station. From there we walked to the Three Self Church. I took a bottle of water and a sprite. Today will be the third day I haven't eaten, but I can't risk being sick on the train tonight. The small building on the ledge of the mountain was full of mostly older women; children are not permitted to attend. One of Jamie's students sat by me on the wooden bench with no back and translated. The building contained about two hundred very poor and uneducated people. I estimated the room to be about twenty feet wide and forty feet long. Two ladies carried in a small pump organ followed by a twelve member choir and two hours of singing the same songs over and over. Annette would have cringed at the sounds that came from that organ, but would have loved the worship as I did. It's the way they learn scripture. I had to keep wiping dust from the pages of my Bible as the wind blew through the open windows. This church has four women pastors, the leader they call grandma. Although I did not understand a word of the two-hour sermon on communion from the visiting male preacher who never moved from his spot, I sensed God's anointing and presence. It was a beautiful service and I praise God for this experience. I will never forget. Jamie says they dismissed early so everyone could eat the food they brought and then help build the new building. They have started digging into the mountainside, one bucket at a time. Everyone was so gracious. I received several gifts, one of which was hand-embroidered inner soles for my shoes.

July 17, 2001—The train station was so crowded. I almost got hit by a van; a Chinese lady pulled me out of the way. We then went to the post office to mail our souvenirs on ahead of us. What an ordeal! I started feeling sick from the heat, so I sat with our bags most of the time. Jamie bought some newspaper to wrap everything in. You have to wrap packages at the post office because they have to see everything you are sending. So Jamie and one of her students wrapped every piece in newspaper. The lady at the window didn't like it. She wanted them to wrap everything in toilet paper, so Lilly went to buy toilet paper while Jamie watched the stuff. After almost two hours at the post office, the box finally got mailed.

Jamie flew with me to Beijing to catch my flight home. We walked around yesterday evening and last night. It is beautiful here, and yes, there are lots of people everywhere. We walked through the Forbidden City. We had to push our way through crowds to see anything, but that's what everyone does here. Jamie got frustrated with taxi drivers trying to rip her off. She refuses to budge with taxi drivers, so we jumped out of taxis a lot and summoned others down. I bet I've ridden in a hundred taxis since arriving here! I did some of my best praying in the backseat of those taxis, because I thought death must surely be imminent. I will never ride in another little red taxi as long as I live!

One thing I learned and remember to this day because I said it so many times was, "Ting bu dong," which means, "I don't understand."

We went to the silk market. Jamie is such a good bargainer. She just walks away if they don't come down to her price. They usually go running after her. We walked by the American embassy which was close by, but the guard would not allow us to take pictures. She loves seeing the American flag. We also went to the pearl market. I bought a necklace. Jamie bought a ring and seven pearl necklaces for her future bridesmaids and herself. I saw several familiar American restaurants, and we enjoyed their food.

July 19, 2001—I am at the Beijing airport now. I hope I'm in the right place. I sure did go through a lot of checkpoints, but everything is okay so far. My flight to Chicago leaves at four thirty.

Let me go back to yesterday. We toured the Ming Tombs Gardens; they were very beautiful. We went underground to one tomb, that of the thirteenth emperor's and his two wives. It was a fascinating descent, but dark, sixty feet underground, and eerie.

The emperors spent many years preparing for their deaths. What a waste.

We finally headed for the Great Wall. Magnificent! We spent two and a half hours climbing the wall and taking pictures. And a climb it was! The mountains are beautiful and so green. The wall stretches for six thousand miles. We went to one of the places on the wall that most tourists go. We climbed a bunch of steps! Walking up a continual incline is a real challenge to the old leg muscles, but it was so worth it. Many parts of the wall to unify the nation for the first time were built around 200 BC by the same emperor who built the terracotta warriors. I know that much blood has been spilled on that wall in battles over many hundreds of years and from the slaves who constructed the wall. Their bodies were just covered over by the stones used to build the wall. It was a grave for many men.

Jamie spotted a Hard Rock Café on our way back to the city and had to stop and eat. She ordered way more than we could possibly eat, but she said it was worth every penny.

This morning we woke at seven. It was our last day together. It was raining, but that didn't matter. We were going to Tiananmen Square. We saw the changing of the guard from a distance. We then headed for the silk market to buy a backpack because I had too much to take back home. Jamie did not want to take another taxi, so we walked in the rain about two miles. "Are we almost there yet?" "Just a little further." I think she was paying me back for all the times she asked me that same question when she was a little girl!

After I leave for the good old USA, Jamie will take a flight and then train for twenty hours to her summer project in the desert for three weeks where she will teach middle school teachers how to teach English. We will not hear from her until she returns to her city. No e-mail or phone calls will be available. I am thankful for the two weeks with her. I was able to hug and kiss her good-bye several times before going to the other side. I could not have had a better time with my little girl.

I learned a valuable lesson on my trip: not every place is like East Texas! That trip changed my worldview. Previously, I really had no clue how most of the world lived, especially in third world or restricted nations. Instead of thanking God every day for freedom, especially the freedom we have in Christ, I took it for granted, not caring about the living conditions of most people on planet earth.

The heart of God is for the lost. It's why He came to earth. "For the Son of Man came to seek and to save the lost" (Lk. 19:10). Jamie truly has the heart of God for the lost as well as the mind of Christ, which she renews daily in His Word. I want that.

Here is something for which I'm proud: I ate with chopsticks everywhere, very clumsily I will add, because I never saw a fork!

# Chapter 13

## *2001 Continues*

July 17, 2001—Dear Aunt Karen and Uncle Gene: Hi. I just wanted to write you a note to say "Thank you" for the love and kindness you have shown to me! Words fall short in expressing how much you both have touched my life. Thank you for letting God use you to impact my life. You've left footprints on my life that have helped me make it to where I am today. Thank you!

I have always admired the way in which you both love Jamie and Janet. There has always been a warmth I have felt in your home. Love can almost literally be felt! I'm very happy that there has been healing in my relationship with both of you because I love you both very much!

I'm overwhelmed with Jamie's love for me which stems out of her love for God that is so deep! God has done a "beautiful" miracle in my life by bringing Jamie into my life again at the right time. I want you both to know I have a love for Jamie deep in my heart and a commitment which is settled to love Jamie, treat her gently, with the respect she deserves! Every time I talk to her, write or e-mail her, I let her know just how special she is and how much I love her! I'm willing to return to her city with her if that is where the Lord leads.

I want you both to know that I will talk to both of you together first before I even think of asking Jamie. I have deep respect for both of you as her parents. I didn't in any way want to rush or push Jamie to the commitment of marriage. I want to be sensitive first to God and to Jamie. She has asked about December when she comes back, and I asked her to consider realistically what she will be going through in reentry here in the States and the time she herself will need to adjust and feel more settled with school and where she will live. We both have agreed that the soonest we would think of getting married will be March, after she returns.

I desire to be transparent with you about our relationship and keep communication open. I'm so glad I came down and talked to you both, and I didn't expect your response. Thank you for your love and forgiveness. It means more than words are able to express! Uncle Gene, it meant a lot that you stopped to eat lunch. Thank you! I want to visit again soon and go to church with you. It will be my first time in the new building. I love you both and thank God for you! (Heb. 6:10).

August 3, 2001—Well, it has been a month since writing in the old journal. When Mom was here, we were just too busy to do it. Luckily she found the time to write *every* minor detail, so I don't feel so bad. She arrived in BJ right on time. I was waiting for her as soon as she came out. I saw her first. She looked so afraid in her little red shirt and blue jeans. Her eyes were looking furtively everywhere for me. Finally she saw me and we both started to cry. It was beautiful. I will never forget hugging her and crying. It had been almost a whole year! Our visit whirled by until I told her good-bye in the Beijing airport on July 19. That was a terrible sinking feeling. It had been so wonderful to see my Mom and talk with her every day. And now it would be another whole year. Very traumatic.

~

August 4, 2001—Jamie has been sick. She was also robbed of all her money, about $260 American money (two years wages for a peasant). "God, help her and protect her."

~

August 6, 2001—I'm in another city (a real dump) to teach middle school teachers for three weeks this summer. I will spare you the details of the absolutely horrible living conditions. I got robbed last week. Someone busted the lock on my suitcase and took all of my money. Evidently they didn't know the value of a US passport. I hate this place (not the country and not the people—just this little town).

On a better note, we have had many interesting experiences here. I taught about a week on literature, and in my packet of teaching materials was the story behind the famous hymn, "It is Well with My Soul." I got to teach the first verse and chorus to the students and tell of the writer's tragedy of losing four daughters in a shipwreck but how he had peace during the time of sorrow. They all thought it would be impossible to have peace in that tragedy. It was really cool to sing it with them.

I also got to teach about the life of King David. Very cool. I talked about God seeing the heart and man seeing the outside of a person. I also got to teach the story of the prodigal son. I explained to them repentance and how Jesus welcomes sinners. They see a sinner as a prisoner or criminal. In other words, they believe people are born good and don't need a Savior. I was able to explain the Christian concept of original sin.

Here's one more interesting note about this place. An old man in his forties (sorry Mom and Dad) was one of our students. His name was Cecil. In the second week, some of his fellow classmates invited our team to dinner, which was fun. Cecil asked one of us for a Bible! It was a very shocking question. He said that when he was in college (probably over twenty years ago), a teacher told him that the only way to get good English was to read the Bible! My friend didn't know what to do. She didn't make him any promises because maybe he was a plant, put there to trap us. She just said, "Maybe." Then we all watched Cecil and prayed about it. We finally decided he was sincere, so on the last day my friend and I went into her room with him. One of the other team members had brought a brand new NIV with him just for that purpose. My friend said, "You asked us for a book, and here it is." When he took it, his eyes glowed, almost like he might cry. He took it with both hands, looked at it, and said, "I have longed for this Book for many years." He was so thankful and happy. We told him to start with the book of John. That moment, the look in his eyes was worth a million dollars to me. I will never forget his expression when he held the Book of Life in his hands for the first time. I pray that one day his name will be written in the Lamb's Book of Life.

August 11, 2001—Jamie called yesterday. She is fine except for chest congestion from the air pollution.

August 24, 2001—I am moving into my new third floor apartment. It's not quite finished yet, but a thousand times better than where I've been living for the past year. I did see something very sad last week from my kitchen window (no one has curtains around here). I kept hearing this terrible screaming and crying. Finally I looked out the window. Others were too. On the ground was a boy of about five years old screaming, "Baba!" (Daddy). His dad was angry about something, and he kicked the little boy. Of course, the boy kept screaming for his daddy. I was so upset by this abuse. I opened my window and leaned over it, hoping the man would look up and see that a foreigner was staring at him. It didn't work. They went into the stairway, the boy still screaming, out of my view. That night I asked a couple of my students if kicking a child is acceptable here. They said, "Yes." It is common for fathers to kick their children and for parents to slap their children in the face as well. Even teachers can slap children. I told them that was abuse in America, not discipline. Perhaps different cultures have different acceptable methods to discipline children? Maybe a kick, so offensive to Americans, is like a spanking here. I've never thought that disciplining children is cultural too. So since the culture sees it as inoffensive to kick or slap naughty children, does that mean it is acceptable to God? It's a difficult question. I'm curious. I never thought about this before.

August 28, 2001—This semester will be interesting. American Literature (seniors) is going to be my favorite course. I gave them their syllabus yesterday. They have to read two novels outside of class and write an in-depth 1,500-word reading journal about each one. Also, we have to cram American Literature into one semester, so we hit the ground running. I lectured on the early colonies and Puritanism. I passed out "Sinners in the Hands of an Angry God," the famous sermon of the Great Awakening by Jonathan Edwards for them to read for homework. It stresses God's wrath rather than His love, but I will try to balance it out next week when I lecture on it. Maybe I'll balance it out by talking about the Quakers. We will see.

These students have never had a foreign teacher before, and I am the only one they will have next year, so I think they will love me. When I walked into the room, they greeted me with applause. That was pretty cool! But after I explained all my rules, they were nervous. They've probably never had a teacher as strict as me. Then again, they've probably never had a teacher to love them as much as I do either.

Great news! A new baby has been born! Sissy. She has been close for so long, but she finally made the decision. Another person has come to faith in Jesus Christ! It's going to be a great year!

~

September 2, 2001—Well, it was an amazing Sunday! Days like today make me wish I could pick up a phone and tell Mom and Dad everything God did, but the phone operators wouldn't exactly appreciate that. Twelve students came with us to church. Of those, six are Christians. Two others were there for the first time.

Following the sermon was testimony time. A woman stood up and told an amazing account. I remember three months ago when she told the church that her son was missing, nowhere to be found. The church fervently prayed for him. She stood with her son, back safe and sound, much to the joy of the congregation.

What happened was this. Her son, seventeen years old, wanted a good job. He was lured away by some people promising him a good job, but he ended up basically being in a slave camp. He was surrounded by walls forced to work for very little in a brick factory. Other children were there too and were beaten, dismembered, and sometimes killed, their bodies thrown into the fire to destroy evidence. As his mother and others prayed several months, not knowing his whereabouts, he was trying to escape. He tried more than once, but could not. Finally, he tried to climb a seven-foot wall for his freedom. Of course he couldn't, but he felt a Strength pull him up and he got over the wall! He went immediately to the police, who arrested the slave drivers and freed the other children. My students were glued to this testimony.

Another lady had a hand that was disabled. God healed it. More ladies stood up, one after another, telling testimonies. Then a man, a doctor, well-dressed and young, stood up. He had been disabled in his leg. God healed him. These are the best translations I could get, but my students were captivated by them, so it is okay.

As we walked to the train station, we talked some more about church. Liz, a team member, walked ahead with a student named Betty. Betty told Liz that she never believed in God before today, but after hearing the testimonies, she believes. Liz told her that belief is the first step. Now she needs to believe in Jesus. We will see when that happens. So, you can see that church was very effective today. Many students' faith grew or came into existence. It is a slow process, but I detect a hunger in the students this semester. *Hunger* is the best word I have for it. It is deeper than curiosity. Obviously, God is moving!

September 3, 2001—Jamie e-mailed us yesterday and told us she is sure about marrying him. Gene cried. We are happy for her.

September 12, 2001—Today was a hard day. I found out at nine this morning that nine hours before, the World Trade Center and Pentagon were attacked by hijacked airplanes. I was doing laundry and praying when Liz came to the door with the news. I had to teach American Literature an hour later—the Declaration of Independence. I walked into class wearing black and told the students to open their books. The words would not come, only tears. I wanted so much to keep a stiff upper lip and show true American courage, but I had to apologize to the students, saying I couldn't teach, gathered my books and ran out of the room. The emotions I feel are too much to put into words on paper. It feels like there's a hole in my heart. I feel like a widow.

September 13, 2001—I start a new journal today, and I'm calling it "A New World." After what happened in New York City and Washington, DC two days ago, America will never be the same.

No more innocence—not that America was free of guilt—but innocence in the sense of that childlike trust and confidence that she is always safe and separated from the world's problems, if not due to geography or technology, at least due to her military prowess and defense system. When the symbols of American finance and military prowess are destroyed in less than an hour, and thousands of people at work die in a single morning, the childlike sense of immunity from danger dissolves, maybe never to return.

The focus of my journals, however, is always what is happening in my new country. So, how will this city and this tucked-away university in the mountains be different after September 11? The answer is simple: this teacher has changed. My idea of American pride is still strong but humbled now. No more die-hard notions of American superiority in this woman. And my idea of evil, my grasp on what it actually is has matured. I have watched the video clip of the World Trade Center destroyed because of evil. Now I can see even more clearly why I must fight the good fight. I will also take advantage of more opportunities to touch students' lives. My time is limited, maybe more than I know. No one, not even Pentagon intelligence, knows the future.

I remember something someone said in a chapel service at my alma mater. "The safest place in the world is in the center of God's will." I have thought about that statement many times, but today it really hit home.

One more note: the children here are so precious! Lately, they have smiled so much at me. Sometimes their whole face lights up when they see me, and I haven't given candy out in a long time. Today, a little girl saw me and winked at me as she walked by with her cute little smile. They love me!

September 21, 2001—Today is my beautiful sister's birthday, but I can't call her because I still have no phone. New apartment—no phone or hot water for the past month, no sidewalks, so I sink into mud when I step outside my building, losing shoes in the process, and it is already so cold that I'm now wearing three layers of clothes. When winter gets here, it is typically seven-layer weather. Most buildings on this campus have no heat. Most students are very poor and have few clothes. They tie rags and whatever they can find around arms and legs to stay warm.

~

September 25, 2001—A team member came to my city today and brought me Dr. Pepper, mayonnaise, and bleach. What more could I possibly want?

~

September 28, 2001—Sue and I decided to go help the church leaders build their new building today. To save money, the church is doing most of the work. That means middle-aged ladies are working their tails off and whoever else can come work whenever they can. We took the bus like always. When we arrived, we found ladies hard at work. They stopped and tried to get us to eat some noodles. We would only drink water; we had come to work. Sue and I shoveled sand and rocks. We literally stood on the side of a hill and threw the dirt down the hill. Digging and slinging rocks and dirt behind you over and over again may not sound like hard work, but it is very tiring. While I worked, I couldn't help thinking about "all church work days" in America. The men do light labor, probably with tools, and the women clean. But here, they are digging out the side of a mountain, with no bulldozer, just one shovel at a time. The church will be on the side of the mountain and above it will be layers of cave houses.

~

October 15, 2001—This afternoon, Sue and I met with three of my students, Lisa, Noah, and Terri. These three have come to know the Lord and are now getting ready to each lead a small group of interested students in a Book study. Sue and I usually join them, but this time they are on their own. Several students are very close. Sue and I usually lead, but once a month we want to sit out so these students can learn to lead on their own. This way, they can talk about difficult concepts in their native tongue. It is important that groups exist on their own without foreigners. In essence, my job is to work myself out of a job and it looks like that will soon happen. Wednesday just might be the day some decisions are made. We talked with them about it, and it was so good to see them planning to do it on their own, taking it so seriously. I was very proud of them. They really want their friends to come through. Wednesday will be exciting.

October 16, 2001—We received Jamie's sixth journal on Saturday. I read the whole thing Saturday night. She is happier this semester with him back in her life. And lots of things are happening spiritually. She is encouraged.

October 20, 2001—My students had their Book studies on Wednesday! I talked to Lisa about her group. She said it was a great meeting. One student asked so many questions about John 3:16. The meeting lasted two hours, much longer than usual, but everyone enjoyed it. At the end of the meeting, this student admitted he was stubborn. He said the more he learned, the more questions he had, and when the group prayed for him at the end, he said, "God, maybe Lisa is right. Maybe I am looking for you. I hope I can find you."

~

October 27, 2001—I'm having more and more excellent discussions. God is definitely up to something. I've also been here fifteen months now, so the students are more comfortable with me and are learning they can trust me. It's all about building those relationships. Having patience is huge here. I can't be in a hurry and try to rush someone to know Christ. It just would not work.

~

October 28, 2001—I told Lisa last night that two more girls want to join her group. These students are hungry. God is stirring hearts. I need to let her lead it without me to keep the size and obviousness down.

~

October 29, 2001—Yesterday, sixteen Christians were murdered at the end of their service when Muslim gunmen stormed the church, shot four hundred rounds of ammunition, killing sixteen and wounding twenty. The congregation had just said, "Amen."

~

November 1, 2001—I feel one of my biggest responsibilities here is to disciple and be an example, a motivation, to the Christians. If I try to do all the outreach myself, I will miss many people, and more importantly, Noah and some of the others won't see the importance of doing it themselves. For this reason, I like to encourage them whenever I can and share with them what I do so they will learn too. But I can't put vision in hearts. Someone else is doing that! Wow!

A couple of weeks ago, I was really struggling with things. Mom told me to hang in there, that things were about to happen. I thought she was probably being too spiritual (sorry, Mom) or was just talking to encourage me. I hoped it was true, of course, but I am surprised at the many things that have happened in the past few weeks. In fact, when she reads this, she'll probably be surprised herself.

~

November 6, 2001—Saturday was busy. Sue and I began by meeting several of our students to climb our first mountain of the semester. It was cold, but fun. It was foggy, so I got a new view of the scenery. We had snacks at the top—fruit roll-ups, apricots, and wafer things. On the way down, we passed a fresh grave, with all the paper flowers around it and many empty holes where bodies had been stolen. At the bottom, we said our good-byes, and I went to the classroom to help students prepare for the American Literature test. They sure were scared. What a great feeling!

That afternoon, I had my portrait sketched. An art student asked Della, one of my students, if she would ask me to let him draw me. We walked to his classroom on the third floor. Unfortunately, my right knee, the one that tortured me last year on my birthday, started acting up, so walking was excruciatingly painful. I think it is somehow related to the cold weather.

In his classroom, I saw a typical art studio—easels everywhere, complete sketches and paintings, and desks pushed against the walls. It just looked free compared to the English students' classrooms with rows of desks and a platform. Of course, the condition of the classroom could not be compared to American classrooms. Black mold covered much of the ceiling. Yikes!

The art student showed me to a chair, where I could be comfortable. Around the room I saw many sketches on easels of the same woman—a Chinese lady who was obviously an assignment for all of them to sketch. I could see they had good talent, but I wondered how his first sketch of a foreigner would be.

He began to sketch and told me I could talk to Della as he worked. Just as I expected, when other classmates came into the room, surprised to see a foreigner being sketched, they started sketching too. Before it was all said and done, seven people sketched me! It was so funny trying to be natural, chatting away with Della, while a row of art students studied my features and tried to draw them. I really had to control my composure because it made me nervous. But it was so fun!

Ninety minutes later, the other students had gone, and there remained Della, the artist, another of my English students who came to chat, and me. The moment of truth came when he said I could look at the picture. All I gotta say is, as far as I know, I have no Native American blood in me at all. But when Chinese see a foreigner, they notice the big nose, just as foreigners notice squinty eyes on Chinese. So, when the artist drew my picture, he drew the nose like he saw it! MawMaw Alegre used to be so proud of my little nose, saying it was like a tiny ski slope—like her nose. MawMaw Allen says it is a sassy nose. But neither of those ladies would have recognized the monster nose on my sketch, only comparable to the stereotypical Indian chief's.

Now I must tell about my experience while I was being sketched. Della, a chatterbox, that can outtalk anyone I know, kept me company, so I wouldn't be bored. We talked about many things. She has been one of my prayer focuses lately. I have been trying to reach her, so I was glad for the chance, but I will never forget (or understand) one of the stories she told me.

Here is the gist of the conversation we had as I was being sketched by people who couldn't understand us. "I heard on the radio that there was this bus in Beijing that was full of people." Immediately I started imagining the bus wrecked off of a bridge or something else that would be logical. She continued, "And a man took off his shoes, and it smelled really bad."

Here again, I was thinking that maybe someone had attacked the man with a knife since they couldn't breathe, or maybe a fight broke out on the bus when someone tried to make him put on his shoes, so that the bus crashed.

She continued, "And there was a student on the bus from Beijing University, and he didn't ask the man to put on his shoes." I kept waiting for the next part of the story, but that was it. No more, no less. I tried to start trying to make some sense of it.

"So why was it on the radio?"

"Because the school is bad."

"Why?"

"Because they didn't teach the student to tell the man to put his shoes back on."

"So the school is bad because they didn't teach the student to tell others to put their shoes on?"

"The school isn't bad. They just didn't teach him well. The student should have told him to put his shoes on," she explained.

"So why was it on the radio?"

"Well, it wasn't on the radio. It was in a newspaper, and the radio collected many news stories from around the country to put on the radio for important news."

"So why was it on the radio?"

"Because the student should have been educated to tell the man to put his shoes on."

"So why was it on the radio?"

"Because the student should have told the man to put his shoes on," she said, getting a bit frustrated.

"I know, but *why* was it on the radio?"

"Maybe for an example to other university students."

"Oh, so if the student was educated, he should have told the man to put his shoes on." She nodded. "So was the man educated?" I asked.

"I don't know," she said. "It didn't give that information."

"So do you think the man should have known to keep his shoes on?"

"Yes, and the student should have told him to put them on."

"What about all the others on the crowded bus? They didn't say anything either. Why is the student to blame?"

"I don't know. Some reporters just put it in the news."

"So why was it on the radio?" She was getting annoyed.

"To tell us the lesson."

"But why was it on the radio?"

"He should have told him to put on his shoes!"

"I know, but *why was it on the radio*?"

Finally, she blurted out, "I don't know! I'm just trying to practice my oral English!" with tears in her eyes.

Yes, this is a true story, and she was telling me what she had read, and somehow our cultural differences had gotten in the way, so that what she had obviously thought was an interesting story was ridiculous and inexplicable to me. I felt bad seeing the tears in her eyes. I really hadn't intended that. That makes three girls in one week I have made cry. Fortunately, the other two were because I was ministering to them somewhat.

I tried to change the subject, realizing she would never help me understand the significance of the story and not wanting her to be upset, I said, "Well, I know how it is on a crowded bus, and if someone takes their shoes off, it is hard to breathe. It would be unbearable." I said this with as much gravity as I could muster.

She took the opportunity to change the subject even further by saying, "And today, people often don't give their seats to old people." So preceded a conversation about respect for the old and other things, and she was okay. However, I am still trying to figure out why that story was both on the radio and in the newspaper, but alas, I guess I'll never really know.

If you read this and think, "Why has Jamie tediously recorded every detail of this conversation in her journal?" I will say, "I don't know! I'm just trying to practice my written English!"

Della is always interesting. She sympathized with me concerning my knee and tried to give me advice. "When I have a really bad cold, if I take medicine, it gets better." (Obviously, since medicine works for colds, it should work for knees too!) She went on, "And if I have a bad stomachache, if I rest, it gets better." (And since stomachs and knees are so much alike, it is logical that resting will help my knee too.)

I love Della and am reaching out to her, but all I got to say is, "Is it possible for a Chinese to be blond?" If it is, then I think she has some blond roots somewhere!

~

November 23, 2001—Happy Thanksgiving! Before you panic, Mom and Dad, I just have been too busy to write in my journal. And when I wasn't busy, I didn't care. The past few weeks have been a blur. I haven't done much e-mailing or letter-writing either. I've just been in survival mode. But today I can finally take a day of rest. I think it will be a very wonderful Thanksgiving Day.

I woke up late (Thursdays are my days off from classes) and just lay in bed thanking God for my blessings this year. Here are a few of the great things that have happened this year: first and foremost, I really feel like I have grown spiritually by leaps and bounds. The same struggles I used to have are so much easier to conquer. I feel an inner peace and self-control that I haven't felt in a very long time. I'm talking about struggling over things for years, sometimes wondering if I would ever get over them. This is my biggest blessing of the year.

Secondly, since last year, three students have come into the family. They have not only become Christians but are growing in Christ and reaching out to their friends.

Third, he is back in my life. This weekend, maybe even right now, he is asking Mom and Dad for my hand in marriage. This is really beyond my wildest dreams. I don't know how I am getting to marry the guy that just happens to be the one I love and admire more than anyone else in the world. I don't know how that happened.

Also, Mom came to visit me this year. It was so special to share my world with her.

I have a *much* better apartment than last year. Yes, the paint may already be peeling; and yes, the phone doesn't work very well for international calls; and yes, it is a fly trap like my old one (where do they come from?); and yes, the door and drawer on my wardrobe are already broken; and yes, I could go on, but it is still way better than my other one—a thousand times better.

Sue is here! I finally have a friend I can really talk to.

I have had so many conversations with students that I haven't been able to record them all. It has truly been amazing to plant seeds and watch them grow.

Our weekly Bible study has grown from three students a year ago to eleven students! I could go on and on. God has been good to me.

Recently a student, who hasn't asked me anything in months, asked me what the difference is between a Christian and other people. What a question! She just kept asking question after question until I told her how to become a Christian, what a Christian believes, how to know if God is real, about the power of prayer, and the wisdom and history of the Bible. She said, "Maybe one day I will become a Christian in my heart. Before, I have read the Bible with my mind only. Now maybe I will try again, reading with my heart."

~

November 26, 2001—He took us to Outback last night. We were there from eight to eleven. He finally asked our permission and blessing to ask Jamie to marry him.

~

November 27, 2001—Here I am with another journal. These journals may make a great book someday. Or they will make great kindling for a fire. We'll see what their fate is, but I must say that they have really helped me document my life here. Whether anyone besides Mom, Dad, and Mawmaw ever reads them is really insignificant.

~

November 30, 2001—One of my students with whom I have never had a private conversation asked to meet with me, so we met in the underground restaurant (literally). I knew she was struggling with personal problems, and another teacher had told her to just "believe in herself." I told her that "to believe in yourself" is the advice most people would give her, but that she had tried it and it had let her down. I told her the only way I knew was to ask God to help her with her problems and to gain confidence.

"Do you believe in God?" I asked.

"I went to church a few times, but the people in my village don't believe."

"Is there a church in your village?"

"No. If there were, maybe I would believe."

I proceeded to tell her that when I have a problem, I pray and God helps me. Because He is with me, I even had confidence to leave my family in America and come here to teach.

"Is God always with you?"

"Yes, and one of His names means, 'God with Us.'" I started to tell her stories of answered prayer, trying to build her faith.

"Magic," she said with wonder.

"No—God," I said. I told her God will help her with her problems if she will ask Him and that He never turns anyone away. (It was amazing how many Scripture verses and things I had thought about this week came to me as we talked. I had been prepared, even though I hadn't realized it.)

She changed the subject, and we continued eating. I didn't want to bring it up again, but suddenly she said, "I have another question for you. How can I believe in God?"

I basically told her three things: ask God to prove He is real to her, read the Bible, and pray to Him every day. I explained to her how to pray. She said it would take time to decide if she would become a Christian. I said that was good, that she needed to take time to be sure, but that God would speak to her, and she could decide then. She said she would do those things.

"Today is a new beginning for me," she said. Wow! Then she said, "I am in the party. Can I become a Christian?"

This surprised me, but I'm glad I hadn't known earlier, or I might not have been so bold. I told her that as a Communist, she could believe, but couldn't be baptized (party rule). But if she became a Christian, then she could decide whether or not to stay in the party. She then asked, "Will God accept a Communist?"

"Yes," I said. This floored her. She had obviously thought that when she signed the paper to join the party, that God had written her off too. She was happy to learn that God loved all people equally. I told her that maybe God would use her problem now as a chance to show her He is real.

"So from one perspective," she said, "my problem is good, because I can find God through it."

"You are right," I said. We walked to my apartment, where I loaned her a Bible, telling her to start with John. I told her we would get together in a few weeks and talk about it together, and she could ask questions if she had any. As she left, she said again, "This is a new beginning for me." Amazing.

December 7, 2001—I went into town on Thursday. Sometimes my trips are uneventful, but this trip was full of surprises. It began with the taxi driver who took me there. He was so taciturn, maybe the only quiet drive in the entire city. Usually they enjoy trying to talk with the foreigner, but not him. He just stared straight ahead, saying nothing, unimpressed by my foreignness. It was like being in the twilight zone; it was so strange.

When I paid the Internet bill at the phone company, I had another surprise. Usually the ladies there are *not* friendly in the least, but as I was leaving, all of a sudden, the lady behind the counter said, "Are you a teacher at the university?" in English no less.

"Yes!" I said, flabbergasted at her English and her sudden kindness. She asked me in English how long have I been here and smiled and said with much feeling and sincerity, "I'm glad to know you." I smiled and left, totally floored. People here just *don't* speak English!

I walked under some construction scaffolding in a dark alley lined with "restaurants" that would be a field day for an American food inspector. At one point during the walk, I almost gagged at the stench of "food." But I didn't stop for a snack. I even passed a cart with some organs of a sheep or pig—not really sure what animal or what organs for that matter. I didn't stop to study them. One could also purchase a bundle of snakes tied together. Hungry?

On the taxi ride home, another odd thing happened; the taxi driver spoke to me in English! Two strangers in one day! A new record! Of course, he asked me how much the university pays me, and of course I said it was a secret. By now, I know the Chinese word for *secret* quite well. He evidently thoroughly enjoyed the taxi ride, because he wouldn't let me pay for it. What a strange trip.

~

December 27, 2001—I received another package from Mom and Dad last week. They consistently amaze me with their generosity. They send me so many packages stuffed with everything I need. And my family, friends, and church family back home are always giving Mom things to send me.

Diane sent me a ton of hot chocolate! Aunt Alice sent me Christmas stockings she made herself to give away. So on Christmas Eve, I gave away stockings filled with nuts, fruit, and candy and delivered them to children of parents I know, also to the little boy who lives at the English department.

The highlight of the stocking adventure came when Sue and I climbed the hill to give the woman who lives in the cave stockings for her two children. I have visited her several times before. When she saw us, her face lit up. I took her by the hand, so hard and worn. I had never felt a lady's hand like that before. I guess it shouldn't have surprised me; she lives a hard life in hard conditions, but it still bothered me. We told her Merry Christmas in Chinese and gave her the stockings for her two little children. She was very happy and wanted to know why we chose them. We told her because she is our friend. She insisted that we come in her cave and eat something, but we had no time. We promised to return. It was a great honor to give her children a Merry Christmas. Maybe one day, they will know the reason for the season.

Christmas Eve morning I gave my last lecture in literature class. It was a wonderful feeling for me, and I'm sure for them as well. The last poem we read was "Stopping by the Woods on a Snowy Evening" by Robert Frost. Of course, the poem is about contemplating suicide. However, the person in the poem decides to continue living in order to do his duties. This provoked discussion. A couple students said it was a person's right to commit suicide. (Sometimes I think they go overboard with their American teacher's emphasis on the rights of the individual.) I listened to them and then decided to get on my soapbox one last time, telling them what Mom told me years ago.

"Suicide is a selfish act. Perhaps the person thinks he is solving his problems in this way, but it causes untold suffering for their family and friends forever." (I didn't know why we were staying on this topic so much, but I wanted to stay on it as long as they did, because they are in a society with very little hope, and I would dread to think of one of them committing suicide.)

A student named Lynne raised her hand and said, "I don't think it's selfish to commit suicide, because it ends suffering." I didn't want to disrespect her right of opinion, so I said, "See, there are many opinions to this topic," and we proceeded to talk about other things.

After class, another student walked with me along the way and told me something shocking. Last year, she and her roommate found Lynne unconscious in their dorm room. She had overdosed on some pills because of a breakup with her boyfriend. They took her to the hospital, and when she awoke, she looked at her friend and said, "Why did you wake me?" No wonder God had maneuvered the conversation about suicide to last so long. No wonder she said what she did. I hope she will think about what I said if she ever gets depressed again. I told them that as long as a person is alive, there is always hope.

I had an interesting meal today. There were few things on the table I recognized, so I had to at least try a few. One of the dishes had cold things on it that looked something like beige grub worms. Biting into it, I found it to be crunchy and not too bad. After the meal, I found out that it was chicken feet. No comment except to say I'm pretty sure there will not be chicken feet on MawMaw's table on Christmas Eve!

A student did ask me again why we celebrate Christmas, and I was happy to answer that question. She also asked the purpose of Christmas trees and smiled when I explained that they are always green, like the life that is forever that God gives us. It was short, but a good conversation to have on Christmas Eve.

December 28, 2001—I had a dream Wednesday night that I believe was from God, and it concerned the hopelessness of the people here. In my dream, I saw many people who had given up and were not eating or drinking because they believed life was so hopeless. I said, "No, this isn't going to happen," and began to feed them and give them water. When I awoke, I had those familiar chills when I know He has spoken to me in a dream.

The meaning is that the people here are surrounded by hopelessness. It is our job to change the situation and give them hope. In fact, their hopelessness is so pervasive that sometimes I start to think that maybe they are in hopeless situations. They don't dream of better tomorrows because they feel it is hopeless. They also often think they are victims of their environmental circumstances and cannot change their future. I have a big job to do. I have never felt such pervading hopelessness in so many people. It really shows me how optimistic Americans are. Poverty is so widespread here. It is just difficult to explain the hopelessness of a third world nation to an American. This is something you have to see and really know people before you can understand it—not something you can understand from a short visit to the country.

# Chapter 14

## *A Resurfacing*

June 11, 2001—Today was one of the happiest days of my life. He, my only true love, told me he still cares for me. He said that it is probably obvious to me what is in his heart: to have our two hearts as one at the right time. He didn't argue with my questions about his previous conduct. He sincerely could offer no explanation other than he wasn't himself and if he tried to explain everything he had done over the past five years, he would just be making up stories because he doesn't remember everything or even have a logical explanation for them all. He said there have been only two deep loves in his life—me and Kristen, the young lady he dated before me who died in a car accident. He said that ever since the day he first saw me, I have been in his heart (a piece of me) as he put it. He has tried at times to take me from his heart, but he never could.

I told him he needs to talk to Mom and Dad if he ever wants to be more than friends, so he asked for their phone number. He said he has been thinking about that anyway. He had a dream last week before this conversation that he was apologizing to Mom and Dad. He even wants to talk to Janet. He just wants to be honest with them about his feelings. I love him. There is no other word to describe me today than "radiant." Everything was wonderful. My happiness is so full that nothing could take it away. The joy and the cherishing are so much sweeter because of the pain and waiting. "Hope deferred makes the heart sick, but a longing fulfilled is a tree of life" (Prov. 13:12).

~

June 12, 2001—Through pain and suffering, disappointment after disappointment, the plant "hung in there," as he would say. Now that the love has returned, after years of drought, the plant is thriving, unable to stay confined to a little, forgotten part of my heart.

~

June 16, 2001—We have a lot of catching up to do. We are missing about five years of each other's life. I want him to know my life, and I want to know his. I see him as a companion to walk through life side by side. If he is really his old self again, then I want him to be that companion.

~

June 18, 2001—Today I stayed home all morning on my day off waiting for his call. No call. He promised he would call Sunday night, his time. I stayed there until 1:00 a.m. Monday, his time.

Actions speak louder than words. He can tell me all day until his face turns blue that he loves me and has changed, but if he doesn't keep even little promises, how can I believe him? He is walking a fine line to gain my trust back. I don't know how long it will take for him to regain it, but I'm not playing games with him. If he has changed, if he loves me, if he doesn't take me for granted, if he wants to "prove how faithful I can be" (as he said via e-mail) then he needs to show me.

He better not think he can take my forgiving and loyal nature for granted. He is on the verge of never having an opportunity to have a cordial conversation, much less a relationship with me again. Yes, I know I sound hostile and demanding, but he has hurt me too much, and I refuse to be like the stereotypical battered wife who always takes her husband back, trusting that he loves her even though he hurts her, and believing for a brighter day. I believe a brighter day is coming, but it doesn't have to be with him by my side.

Yes, I know that accidents happen and the best purposes of mice and men come to naught sometimes, but I see a pattern of promises from him, trust from me, broken promises from him (usually with "good" excuses), and disappointment, hurt, resentment, and anger from me. I don't want this all too familiar cycle in my life. That means he must change.

June 20, 2001—He called this morning. He had stayed up until 3:00 a.m. cleaning his community and had slept through his alarm clock.

His e-mail to her: Jamie, sometimes I have a hard time realizing that you want me back. I'm overwhelmed. My heart is very happy. It's an awkward feeling because I know you well, but like you said, it's been almost five years and we do have a lot of catching up to do. I want to give you my friendship now because you've waited so long and have always given me yours. Words fail to express what is inside my heart for you and I wish I could, but I will show you because that's what you need right now. I want to show you by my actions that I'm not the same guy, and that will take time. Thank you so much for giving me a chance to show you that, Jamie.

Her e-mail to him: Thank you so much for calling me this morning and for the beautiful e-mail. You are so sweet. I am glad you are happy. I am too. I told someone today that you are the only person in the world I would have a relationship with across two hemispheres. I think it will take time to build the trust back, but I am willing to do that.

His e-mail to her: Dear Jamie: Thanks for your e-mail. Thanks for thinking about me yesterday while I was with your parents. I'm so glad that I went down to meet with them. They were, as you said, very straight forward with me, and I completely understood why they were and respected everything they had to say because it was from a parent's heart. Jamie, you have wonderful parents and they deeply love you. I asked them to forgive me for hurting them, asked each one of them separately. Your dad told me that he has been angry with me and asked me to forgive him too. The response from your parents made me melt inside. Your dad stood up and shook my hand and told me that he forgives me right there and gave me a big hug. Janet told me that she forgives me too, but I must treat you well. She loves you very much. Your mom forgave me too. She fixed such a nice meal for us. Jamie, you are a precious gift and such a blessing to everyone your life touches. I'm so blessed to have someone with a heart of gold and as beautiful as you who wants to be with me. I've reflected on the many ways in which you have touched my life, and words fail to express my thanks and the way in which you've helped hold me up through a difficult time. Thank you, Jamie.

From her journal:

Wow is all I can say! I am so shocked that my parents had a good discussion with him. Mom sent me an email saying that he was sincere and really cares for me a lot and promised never to hurt me again. He also promised to be accountable to Dad for a while. Dad will call him every once in a while to check on him. They say it will take a while to trust him again, but they see no red flags and if I want to pursue a relationship, they support me. I am so surprised! They all three agreed, even Janet, who said she felt as if she were talking to the old person again. I had hoped the results would be good, but I never thought they would be this good. For my very cautious parents to agree 100 percent with Janet that he is healed and safe for me, surprises my socks off!

June 21, 2001—Today his e-mail promised me that he had made up his mind to hang on to me. He wants to marry me! I love him so much.

July 17, 2001—His e-mail to Jamie: Hi Gorgeous. Thanks for your email and kind words. I love you, Jamie, and I want you to know that I'm settled in my heart to be with you the rest of my life. I have an overwhelming peace that is new to me in that I haven't experienced it like this ever before. It's hard to explain in words, dear, but it's accompanied by a happiness I've never quite had like this before either. I still often find myself crying because I'm so happy that you want to be with me, someone so special like you, dear. Thank you for taking me back.

When I visited your parents, I had a good heart-to-heart talk with your dad in the garage. I'm so happy because there has already been a big improvement in our relationship, a friendship in which I feel as if I can share anything with your dad. I feel comfortable too. I love your parents. They have touched my life in ways they will never know. I told your dad that I desired to keep open communication with him and would not hide anything about us from him, but would be transparent with him about our relationship. He gave me a big hug before I left after our talk and told me that he loved me. I told him the same thing of course. I'm so happy. One of my heart's desires has been that I would have a restored relationship with your dad and mom, and I see those thoughts coming true and I'm so thankful.

Jamie, you're a miracle in my life. I'm very thankful that I'm healed inside and my emotions are healed. It's been hard and I've longed to be like this. Sometimes you can't speed up the grief process when someone so close to you dies. I believe you can understand that, Jamie.

Her e-mail to him: In your email, you asked me to forgive you for hurting me. I forgave you a long time ago. The pain was really bad and deep and lasted for a long time, but I survived. I do want to know what you mean by saying you feel like you are back to your normal self again. Can you explain? I know the pain you caused me was unintentional. I hope you are really better now. To be honest, it is very hard to trust you. So many times in the past couple of years you made promises that were not kept, whether they were little like going to get coffee or whatever. So I finally got into the habit of not believing your promises to protect my emotions.

July 23, 2001—Dear Jamie: Hello dear. I have been carrying you in my thoughts all day today. You're on my mind and in my heart! I love you, my Jamie! I have been talking to Father today and thanking Him for letting you come into my life again. I'm so happy and so blessed, dear, to have you back for good I believe in my heart! I find our love to be amazing. It's the only way I can express it. It's wonderful, a miracle, dear! You are beautiful to me beyond what words can describe!

Jamie, I want to encourage you today to keep your head up, keep walking straight ahead. You're going to make it, dear. You're strong, and Father is helping you! Know that I think about you when I wake up and during my day, and before I go to sleep, you're one of the last thoughts in my mind! I love you with my whole heart! You are a beautiful blessing and precious gift to me!

Thank you for always being there for me when Mom died. I can clearly remember the times you sat with me and put your arms around me and cried with me. Those times mean more to me than you will ever know, dear! Thank you!

You are so special and I'm so happy to be back with you and I just want you to know you're stuck with me. I'm yours completely! Jamie, I love you so much and I'm looking forward to seeing you, hugging you, kissing you, talking, listening, sharing, catching up, knowing you better! I love writing you and will continue to until you come back, and by the way, after we are married I won't stop writing you notes!

Jamie, thank you for taking me back. I have never been as happy as I am now. I still cry for joy because I have the most beautiful lady in the world in my life and it will be an honor and a privilege to spend the rest of my life with you, dear! Jamie, I'm thinking about you every day. I'm counting the days until I see my sweetheart, my sunshine, my rose! I love you more than words will ever be able to express, my Jamie! You hang in there. I'm so proud of you, dear. I love you.

October 24, 2001—Jamie's letter to him: Dear Darling: Just a little note to say I love you. Today you told me about your consumer debt, and we made the difficult decision to delay our reunion and engagement until July. I forgive you for what happened over the past few years you got into debt. I am thankful you are actively changing the situation by changing your spending habits and getting help from a professional. That shows me you want to change. We must always remember this difficult time and avoid buying things we can't afford.

Do you know how much of a dream come true you are to me? Do you realize how many times I have imagined my husband or pretended I was getting married as a child? Do you realize how much you fit my desire for a husband? You are the one, the one I have literally waited for my whole life, the one I will be able to give myself fully to not so far away from now! The one I will make a family with, the one I will share my dreams with, the one I will work side by side with. I love you, Darling, faults and all.

Can I ask you one favor? Don't do any get-rich-quick schemes—things like that water purifier you sold for a while. You have enough on your plate, and those things are more trouble than they're worth, though the promoters make them sound good.

My Note—After reading literally hundreds of his cards and letters to Jamie, I have come to the unmistakable conclusion that if you've read one of his overly crowded, beautifully artistic scripted pieces, you've read about 95 percent of them. The highly noticeable and dominating characteristic of every card and letter is repetition. But she loved him and must have loved reading the same words multiple times, because she never threw anything away.

# Chapter 15

## *2002*

January 3, 2002—Here I am at the beginning of my last calendar year in this beautiful land. I can see that the last six months of this two-year stint will be much harder than the first, but His grace was sufficient then, and it will be now.

January 19, 2002—Lisa wants to leave the party, which is a very serious situation for her and her family. I am unable to help her in any way. The authorities suspect me of influencing her. In talking to my team leader, he said something may happen as a result of this and that I will be the fall guy if we get blamed for anything. Although I did nothing and didn't know about the situation for several weeks, it is best that if someone has to take the blame, it be me, since this is Liz's career and Sue has another year and a half left. So if anyone goes home, it will be me.

January 22, 2002—I found out some more appalling information about the cheating in the educational system. On the big Band 4 tests of English that every college student must pass in order to graduate, cheating is very common. Noah said that all of his roommates went out of town recently to take an examination of English for others. This is how they make money. According to Lisa, it is even easier to cheat on the test to enter grad school. The teachers who proctor the test often tell students with whom they have a relationship what to study because they have seen the test. They sometimes even tell them what will be on it.

Cheating is quite acceptable here, but not in my classes. I'd fail my own mother if she was in my class and didn't do the work! (Sorry, Mom!) I try extremely hard to instill honesty, integrity, and responsibility into my students and freely give "big fat zeros" when there is obvious cheating or plagiarism. In a society where scores are overrated, this should not be tolerated.

Cheating isn't limited to students. Teachers more often than not never grade papers; they just give the students the grades they want them to have. Last semester, when they graded college English exams, too many failed; so the head teachers changed grades so not many would fail. The worst thing is not enough students failed the listening exam. So the teachers chose a few students to fail. Yes, they actually took some low-scoring students who passed and failed them. Now the students will have to take makeup tests and will be disqualified for scholarships because they "failed." I have talked with students after they failed. They are very disappointed. But now I wonder how many "failures" actually fail. How can these teachers sleep at night? It's all they've ever known.

Now, for something funny. Daddy will love this. One night Sue and I were staying up late grading papers, when lo and behold, we heard a dog howling at the moon. This wasn't some pathetic little dog; this sounded like a big country dog, the kind I used to hear when I visited MawMaw and PawPaw Allen in Colmesneil. I said, "That dog better be quiet, or they'll find him and cook him." Sue burst into laughter. Then she told me that when she visited this country before, she and some Americans decided to order dog at a restaurant and were told that dogs weren't in season at the time. That's interesting. The thought of dogs being in or out of season was highly amusing to us in the wee hours of the morning. But there's more. Recently I was teaching middle school students some English sayings, and one of the quotes was, "A dog is a man's best friend." So I had to ask, "Why is a dog a man's best friend?" One student raised her hand and guessed, "Because you can eat it?" The student was just as serious as could be, but I did inform her that it would not be good to eat your best friend.

Before I continue, I want to tell you what Sue and I did on Tuesday night. After our two nights of traveling by train for a total of twenty hours, we arrived at a city of 5 million people, Lisa's home city. She took us to an underground church. She said there are many Christians here and that it was okay for us to go.

We walked together down the dark, cold street to a small street, and through a maze of alleys running between houses, all very dark. A barking dog found us and was threatening, but the owner stopped him from chasing us. All else was quiet as we walked through the maze, finally reaching a doorway. We walked into the empty room and out into a courtyard. On the other side was a closed door. Lisa opened the door, and I saw a lady reading a Bible to forty-five women and children, sitting on little stools circling a potbelly stove. The living room was clear of furniture as the only remaining pieces were pushed against the wall. The ladies made room and stools available so we could sit, right next to the fire.

I could see through an open doorway where men were listening too, but I couldn't see how many there were. The lady spoke about Solomon and read passage after passage about him from the pure and unadulterated holy Word of God. The ladies listened to every word and one even helped me by showing me the place to look at in her Bible by pointing to the chapter numbers. Another lady sat behind me and picked the hair off my coat. (Either my loose hairs annoyed her, or she was very kind.) They took notes and listened diligently and were so warm to me. I sat there and was amazed at their dedication. It wasn't even a Sunday, but a Tuesday night Bible study.

The speaker talked of persecution, reading from Revelation, and I knew these ladies could understand it. The teaching lasted an hour and twenty minutes followed by prayer (reciting the Lord's Prayer at the end) and then everyone went home. I really admired their faithfulness and faith. It was an honor to be there among them. They and their families have endured much for their faith. Sitting there, I wanted to spend the rest of my life in this country that I have grown to love so much. We will see. They are proof that fruit does come and last even after the workers, like Hudson Taylor, are long dead.

By the way, just for the record, this was a registered house church, which means the government knows about it and allows it to exist. So it was okay for me to attend. Actually it is called a teaching point. I never want to hear another American complain about the facilities of an American church. An unforgettable experience, Tuesday night will always be special to me.

In this city, there is absolutely no trash on the ground. However, the air is so polluted that you can't see the mountains just two hundred yards away. This city is lodged tightly between two mountains. Sue and I were only there Monday through Saturday, and we left with congestion and coughs all because of the air.

January 25, 2002—I am now in one of the largest and most modern cities in the country. Sue and I will spend one week here on a project. This city is massive! So many tall buildings neatly lined up. It has a lot of air pollution, but as the plane approached the ground, I was amazed at row after row of buildings. It reminded me of New York City in size and height of buildings.

Our hotel is...unforgettable. We asked our travel agent for something affordable. She reserved us a room in a very old hotel. The internet said that in the 1930s Albert Einstein, Ulysses S. Grant, and Charlie Chaplin stayed here. Sure enough, their pictures were in the lobby. It's old, and they obviously want to keep it looking old. And our room has hot water for showers! We're excited! This is the most beautiful city I have ever been in at night—even better than New York or Paris.

February 1, 2002—Sue and I traveled to another smaller city. What did we do when we arrived? Went to Walmart! We haven't been in a Walmart in so long. We walked on every floor, loving every minute—except for the "deli" section. They had dried pig heads. The pig heads were flattened, like an empty rubber hot water bottle, snout pointing to the floor. They also had a bunch of eels just lying there, ready to be taken home, but we left them right there. What would Sam Walton do if he knew he was selling pig head? And what exactly do you do with a pig head?

February 6, 2002—We are officially on vacation and enjoying the freedom and the church services. What has God done for me here? He has reminded me over and over that His grace is enough and His strength is made perfect in weakness. I should just walk day by day trusting Him, and He will get me to the place I need to be, and my faith will grow.

It has been a very encouraging time. I have especially loved hearing testimonies from team members. One spoke of his friend, a seventy-year-old pastor, whose church decided he was too old to be their pastor. So he went to India and lived the rest of his life, serving God in that land until he died there at the age of eighty-eight. That is what I want. I want to spend my whole life in the land I love so I can see the fruit of my labors.

The last night of the retreat ended with prayer for my country. There was a prophecy given which said we are right where we need to be, and right now there are many burning coals, just patches of His fire, spread throughout the land. However, when the church is ready, God will set the land ablaze. I hope I can see it happen.

February 16, 2002—I fly back to my country tomorrow. I cannot describe the heaviness and somberness that settles over me as I think about returning to my new home. I love that land. I love her people. I love serving there. But words cannot express the feeling in the air of a country that is not free. Words cannot express it, because there are no English words to describe a country with no freedom. Freedom cannot be understood by someone who has never left America. It cannot be valued until it is taken away. Until it is taken away, one has no idea how dear it is.

Before leaving America, I used to be thankful I was a woman, if for no other reason than I would never have to serve in a war. But I understand freedom now, and I see that it is worth bloodshed to keep freedom. I must say that this journal will be kept under lock and key when I return to my home because of the lack of freedom here. Political freedom, as great as it is, can never be compared to spiritual freedom in Christ; and that is my motivation—to bring true freedom to a land where the people lack the freedom to hear and know the Truth.

February 24, 2002—I went to the home of one of my students for dinner yesterday, because her father knows what foreigners like to eat. This was the menu: fried mushrooms, boiled mushrooms, pig's stomach, and pig's ear. (I sure am glad he knew what foreigners like to eat, or it's no telling what we would have eaten!)

Next it was time for hotpot. "What kind of meat would you like?" Lilly asked. "Dog, lamb, or chicken?" What kind of a question is that? Maybe it was the result of the pig stomach or maybe pig ear does something to the brain, but I said, "dog," noticing Sue's nervousness. Suddenly I just wanted to try it, so that I could tell everyone I had eaten dog. The only problem with that is that one bite is never enough to please your host! They put plenty on our plates for us, and we chomped away. It really didn't taste bad; it's just the thought of eating dog that is gross. I couldn't tell what kind of dog it was. It was cut up, still on the bones, boiling in the pot in front of me. It must have been a big dog, though, because there was a lot of it—plenty to go around. No, it doesn't taste like chicken! It is very stringy and bony, unless you get an organ. It reminded me of mutton, and the meat looked like roast beef.

I should be ashamed of myself for making fun of the dinner. I know they spent much more than they should have and were treating us the best they could. I was very grateful to them.

Last night I received an e-mail from a young lady I met in my travels. She wrote that she has thought a lot about what we talked about, and especially what I said on the train. I told her that I wanted to be remembered when I die as a person who really loved people and helped people. (I couldn't mention God at that point.) In the e-mail she said she had told some people what I said and said the world would be better if more people had that goal. She said she will always remember my words. This was very encouraging to me, because I had been disappointed that we had not had a "good" talk when we were together. You never know what God will use to touch people…

March 13, 2002—I stand here after being on this continent twenty months and one day. I am very happy with the four people who have come through and made decisions and the growth of many people I have been able to assist, but suddenly I am nervous. So many are so close, and now I face the possibility of being kicked out. I hope I can stay here until the end of my commitment.

The difference between a Christian here and an American Christian is these people will study the Bible, ask many questions, and spend a longer time analyzing it *before* making a decision. The American, however, may make a decision to believe in Jesus Christ on the spur of the moment in a church service; then the discipleship begins. A Christian here has already learned a lot of Book knowledge and will not be easily swayed later, so I am willing to wait patiently for their decisions.

~

March 14, 2002—I want to comment on freedom or the lack thereof. Recently I was asked by a student very naively, "In America, can people have more than one child?" Another student at another time asked, "In America, if you disagree with the government, can you announce it publicly?" Another student was surprised when someone mentioned that their government had imprisoned Christians. And still yet another student asked me, "In America, can political leaders believe in God?"

These questions show their naivety. They have never experienced freedom, so they assume they have it, and assume their way of life is normal. They don't know what freedom is until they see someone else with it. When I told the student, "Yes, if you disagree with the government, you can do so publicly without fear of losing your job or other ramifications," she said, "*That* is freedom," realizing she didn't have it. Perhaps this is why the government here makes it so difficult for common people to travel abroad, and perhaps this is one reason why they watch foreigners as if we are felons.

On another note, last night I dreamed I was in an American Walmart stocking up on paper clips, Ziploc bags, liquid paper, and shoes. Oh, to be in a country where I could buy paper clips, Ziploc bags, liquid paper, and shoes!

Today showed me once again that God is doing something big in this city—way bigger than me or Sue. We are a tip of the iceberg, but our students are melting away strongholds just by "being a light." I don't know when exactly they all changed from the selfish stage of being thankful for their salvation and not seeing the need to share Jesus with others, to a stage where their light and passion are blinding! I think with the students doing what they're doing now—so naturally, passionately, and independently of us—the "work" here is about to explode! The promise God gave me on my first day in this city, "Shout, for God has given you the city," is coming true, and I am being mercifully allowed to see its beginning—like Moses being able to peek at the promised land. If we get kicked out, what's happening now (and the students aren't telling us everything) can only get bigger!

Now I have eaten many different animals and animal parts since I've lived in this country, but I draw the line at chicken blood. My momma didn't raise me to drink blood! Actually, this would have been eating, because it was coagulated, not liquefied. (Sorry, Dad, but that detail is important for posterity!) However, I was informed that even though chicken blood is healthier, lamb's blood is tastier.

March 24, 2002—I have some big news! On the walk back from church, a student named Kay told me she believes! She has ever since December; she just wasn't ready to tell anyone. She said that when she went to that job interview in December, she prayed for confidence, and she *felt* the confidence. After that prayer and getting the job, she decided to follow God the rest of her life. She said at that time though, she understood very little; she just believed. But now she understands. So, 6/7 is now here, with two others about to come through any day, if not already! God is so awesome!

The crazy thing is that a non-Christian hasn't asked me anything in a long time. There have been no big conversations with any of them (except one) this whole semester. But God is moving in people's hearts, and He is using their own people to reach them. I am finally doing what I'm supposed to do—equipping nationals to reach their own. This is how it should work.

April 9, 2002—letter from Jamie to him—I read something in a novel by George Eliot recently which explains how I feel today. It said:

> Again and again his vision was interrupted by wonder at the strength of his own feeling, at the strength and sweetness of this new love—almost like the wonder a man feels at the added power he finds in himself for an art which he laid aside for a space. How is it that poets have said so many fine things about our first love, so few about our later love? Are their first poems their best? Or are not those the best which come from their fuller thought, their larger experience, their deep-rooted affections? The boy's flutelike voice has its own spring charm, but the man should yield a richer deeper music.

Thank you for listening to me tell you about the struggles I had. I knew I would have to tell you, but I didn't know when I'd be able to. I was afraid you'd abandon me, but you didn't. And now I feel like the healing process from all the struggles is even better because you are fighting with me. I love you. You are such an amazing gift to me, beyond my wildest dreams, the man I have waited for all my life, the man in my mind I had feared was too good to hope for. I will treasure you always.

~

May 30, 2002— It has been a busy week and a lot of good times with students. I met with Lilly on Wednesday in the garden because she had some questions about Acts. She wanted to know more about the Holy Spirit and what He does. I was able to explain about the comfort, wisdom, guidance, conviction, and power He gives. It was an honor. God has really changed her. Just yesterday her roommate told me, "Lilly has changed." Another girl saw Lilly's Bible and told her she has wanted one for a very long time. Lilly had two because she has the Full Life now in her language. She immediately offered to give her friend her Bible. She was happy to be a light.

~

June 3, 2002—Jamie called Sunday morning (her Sunday p.m.) and said she had just experienced her most dangerous day in Northern Asia. She went home for the day with one of her students, a very dangerous, treacherous two-hour drive to a very remote city and cave home. She could say no more, but she was glad to still be alive! Praise God for protecting her while we slept.

~

June 14, 2002—So what have I been doing these past few weeks? Students I have spent time with are inviting me on outings—people who want to say good-bye. At times, the emotions are almost impossible to contain. It has been hard, and I expect it to get harder. But in three weeks, I'll be headed home!

~

June 20, 2002—One thing strange about going "home" is that I will lose my celebrity status. I must confess, the fame has been nice—at times. I know in America, I will never make a TV advertisement or have my picture on the wall in a restaurant or get free things because of my foreign face. I'll never attract crowds when doing common things. People suddenly won't care what is in my shopping basket when I am at the grocery store. They won't curiously gather around when I buy vegetables. Nothing will happen like the other day when I bought tea from a tea lady on the street. A crowd of twenty-four people (I counted) gathered to watch my student bargain for the tea and I inspect it before buying it! Nothing will happen like the five or six little boys who gathered around me at the grocery store as I paid for my juice, just to see what I bought and talk to me. By the way, I didn't know any of them, but one of them told his buddies that Sue and I were teachers at the university, and another said we were on TV for the American restaurant. And when I got in the taxi, the taxi driver knew we were university teachers here also. My days of fame are numbered.

I have another incident, one that will shock my readers, one that illustrates the stupidity of this university's leadership. (I never mince words in my journals.) The four American Literature students were scheduled to take their makeup test, the one I missed church for because the department gave me one day (eight hours) to make it. But one student didn't know where to take it (another communication problem). She waited in her classroom at the appointed time to take the test, but the test was in a different building, so she missed it. The department told me I had to make another makeup test for her—that day. So I did, and she took it. When the department leader gave the four tests back to me to grade, he said I had to pass them because it was their last chance! They made me make two makeup tests for something they forced me to pass the students on anyway! Ugh!

July 8, 2002—I'm home!

# Chapter 16

## *My Foreign Teacher*

From a book compiled by her students when she left to return to America in July of 2002:

Introduction: This volume is dedicated to Jamie Norton, a proud Texan and devoted teacher. Jamie embarked on the journey to NA in the summer of 2000, and after two years, will now return to America.

Though the road has been long, and at times more than a little bumpy, the two years she spent teaching in the Foreign Language Department have left a lasting imprint on all those she met. Whether foreigner or Chinese, teacher or student, Jamie has touched hearts and lives.

The following is a collection of letters written mostly by students (83 to be exact) that express their gratitude and love for Jamie. Some recount specific days that students remember spending with Jamie, and some detail the overall impression of gentleness, compassion, and faithfulness that characterized Jamie's time in our city. Many letters speak of Jamie's ability as a teacher—responsible and strict, but also warm-hearted and fun.

Regardless of the specific content, all the letters reveal the special qualities that made Jamie such a respected educator and valuable friend to all of us. Her teachings of literature, writing, and conversation will help her students greatly, but even more important are her examples of openness, generosity, and love.

Jamie will be missed greatly, but as can be seen from the following writings, she will never be forgotten.

We love you, Jamie!

—Lilly, Noah, and Sue

It was a summer dusk, very hot. Under the big trees, along the small road, I was walking with my best friend. At that time, we were grade two students. Suddenly, we saw a beautiful girl, wearing a long black dress. Nearer and nearer, we recognized that she was a girl from western country. Her hair is a bit yellow, her eyes are very big and beautiful. She was smiling, and her smile is sweet. She went by us and left us a beautiful shadow. We thought that she was a college student who came here to travel, but two months later, she became our writing teacher. She is so beautiful and kind. We enjoyed ourselves during the two years.

Dear Jamie: Do you remember the first time we met together? I went to café and wanted you to give me an English name. I was very shy and dared not speak to you that night. One of my classmates introduced me to you. I still remember clearly how beautiful your smile is and how sweet your voice is. You looked at me kindly with a gentle smile on your face and in your eyes. This let me feel a little ease, but still my face turned red when you asked me questions. One of your questions was what I want to do in the future. I told you I want to be a teacher. You thought for a little while and then gave me the name, "Heather." You told me that heather is a kind of wild flower that is indomitable and has great vitality and can live under very hard conditions. It seemed that you had known the disadvantages of my character. Then you told me to be brave and encouraged me to learn from the wild flower. Jamie, thank you very much for giving me the name. I will never forget your words, because they gave me great power to improve myself.

It was my first time to have dinner with a foreigner. I felt excited, but nervous. We ordered many kinds of foods. "Cheers! Congratulations!" Jamie said loudly. During eating, we explained the names of foods for her and also she learned them in Chinese. It was so funny. Sometimes she could do very well, but sometimes her pronunciation made us laugh. She was a shy girl. At that time, there were red clouds on her face. It was a surprise that she could use chopsticks. Although she couldn't do very well, it was better for a foreigner. We talked about American and Chinese culture and foods. How delicious and how rich! After finishing, we all have a round stomach.

In the winter semester of 2001, Jamie was our oral English teacher. She gave us every class very carefully and patiently. At the end of the semester, we were given an oral examination. Every student must give a speech one by one. Jamie gave us five minutes to prepare for the material. At first, I was so nervous that I had no idea about the topic. It was clear that my oral English was very poor, and I was always afraid of speaking English. But then I calmed down. I was full of confidence and started speaking. Jamie gave me encouragement. There was a sweet smile on her face. I felt very happy and excited. Then I completed my speech fluently. Finally, my speech got great success. I gained the score of 92. I was much too stimulated. In my opinion, this was the most unforgettable thing during those days that I was with Jamie. She gave me great courage to study. In my life, Jamie was my best teacher and best friend. I'll appreciate Jamie forever.

In my life, Jamie Norton is my most impressive foreign teacher. During these two years we got on very well with each other, and we established very deep friendship. Jamie is not only my good teacher but also my good friend. Actually, there are a lot of stories about my dear teacher Jamie in my mind. If I have enough time I could write a book about Jamie. All in all, Jamie is very beautiful, gentle, educated and kind lady. I've never met this kind of foreign teacher, very wonderful, excellent foreign teacher. Tomorrow I'll be a teacher. I promise to be an excellent teacher like her. I'll never forget my dear teacher, my dear friend.

At this very moment, I don't know what to say. I hope you will be happy forever. Thank you for your friendship. Thank you for coming to our dormitory and telling us your beautiful love story. I have a great decision that if I have a daughter one day, I'll call her Jamie. Please remember the happy times we have spent together. I'll miss you every day.

Jamie is my first foreign teacher who teaches us oral English. We all like her very much, not only because of her way of teaching us, but also because of her vigor. Every day, she shows you her endless energy for life. Talking with her, you will feel very comfortable. Jamie is very beautiful. In her class, your curiosity can be aroused. She usually provides some very interesting topics to us. But to be honest, she is really very strict with us. We have quizzes frequently, so we must study hard. Actually, she is an excellent teacher. We've learned lots of knowledge from her. Now Jamie will go back to her motherland. We really do not want her to leave us. I think we will all remember our first foreign teacher.

Jamie is a special teacher. From her, I get a lot of English knowledge. But the very important thing is I have changed a lot of old ideas in my mind. I come from a little village. I didn't see any foreigners until I came to university. I thought maybe foreigners are very cruel and strict, but from Jamie I know foreigners also are very kind, friendly, and easy going. Jamie, a good person to remember.

Many thanks for your help and advice. I really learned a lot of things from you. I am exceedingly grateful to you for your kind advice on my study. Do you still remember the first time when I talked with you? I still can because you gave me the name "Liza." I just can't believe that Jamie will leave. She is my teacher, my good friend, and I'll remember her in my whole life.

Jamie is a beautiful, gentle, and soft lady. She can always make her classes interesting, and we all enjoy them very much. Not only can she teach us much knowledge, but also endless happiness. Her methods of teaching are very special and quite different from Chinese teachers. We can accept them, and learn quickly within them. Jamie often shows us some wonderful plays in order to help us learn more customs of foreign countries and practice our listening. Then we talk about the stories and the leading roles. It is very useful and interesting thing. Well, it is utterly valuable to keep every droplet of Jamie in our hearts. And we'll always remember this kind-hearted lady and the good days she brings to us. We all wish her a happy life in the future and want her to know that we'll love her forever.

Jamie loves the children very much. She greets the little and maybe dirty children whenever she sees them on the way. Once she told me that one day a little girl, complete stranger, greeted her and then asked her to visit her house. She agreed without hesitation, and ate a plain meal there. When in café, she talks much with us students, no matter how good or bad our spoken English is. She always tries to help us improve our spoken English. She tries to talk with everyone around her without leaving anyone feeling isolated. I'm deeply thankful to her at this. She also shows great patience when answering our questions. She can explain to us again and again without being troubled. The only chance we stay close together was that time when some others and I accompanied her to church. By the way, it has been a rule for her to go to church every weekend, but it was the first time for me. When I was puzzling, she greeted me and inquired about my name and other things warm-heartedly. I was moved and grateful to her. On the way she talked with me actively. I felt unforgotten. Since then I thought I knew her even better. Another thing which moved me deeply was that she told me she believes God and Bible, the good book, which purify her soul and make her love all. She has a beautiful mind, which is really precious but hard to be possessed by all. Because of this I respect her and I love her.

Jamie, are you happy? Do you still remember the beautiful things about this place, your students and your friends? Although you are on the other side of the sky, our hearts will stay together. We are good friends. I wish we meet again sometime. Best wishes.

Time flies! I can't believe that two years have passed so rapidly. During this past year, we went to church, climbed the hill two times, and had a party at Christmas. I really enjoyed the time with you. I'm glad to know you. Since we met, I learned a lot from you; the most remarkable thing is honesty. Before doing the paper questions for my friend, I always did everything by my own standard. After the talk with you, I know I was completely wrong. What you said made me feel guilty. I asked God to forgive me, and I promised I'll never cheat again.

Jamie, to be honest, I hate you sometimes for you are mean. One time you cut ten points from my score just because I forgot signing my name. You won't grade our papers only if we made boring introductions. Today when I think about these things, I appreciate you a lot as I am not careless and I and all my classmates have improved our writing. Jamie, I have to say you are the kindest teacher I've met. Through our journals you always give us encouragement and loving care, so students and you understand and respect each other deeply. You went to see the waitress when she was sick only because of her hospitable service. You always collect drink bottles to give the old lady who collects rubbish. There are too many things you did that I can't remember. The only impression is that you are a warm-hearted lady. Today, I know you will leave very soon. I felt sad, only sad because I can't see you anymore, never. I don't know it's a good or bad thing to know you in my life. Once I asked God, "Since you let Jamie come to our city, why do you let her leave? Don't you know her leaving will always make students' hearts ache? But God never answered me. I have said too much. I'll stop here. May you always be happy.

One day we went to fly kites at the airport. The most important thing happened on the way home. The bus which we took was number eight, and I guess there must have been many peasants on the bus. When they saw Jamie, they were surprised. They all stared at us, especially at Jamie. However, Jamie is a shy girl and this embarrassed her a lot. After we got off the bus we walked on the street. Jamie decided to conquer her fear to settle this awkward situation. She did a surprising behavior. Guess what she did in the street? She danced and sang! But to my surprise, many people also stared at me. They might have thought me a foreigner, too, maybe Japanese. What I only wanted to do was to escape from the people and the street.

Dear Jamie: I don't quite know how to put this. I meant to write something happy and touching, about our happy times together, but whenever I thought that you are leaving, I just couldn't come up with anything. Although we've had many happy times, the support and love that you gave me when I had my trials are most unforgettable. I remember you were always there when I needed you. You always knew the right words to say and the right thing to do. With all your sincere compassion and love, you've made yourself a very dear friend, but to me you're more like a sister than a friend now. My letter may not be the sensational one, yet I wish these lines will become a warm ray of sunshine or a sweet fragrance of a rose. When you read them, I wish that your heart will smile a smile that even makes the air around you joyful. Remember that I will forever be your sister and friend. I will support and love you in my own way. Remember that you will always have a very special place in my heart. Love always.

~

Jamie is a good teacher. The way of her teaching is acceptable and lively. I think she has given many wonderful performances either in the literature class or in the writing class and European culture class. In this way, she imparted the knowledge to us in an unforgettable way. That is the reason why I never lose my mind in her class. Jamie is much more strict about her teaching than any other teachers in our department. She takes cheating seriously. The most famous speech she gives us before the test every time is her Cheating Speech. I remember it clearly although I've never cheated in the test. I think it's a good way to get rid of cheating. When I become a teacher, I will adopt it as one of my teaching methods.

Life is a river
which flows through
many turns
and changes.
But even when that river
takes the two of us
in different directions,
we will always find
each other again
just around the next bend.
For our friendship
is forever;
Our friendship
runs strong and deep.
Thanks for your friendship, Jamie.
My love to you always.

You could never imagine how long and how many times I have written this letter, because every time I just can't finish it. Whenever I am writing, and I look back to the past days, I shall always not be able to control myself and just want to cry, so I stopped many times. I really like our little talks either the silly ones or serious ones. There are just too many for me to choose something specific to write about, but I assure you I shall remember each one and every one as clearly as it just happened. I really enjoy everything that we've done together. For always I think it is such a wonderful thing for me to meet you and come to know you and be your friend. I shall always thank you, and remember your help and guidance. If it were not you, I would not be what I am right now. I can't imagine what a life of darkness, helplessness, unhappiness I would be living if you just did not come and show me the Light. How much I shall for always treasure your guide and lead. How dearly and sincerely I wish that you could stay longer even one more day and spend longer time with me. I know that is never possible. I can't imagine who I am going to talk to when you are not here with me. Who am I going to call when I am too depressed and stressed? Sometimes I am so afraid and worried to face my last year here without you. How much I shall miss you!

Precious Friend,
God bless you, precious friend of mine
for all you've been to me,
for deep enrichment to my heart
and pleasures real I see.
There is no way that I could tell
the courage that you lend,
and yet somehow I still must say
I'm glad you are my friend.
God bless you for the tender faith,
for every word you speak,
the comfort that you always bring,
so much I fondly seek.
Mere words alone can never tell
how quickly smiles are mine,
and I do hope you understand
you've made my days sublime.

Like a fresh air,
you brought America to us.
It's way of living,
eating, dressing,
working, playing,
the most important
it's way of speaking.
Your kindness and hard work
won the respect of the Chinese,
bridged the gap between
west and east.

It is easy to see Jamie lives a life of love and is constantly giving to her students. She is an extremely intelligent and dedicated teacher, who is unwilling to compromise, even in the most challenging of situations. The students adore her, and I know to many of them, she is a beacon of light in what would perhaps otherwise be a dark and dreary existence. Images come to my mind of Jamie talking with students, patiently explaining things; Jamie stopping on the sidewalk or on the bus to speak to small children and offer them candy. I think of more relaxed moments of Jamie eating jiaozi and drinking a Coke, Jamie playing Nerts, all the while spouting off stories of pure Texan pride.

—Sue

Dear Jamie: I can't make this a long letter, so I'll pick the most important things to write. First and the most important is that you'll always be my precious and dear sister, and you'll forever have a unique place in my heart. Secondly, I promise that I'll focus on Jesus, and I believe with His help, I'll come through. Jamie, I'll always pray for you and write you about things going on here. I know departure is hard. I know that we'll all be sad, but

I also know that our Father has really given this city to you, and you have made a great difference here. I'm sorry this letter is too short, yet I believe it will be meaningful to you. Have a nice trip.

Love, Terri

# Chapter 17

## *One Dream Realized*

July 13, 2002—God has already given her a job. On Thursday she found out she will be the new ESL teacher at Lufkin Middle School. God is so good! So he will move to Lufkin now.

~

July 15, 2002—Jamie is still battling her thought life even after two years overseas. Satan fills her mind with doubt, fear, and lies to the point of overwhelming. Gene and I prayed for her last night.

~

July 27, 2002—They are in Waxahachie packing his things to move to Lufkin. She called at midnight. He proposed and gave her a ring! She is so happy. She has waited a long time for this.

~

August 3, 2002—He got a job at Coston Elementary as a special education teacher's aide.

November 29, 2002—Last night I cried because of how much money he owes that will keep us away longer. I added things up, and we've paid about $5,000 since I got here. And we owe about $39,000 more. If he doesn't help me more and take more responsibility for things, we're going to have trouble taking care of our commitments. I prayed that God will do a miracle. Then I started crying because of all my friends in Northern Asia. I decided to make something of my sorrow, so I prayed for my friends. God gave me peace.

I am frustrated because I have to go through more preparation time before I go back because I am getting married. At the age of twenty-six, I should be about ready to go back, but marrying him pulls me back. I asked God to give me one more sign that I'm to marry him, and to give me the right attitude. Right now I see marriage to him as something that will hold me back and put a heavy burden on me, not as what I used to see it as. If God would do a miracle, though, I wouldn't see it that way. If He would tell me one more time for sure, I'd never doubt again. I feel like this preparation for marriage/wedding time is so wasteful. I don't want to waste days upon days preparing for a two hour event. What about souls? This is how I feel.

And more than getting married, I want to return to Northern Asia. But we've already put down so much money (Mom and Dad have). The wedding will happen March 8. I just hope I have the right attitude by then.

November 30, 2002—"Whoever watches the wind will not plant; whoever looks at the clouds will not reap…So you cannot understand the work of God, the Maker of all things" (Eccles. 11:4–5). Always waiting for good perfect conditions or safe, less risky conditions will accomplish nothing. You can't wait for the right number of kids or a "safe" place to go before you follow Jesus. You must "just do it," or nothing will get done.

Today MawMaw Allen told me I could spend up to $1,500 on bedroom furniture and she will cover it! And that is such a blessing. God is giving us $1,500! Praise Jesus!

~

December 1, 2002—For the past few Sundays, I have been so thankful because I see growth in my inner thought life. I just praise God during the singing for deliverance. Yes, it is still hard sometimes, but it is getting easier as my mind gets more renewed. It's as if prayers which have been stored up in heaven, calling for deliverance for years, are being answered! God is good!

I remember those two years in my home across the ocean. At times, I could hardly stand spiritually. I felt for my spiritual survival, the most logical thing for me was to return to America to get built up. But I knew that though that seemed logical, God had called me there. I felt like it was similar to spiritual suicide to stay there and keep giving out; but I kept on, by God's grace. Because of that persistence, God blessed many lives, and showed me He never leaves us or lets us slip out of His hand. It is amazing the things we consider "impossible" that we can do, when we just do it by Jesus's power. Praise God!

~

December 2, 2002—I have more peace about marrying him. I love him, and I'm not going to worry about his faults. We are doing premarital counseling, and that will help. God will help us.

~

December 4, 2002—Today I had a very hard struggle. Last night I repented in Jesus's name of everything, but it was so hard today. However, He reminded me of Philippians 1:6: "Being confident of this, that he who began a good work in you will carry it on to completion until the day of Christ Jesus."

"That is why, for Christ's sake, I delight in weaknesses, in insults, in hardships, in persecutions, in difficulties. For when I am weak, then I am strong" (2 Cor. 12:10).

~

March 8, 2003—Dear Mom and Dad: Well, the day is finally here! The day some of us have anticipated and others have dreaded since the day I was wrapped in a blue blanket (the hospital nursery got it wrong)! Thank you for loving me so much. I have never doubted your love for me. I appreciate your godly example of how a marriage should be. And yes, even though I am getting married today, you will always be my parents, and I will always be your little girl. I love you! Love always, Jamie.

~

March 19, 2003—We want to thank you again for our lovely wedding. We know you sacrificed so it would be just as we wanted it. We really don't know how to thank you enough for everything. But that is how it's been all my life. I love you so much. Jamie

Dear Mom and Dad: Thank you for your love, care, prayers, kindness, generosity, and your support throughout our relationship. Words are not adequate to relay how Jamie and I feel in regard to how much you have given and sacrificed to make our wedding a special day, beyond what we ever dreamed. Thank you for raising a godly wife for me. I love you both dearly.

~

July 12, 2003—From Jamie's Journal:

Everything changes. The only One who absolutely never changes is God. He went with me to Northern Asia three years ago, was with me the entire time, came back with me to America, and remains with me. In life, He is the only constant.

We've been married four months now, and the act is still so painful. What's wrong with me? This has been the hardest part of marriage—having the "right" finally—but not the ability. It makes me feel less than perfect as a wife. I cannot meet his need, and that worries me. Why God? Will the surgery be successful? I know God will take care of us.

July 13, 2003—Today I spent two hours listening, praying, and reading my Bible. God really spoke to me! Here are the things He impressed upon my heart:

1. When I get busy or overwhelmed, I tend to drop my time with Him.
2. I don't trust my husband with finances and organization, and I should.
3. I have no "secret place" where intimacy with God occurs often.
4. My prayer time has become a ritual, a habit, instead of fellowship.
5. I don't trust God enough, but I must. He is my keeper, the shade at my right hand.
6. I'm too legalistic with myself and others.
7. I am to evangelize all nations.
8. God isn't through with me yet.
9. "For who is he who will devote himself to be close to me? So you will be my people, and I will be your God" (Jer. 30:21–22).

July 26, 2003—Jamie had surgery yesterday, a laparoscopy and uterus suspension. There was no evidence of endometriosis. But her uterus was tilted forty-five degrees. He pulled it back into the right position and attached it. She should not have any more pain. We praise the Lord once again for answering prayer.

~

July 30, 2003—Well, I survived my surgery. My recovery has gone well, although I felt really bad the first twenty-four hours. I want to record a dream I had the night before my surgery, when I was nervous, and prayed for a good surgery and for peace. That night I dreamed I was in Dallas with him and others. We made a wrong turn and ended up at a house with an old lady. She was so nice to everyone, but especially to me. She begged us to stay and visit her and gave us flowers, more to me. Before we left, she asked me to stay behind. She opened up her Bible and read about Shadrach, Meshach, and Abednego. Then she looked directly at me and said, "Just as Jesus was with the three Hebrew children, He will be with you." Wow! I woke up with such peace! Thank You, Jesus!

~

July 31, 2003—I got afraid today as I walked through Walmart. What if we can never do it? Am I to live a life unable to enjoy what everyone around me says is so wonderful? Will our marriage survive if we can't benefit from the "glue" of marriage? I started to get depressed and foresee a future full of unmet desires.

Whatever happens, I will please Jesus to my utmost ability. He told me again, "My grace is sufficient for you!" He can use this struggle to make me stronger and improve our marriage. Whatever Jesus wants is what I want. By the way, I don't have to reconcile myself to depression because of this, and I don't have to accept a less than perfect marriage. I will not give a foothold to depression or resignation. I will not allow my joy or effectiveness to be stolen. God is my sufficiency.

On another note, I watched a beautiful video today from my home far away. Four of my students talked to me. It was a treasure! I cried as I listened to them talking about God and His plans for their lives. And they thanked me for helping them and praying for them. It was a great reward. I lay it all at the feet of Jesus and ask Him to keep them.

Here is something praiseworthy! There are thirteen new babies now from that first two years in my city. Thirteen! God is so good! It was so worth it because I was in God's will. I decided again today after watching the video to always do whatever Jesus wants me to do—regardless of the cost. Northern Asia is one piece in the puzzle that God is making of my life, and I was one piece of the puzzle in the ministry taking place on that campus and in that city. Praise the Lord!

August 1, 2003—Last night, we tried again. Once again—pain and tears. He tried to console me. I was very comforted in his love, but I hurt so much emotionally. All my life I was told, if I waited until my wedding night, it would be worth it. I was told how beautiful and wonderful it would be. I waited until March 8, 2003, at the age of twenty-seven. But this has been so disappointing. I am totally happy with my husband; he is wonderful. But this sex thing is so hard and so disappointing.

I woke up today to a beautiful card written by him, assuring me of his undying love. It comforted me, but I still cried over the disappointments of almost five months now and following years of anticipation. But in the midst of a flood of tears, I felt God's peace. He comforted me, and I will make it. God is big enough, and He will be by my side.

August 11, 2003—God is able to keep, restore, and use me. If He could use the murderer Paul, He can use me. I will never be proud of my accomplishments or "righteousness" again. Everything I am and ever will be is a gift of God. I have seen how utterly sinful I was before He touched me.

Yesterday, we tried again, and it didn't hurt! God is so good! I can finally say it was worth the wait!

August 15, 2003—Things have been stressful lately. Dealing with insurance from a minor car accident he had, red wasps in my classroom, PMS, and his job situation, I felt negative and discouraged and wanted to give up on trying to go back on the field. He even has an ingrown toenail!

But last night, I was so aware that God is with me. He has given me peace, and that means so much to me. He reminded me of several Scriptures. "And without faith it is impossible to please God, because anyone who comes to him must believe that he exists and that he rewards those who earnestly seek him" (Heb. 11:6). "You will seek me and find me when you seek me with all your heart" (Jer. 29:13). I really want to know God intimately. I know so much about Him and His Word, but I want to know Him.

October 17, 2003—Jamie confided in me that she still experiences extreme pain when they are intimate. The surgery she had in July did not help. She is going back to the doctor. We prayed. She may go back to her doctor in Houston.

~

October 31, 2003—Jamie saw her doctors in Houston. Her pain is all related to the endometriosis. It has produced stomach and colon problems in the way her body processes food. She is on a strict diet.

~

December 2, 2003—Jamie saw her doctors again and received a great report. Praise the Lord! Her colon looked 70 to 80 percent better, and her pain level has gone from ten to one! She lost nine pounds in one month and feels great. Thank you, Lord.

# Chapter 18

## *A Good Report*

Jamie wrote a personal history of her life in the early part of 2004. She tells her life story better than I ever could.

My parents, Gene and Karen Norton, reared me and my younger sister in a home centered in love. We never doubted their love for us because they showed it to us regardless of our behavior and treated us equally. We were also always able to talk to them about our problems. My parents had high standards for us girls, always encouraging us to "live a life above reproach" before the world. God was always the center of our home and family activities. We were in church whenever the doors were open, and often helped our mother do ministry work. After my sister and I were grown, my mother told us that she had raised us "for the ministry." She knew for a long time that I would be a missionary and Janet would be a pastor's wife.

Today I have a close relationship with both of my parents. They reared me to be independent, and although we live in the same city, they try not to interfere with our lives. They only give advice when we want it, and because of this we have been able to "leave and cleave." I now consider them my dearest friends, the ones whom I can share more with than anyone else in the world besides my husband.

Although we have a close relationship, my parents have never tried to hinder me from going overseas or from doing anything God has called me to do. They have always been very supportive of me—verbally, prayerfully, and with their actions. When I went to Northern Asia for two years as a single woman, it was heart-wrenching for them to watch my plane take off, but they told me that they would never want to come between me and God's call on my life. They still show that same attitude, now that my husband and I believe we are to spend the rest of our career overseas.

My father is a man of integrity. Honoring his commitments and speaking the truth is priority to him. He served as a deacon for sixteen years and has taught many Sunday school classes along with my mom. Many men in our church look up to him as a godly example. I can say as his daughter that my dad is the same at home as he is at church or anywhere else.

He is very laid-back and flexible. People love to be around him because he shows genuine love for them, and he has a great sense of humor. (As children, my sister and I thought he was corny, but now we love his humor!)

My father and I have a great relationship. He always made it clear as we were growing up that his family was more important to him than anything else except God. As the father of two daughters, he made us feel special. As I was growing up, others would often tell me about how he had been bragging about me or my sister. He lavished praise on us face-to-face as well.

When I turned fourteen, my father took me on my first date. That night he gave me a small gold and diamond heart ring. He told me that I was a lady, and that my heart belonged to him. He said that it would be his until he gave me away at the altar, and that I could call him anytime day or night if I ever got into a compromising situation. On that night, I promised him that I would save my virginity until my wedding night, and the ring was the symbol of that promise. In the following thirteen years until my marriage, that ring comforted me, reminding me that my dad would always be there for me. On my wedding night, I gave the ring, a symbol of my virginity, to my husband.

Today, I am still a daddy's girl. My dad still gives me hugs and kisses every time we are together. Though he knows that he isn't the main man in my life anymore, he cherishes me, and I cherish him. I couldn't ask for a better, warmer relationship with my "daddy."

My mother is a woman devoted to ministry. All of my life, she has awakened early in the morning, often at four, to pray and study the Scripture. Her whole life revolves around God and church, so our family has always revolved around those things as well. She has worked in the church for over twenty-three years, beginning as a secretary, and ending up as the Christian education director, as well as a licensed minister with the Assemblies of God. Growing up, my sister and I spent a lot of time after school at the church helping her or playing while she finished her work. Now that we are grown and married, my mother can devote even more time to preparing seminars, organizing small groups in the church, overseeing Sunday school, and the list goes on.

While my father is laid-back, my mother has been described as the Energizer Bunny. She can do more between 4:00 a.m. and 9:00 p.m. than anyone I know. She is very organized in her work, and can manage a household well. I'm not sure how she does it, but her house is usually very clean, and she has good meals on the table for my father, while at the same time ministering at the church so well.

My mom began reading to me at an early age. Every night we would say Scriptures together and pray together. By the age of three, I could quote the twenty-third Psalm and the Lord's Prayer thanks to my mother, and my love for memorization never stopped. I was a Missionette Star and a top North Texas Bible

Quizzer in the seventh and eighth grades. All of this started with my mother's nurturing and teaching.

While I was in Northern Asia from 2000 to 2002, my mom showed me in a very clear way how much she loved me. Although she was busy, she wrote me at least once every week while I was there, and sent me over seventy packages during my two-year stint! Often the postage cost more than the actual much-needed contents. She constantly reminded the church to pray for me and even wrote my quarterly newsletters for me based on information I sent back to her. She is the ultimate supportive mother and has been all of my life. I will never forget her and my father's sacrificial support while I was overseas, and that has made them both even more precious to me.

Though she has many important ministries in our church, my mother has made it clear throughout my life that she always has time for me, and that her family comes before her ministry. Her priorities are right, and she is willing to sacrifice anything for God, her family, and ministry. She is my role model, the woman I hope to be like one day. And as a married woman, I am thankful to have her as my friend.

Janet Yancey, my sister, is twenty months younger than me. I am thankful to say that both she and her husband Jeremy are very healthy and have been happily married for almost four years. They serve as youth pastors for over two hundred teenagers in an Assemblies of God church in Wichita, Kansas. Janet and Jeremy love ministry and have a big vision for God's work. They are also not afraid to work hard for their teenagers. Along with helping her husband, Janet works full time as a recruiter in a Wichita hospital. They have an infant daughter, Sage Elizabeth, whom we are very proud of.

Janet and I were like night and day growing up. She was the "glamorous," well-dressed trendy sister; I was often the out-of-style average sister. Janet loved to talk on the phone for hours to one friend after the other while I was in my bedroom studying.

She loved to have fun; I was more serious. She was outgoing; I was introverted. We were each secretly envious of each other for years. Janet always wanted to be like me, and I always wanted to be like her! My mother, in trying to explain our sibling rivalry, once told us that she thinks that because we were so close in age, each of us tried to be different from the other to assert our individuality. I think that is a fair observation.

When I went away to college during my sister's senior year in high school, Janet and I missed each other and began to realize how much we loved each other. We became friends that year, more than we had been before. The next year when she came to the same college as me, our friendship deepened. We realized what a special bond we had as sisters. We also realized that friends come and go, but sisters are forever.

It was hard for me to watch her get married three years before I did, and it was hard for her to watch me go to Northern Asia soon after her wedding, but we have never lost our closeness. I am happy to say that her husband, Jeremy, fits into our family as if he was always meant to be there, and I thank God for my sister and her family.

As a child, I was the "smart kid." My parents enrolled me in kindergarten at the age of four because by then they had already taught me to read. They had me repeat kindergarten the next year because they didn't want me to be a year younger than my peers for the rest of my school years. I loved school, and my sister and I often played school at home. In the fourth grade, I was enrolled in the Gifted and Talented program in our school district in which I stayed until high school, where there were other advanced classes available. When I think about my elementary school, I think of the love of my teachers and principal. The adults at that public school just oozed love, making it a warm and happy place to learn. I had several close girl friends in elementary school, one of which was a bridesmaid in my wedding. I must admit that I was cocky as a child because of my intelligence. I also thought I was "better" than most kids because I was a "good" kid. I have since learned that I have no reason to be proud because all of my gifts are from God, and it is only by His grace that I can be righteous.

In junior high, my life was very busy. I continued competing in the Angelina County Spelling Bee, which I had begun doing with my teachers in elementary school. I also began competing in Teen Bible Quiz. My Bible Quiz coach, Lawrence Purke, developed a strong relationship with me, and throughout my life has kept up with me, checking on me and offering his prayers, love, and support. Another thing that I enjoyed doing in junior high and continued to do through my senior year of high school was play the French horn in the band. But in my opinion, my biggest achievement was co-starting Cougars for Christ, a Christian group that met once a week before school. I had the approval of the school counselor and principal to lead this group in my public school. To my knowledge, the group was in operation several years after I left junior high.

Most of my friends in junior high and high school were fellow "band nerds" like me. I made two close friends who became lifelong friends and were also in my wedding. I am thankful to God for parents who taught me the importance of choosing friends with good morals early in life. Because of the friends I surrounded myself with, I never had to face peer pressure even in high school to try things such as drinking, smoking, or doing drugs. It was just something my friends and I never would have considered.

In high school, my school life was centered on two things: band and academics. I loved the French horn and competing for first chair. My friends would laugh at how competitive I was. I wasn't a good loser either. (I still like a good challenge, but I hope I am a better loser!) I also pursued my lifelong dream of becoming valedictorian and following in my mother's footsteps. I fell short of my goal, only graduating third in the class (summa cum laude) after many hours of homework and studying. But in a graduating class of 376, a third place ranking was good enough to help me get financial aid for college.

During high school, I was also very involved in church activities. I coached a Junior Bible Quiz team four years, combining my love for competition, my love for memorization of God's Word, and my love for teaching one-on-one. I also served on the youth Servant's Council, assisting our youth pastor, Russ Madill, whose example in ministry had a great impact on my life. Once, he took some of us on a ski retreat, and while I was there he mentioned to me that he didn't like to ski. I was astonished and asked him why he had come. He looked at me and said, "When you are in ministry, you put the needs of the ones to whom you are ministering before your own." His words stuck with me and have influenced my decisions in ministry ever since.

After my high school graduation, I enrolled at Stephen F. Austin State University. I didn't go there because I felt it was God's will, but because the school was nearby, and it was completely paid for through scholarships. That was a miserable year. Although I made excellent grades (3.844 GPA), I had a thirty-minute daily commute and was unable to make good friends. I walked around the campus in misery. That spring semester I knew I had made the wrong choice for college because I hadn't sought God's will enough. I decided that I would go wherever He led me the rest of my life.

After one visit to my alma mater, I knew God wanted me there. The next three years were vital to my spiritual development. Through my relationships with strong ministry-minded Christians, my love for God and ministry deepened. I served as a Resident Assistant, taking care of the spiritual, social, physical, emotional, and academic needs of freshmen on my hall. This position was a twenty-four-hour-a-day commitment, but it was worth it. I learned how to pour myself out into others as an RA, often counseling young women into the early morning hours. I also received valuable experience in working under the leadership of my dorm pastor who taught me what loyalty and associate pastoral ministry were really like. I also received the honor of being elected Resident Assistant of the Year by my fellow RAs.

After graduating with a BS in secondary education (3.95 GPA) in 1998, I enrolled in graduate school at the University of Texas in Arlington, where I pursued a master's in linguistics. I did not complete it after two years of coursework, but I did receive a graduate level certificate for Teaching English as a Second or Foreign Language. Studying linguistics was good for me because I learned much about language development and language teaching. I also had the opportunity to work full-time as a teacher in the English Language Institute, UTA's English language program for international students. There I taught students ranging in age from sixteen to forty-five from over twenty countries. And there I developed my teaching style and love for international students.

In the fall of 2000, I did not continue my master's work; instead I followed God's open door to be a missionary associate in Northern Asia. I left UTA graduate school with all As and two Bs, lacking eight hours from finishing my master's in linguistics. I understand that missionaries are often able to complete a master's degree while on the field. It is my desire to earn an MA perhaps in Christian education to help me better serve in Northern Asia.

I was four years old when I was born again. I do not remember the experience, but my mother tells me the story in this way: "We were kneeling at your bed one night praying. I was praying, and then you said, 'Be quiet, Mommy. I want to pray.' Then you proceeded to ask Jesus into your heart."

From that time on, I have walked with Jesus. I have not been perfect, but He has never left me. He has always been and always will be with me and me with Him.

At the age of seven, I began to desire the baptism in the Holy Spirit. I knew that it was a gift that God had for me, and I wanted everything I could have. I began to pray for the baptism but did not receive it until I was eight. That Valentine's night, Evangelist Don Brankel called for people who wanted the baptism to come to the altars. Our senior citizens' pastor "prayed through" with me, simply telling me, "Just tell Jesus you love him." I did, and Jesus baptized me in the Holy Spirit, and I began to speak in another language. I was so excited. To an eight-year-old child, waiting for a few months for something seems so long. I was so happy to receive the gift that I continued speaking in tongues in the car as my parents drove us home, and even when I was brushing my teeth. I just didn't want to stop! I was happy that God had given me the precious gift. And I had an immediate boldness after receiving the baptism.

When I was thirteen years old, I was lying in bed one night. All of a sudden, I knew that God had called me into the ministry. I can't remember it all clearly, but I do remember knowing beyond a shadow of a doubt that I was to be in the ministry. I was excited to think that He had something special for me to do.

God didn't tell me what He wanted me to do for years after that. Finally in 1995, He told me where to go to school and I majored in secondary education because a female faculty advisor told me that majoring in Christian education wasn't very practical. She said that it would be difficult for me to find a church that would hire a female Christian Education Director. Though I was disappointed, I followed her advice.

I later determined to change my major to something more ministry-related, like pastoral ministries. But God spoke to me clearly my first year at the university and told me to continue majoring in education, so I did. While there, He opened my eyes and my heart to the mission field. Before then, I just hadn't realized the enormous harvest field that existed outside of America. During my second year at the university, God began to deal with me specifically about going to Northern Asia. By the time I graduated, I knew that God wanted me to spend at least two years in

Northern Asia as a university teacher. So in July of 2000, I left my family, friends, and country to follow Him, a decision that would forever change my life.

I went to Northern Asia out of pure obedience. It's not that I had always wanted to go there. It's just that I knew God wanted me there, and I knew that the safest and best place to be in the world was in the center of His will.

I wasn't there very long before I recognized the overwhelming need of the lost people around me. I was surrounded by a multitude of people with long, dull faces who had never heard the name of Jesus. Sometimes the lost mass of humanity in the streets was unbearable for me to think about, for I knew that most of them were headed to hell because they did not know Jesus.

I began to pray about God's future plan for my life. I knew He had called me to full-time ministry at the age of thirteen, but did He intend for me to spend my career in Asia? The more I prayed, the more I knew I was created to serve in Northern Asia for the rest of my life.

We were married by Dr. G, former president of my university and missionary to Asia. Before the wedding, we made it clear to him that our plans are to go to Northern Asia as soon as we can. He spoke of our call in our wedding ceremony, speaking about how God has a great divine purpose in our marriage. We both believe that. We believe that "two are better than one," and we are anxiously waiting for the day when we can help more Asians find Jesus. This is our passion.

Our call to Northern Asia has been confirmed several times. After I accepted the call, my mother told me, "I always knew from the time you were a child that you would be a missionary." She just hadn't told me because she didn't want to play God in my life. Also, at our wedding, our associate pastor at the time, Andy Salagaj, saw a vision of a woman standing in a black ocean. The woman looked Asian, and she was calling for someone to come to her. The more clearly he could see the woman, the more he realized that she was not standing in an ocean, but in a great sea of people. He told us after the wedding that he interpreted the vision to pertain to our future. These confirmations from God's people are great reassurances to us of His calling and plans. We believe that God's plans are great because He is great!

Although I have never been on a church staff, I have much ministry experience. I helped in Vacation Bible School five years, teaching classes with up to twenty-five students. I coached Junior Bible Quiz for four years (1990–1994), teaching students from grades three through six, and being responsible for between four and twelve students during that time. I also coached Teen Bible Quiz for two years (1994–1995 and 1999–2000). This was one of my favorite ministries. It was great to see teenagers have fun learning God's Word.

I have been a witness in public schools. As I already mentioned, I co-began and lead Cougars for Christ, a Bible study in my school. Here I discovered my love for giving devotions to groups of people. I also served as the chaplain for my high school band, leading the band in prayer before trips and football games my senior year in high school.

I served as a camp counselor for Dallas Metro, an A/G ministry to inner-city kids in 1996. This was the first time I had a lot of close contact with people of another race, and it opened my eyes to some prejudice in me toward them. I believe God has helped me with this after showing me that weakness in my life. I also served as a summer camp counselor for our church youth group in 1996, being responsible for about eight junior high girls. By doing this and by coaching teen Bible Quiz, I learned a lot about junior high students and how to love them.

While I was a freshman in college, I wrote a discipleship tract entitled "What Next?" for the church to give to new converts. During this time of my life, God impressed on me the importance of following up on new converts.

I worked in the office at my church in the summer of 1996, helping my pastor organize the mission's material and the library and writing a history of our church.

While in graduate school, my roommate and I taught third grade Sunday school for a year. These children were a bit too young for us, but we finished our commitment to teach for a year. Also, while in graduate school, I helped begin All Nations Church in Arlington, Texas. I invited people to the church, led the first convert to God, and helped them start their English as a Second Language program. It was so exciting to be a small part in this church planting ministry, but I could not participate for long, because I soon had to focus on my preparations to go to Northern Asia. The final ministry I did while in graduate school was tutoring two Saudi Arabian women in their home in the spring semester of 2000, trying to reach out to their families with the love of Christ. What a love for Muslims I received from doing this!

Since returning to the States in 2002, I have served as a pastor's prayer partner, led monthly mission's prayer meetings, and helped in several outreach projects in my church. I have also spoken from God's Word and about my work in Asia to at least seventeen groups of people. The groups include my entire church body, various groups of young people, college groups, our church's senior citizens' group, home groups, various children's groups, four other church organizations, a junior high group at a public school, and a jail ministry.

My husband and I have also started teaching fifth and sixth grade boys in Sunday school. I believe we can relate to preteens better than younger elementary students, and we are going to learn how to reach this age group better by serving in this ministry. We are also starting to serve in weekly hospital visitations under the direction of the pastoral staff of our church. This is particularly exciting to us, because we love visiting hurting people. One-on-one ministry is our strength, and we are greatly looking forward to helping God's people who are in need of encouragement and prayer.

When I was in Northern Asia as a missionary associate, I was assigned for two years to a small city where there were only two foreigners, a career missionary and myself. The career missionary was a single woman from Great Britain who had lived there for several years. She was about thirteen years older than me, and while she helped me find my way around the city and helped get me set up at the university, she offered me little to no emotional support. I was dealing with culture shock, homesickness, and extreme loneliness, and the students at the university took around six months to consider me a friend. Even then, because I was ministering to them, I couldn't confide in them completely.

That was a long and lonely year. We were eight hours away from the other missionaries on the team, so I had no one nearby to listen to me, support me, and be my friend. Culture shock is hard enough, but facing it alone was very challenging.

Of course, I was not alone. Jesus had promised that he would be with me to the ends of the earth, and He was certainly with me during that lonely year. He took care of me, and I was able to develop telephone friendships with other team members far away. My mother also became my sounding board. She and my father listened to me talk about the loneliness and offered much emotional support from across the ocean.

The first year came to an end, and another team member came to join us. The new member and I became very close; she was an answer to prayer. I was stretched in my first year in Northern Asia, but it was yet another chance for God to remind me how His grace is truly sufficient for me.

I believe my greatest gift is working one-on-one with people, befriending, mentoring, and teaching them. I love coming alongside people and showing them God's love. I am a good listener, and love encouraging others in the Scripture. God has also gifted me as a classroom teacher. He gives me creative ways to teach others.

As for my character traits, I am a very persistent person. I strive to be committed, not backing down on a commitment or giving up when things become difficult. I don't need to see results to be motivated to keep doing what I believe God wants me to do. I developed this by watching my parents' faithfulness in ministry. Finally, I am flexible. When changes in plans occur or glitches happen, I can roll with them and make changes as necessary. Living in a developing country, I found that this is a good trait to have.

In my personal life, I still need to work on patience. Living overseas, I was able to develop my patience more, but I still need improvement in this area. I also have a tendency to worry, but I believe God is helping me in this area as well. He continually brings me through things, step by step, and reminds me that I don't need to worry. The more I walk with God, the easier it becomes to trust Him with things that are beyond my control.

I went to Northern Asia at the age of twenty-four, from July of 2000 to July of 2002. With strong prayer and financial support from my home church, I was a missionary associate from North Texas. I served in a small "city," where thousands of people still live in caves. I lived and worked at the university, where I taught foreign language majors English. While I was there, the number of converts rose from two to seven. Since then, there have been other converts. The number of converts is a small reflection of what God did during those two years. I was able to spend many hours with students, developing relationships, pointing them to Christ when allowed and discipling believers. I was also able to participate in a Bible study with several students weekly. I believe that God is still doing a great work in that city.

As I listed above, the outreaches I have been involved in were through my local church, rather than through the district. Some of the events include a Thanksgiving meal for the less fortunate in our city, a visitation project inviting people to church, Fall "Famtastic" Night, and a Christmas gift outreach to underprivileged children.

God is growing me. He has brought me to a place where I have seen His faithfulness so many times that it is becoming easier to trust Him with things beyond my control. Also, when I think about the tremendous sacrifice Christ paid for me at Calvary, I can better understand His love for me, and I want to be closer to Him and to have every impurity wiped out of my life.

I have consistent prayer and Bible study time daily. I typically spend at least forty-five minutes a day with the Lord. Most of my prayer time is usually spent in intercession for others, and lifting up Northern Asia is one of my regular habits. I pray for those I met over there, both nationals and foreign workers. I also lift up my pastor and church leadership along with my family and friends. After praying, I read the Word. I am presently working on reading the Bible through again this year. It is dear to me to see how God can speak to us in different ways at different times in our lives with passages that we have read several times before.

I am my biggest critic, but God is showing me that He can use me despite my weaknesses; in fact, His strength becomes perfect in my weakness.

# Chapter 19

## *2004–2007*

January 3, 2004—God has been speaking to me lately, and I want to write down what He is saying. He is like a big old white house tucked away in the forest. The house is warm and light glows from the windows. It is always open for anyone to enter. In the house is everything we need—provision and plenty of food in the fridge, security (it is always safe there), and unconditional love. We are never put down or abandoned there, but encouraged, uplifted, and re-energized to do the task before us. It isn't a house where we just go to get "pumped up." It is a house where we can abide. It is the house of His presence. There is only one way in which to enter—a straight sidewalk that leads to the house. The sidewalk is Jesus.

We must point others to the sidewalk that can lead them to so much love, provision, comfort, and safety. Not only should we be signs pointing the way to Jesus, we must also be big white cozy houses for the hurting. We should abide in God's presence so much that we become people of His presence. We become a safe place where hurting people can go. We become a place where the lost can find unconditional love and safety. We become a cozy home where the fire of the Holy Spirit burns within us. God isn't only a warm home for us; He wants us to become a warm home for others that will help them finally "come home." This metaphor is changing how I see God. It makes Him easier to trust and approach, and it encourages me to be more like Him.

The closer we are to God, the less the attractions and distractions of the world affect us. Going into God's presence cures many of our problems.

Also, when God told Noah to build the ark and put every kind of animal inside, he did. He didn't question, "How in the world am I supposed to round up all those animals?" He just started building. For a hundred years he built and obeyed God. In the end, the animals came to Noah. This is how God works. He calls us. We go to work, and He takes care of the rest. There may be parts of His instructions that seem impossible, but we are to obey what He tells us and let Him take care of the details in His time. Don't sweat the small stuff!

February 28, 2004—Jamie saw the doctors again in Houston on Thursday. She was doing well, except she needs to stick closer to her diet and lose nineteen more pounds. She was also referred to a third doctor who did a biopsy on abnormal cells (unrelated to the endometriosis); the results should be back in a few weeks.

March 17, 2004—Jamie went back to the doctor. She has Human Papillomavirus (HPV) that will require laser surgery and six weeks of injections.

April 7, 2004—I talked to Jamie. Her insurance will not pay for the injections she must have, and they are very expensive. Also, more things are coming back on his credit report of money he owes. They need healing and a financial miracle.

~

April 15, 2004—Jamie starts taking the interferon injections today. This is a type of chemotherapy and can have horrible side effects. "Dear God, please take care of our Jamie, protect and heal her."

~

April 18, 2004—We have now been married over thirteen months, and we still cannot have physical intimacy without extreme pain. Surgery didn't help. The books we've read haven't helped.

On our wedding night in our hotel room, I gave him a little gold heart ring, the ring my father gave me when I was fourteen years old. It was a symbol of Dad's promise to take care of me, and of my promise to "do the right thing and wait for the ring." I saved myself for my husband. Then came the many tears and disappointments. I felt like a loser wife, a defective wedding present. He assured me I was not. I felt inadequate, but he always loved and encouraged me.

"Why is this happening to me? So she went to inquire of the Lord" (Gen. 25:22). It's okay to ask, "Why?" God can handle our whys. But we must follow that up with seeking after God.

~

April 24, 2004—It dawned on me that even though I don't know why, how, when, or where I was infected with HPV, God does. In fact, God, who takes care of me and who owns me had to give permission for the infection to occur. I thought HPV was a sexually transmitted disease!

The other day I felt God's hand on me in a very powerful way. The key to all of this is agreeing with God's people in prayer. We have used every penny we have and then some on medical procedures and medicine, injections, vitamins, and minerals. We have gone to five doctors; I had an outpatient surgery, a laser procedure, an extreme diet, and dangerous medications. We have told many people so they will pray. We have requested prayer at church on more than one occasion and have been anointed with oil. Many are praying, but we have no other resources.

On the cross, Jesus purchased my healing. The woman with the issue of blood for twelve years spent every penny she had and still no healing. All she had to do was touch the hem of Jesus's garment. And that is all I need to do. The sense of aloneness from people (not God) is hard to accept. No one, not even Mom and Dad, understand what we face. I tell them I am very sad, and they assume it is the medication, which can cause depression. But they don't know what it's like to be disappointed and frustrated over and over again for thirteen months.

May 9, 2004—This week has been hard. My hair is falling out from the injections. I am also experiencing depression, moodiness, and cold symptoms. I talked to Nathalie today, and she said the devil kicks us when we're down; God never does. He allows things to happen to us to grow us, but we can't give up on God and His calling. Also, God sends His cheerleaders our way to encourage us—sweet cards in the mail, phone calls, and people who walk up to us and say they are praying for us.

May 17, 2004—A letter from Terri:

Dear Jamie: I can't describe how much I miss the time when you were here. Both of us were pretty much open in talking about everything, and you have no idea how much you have influenced my life. Nobody can replace you. Although I have other American friends as well as Asian, none of them have the same kind of influence on me as you have. One thing so special about you is that you never failed to encourage me, even though I knew

I wasn't doing a great job, or being an amazingly nice person. I simply wish that you could come here again.

~

May 25, 2004—God has blessed us in so many small ways financially that add up to a lot this month! I have wanted to go to Kansas to see Janet, but we didn't have the money for gas. Mom gave us a hundred-dollar Walmart gift card (I know that was a sacrifice for them), so now we can go! Our church family here in Lufkin has blessed us in so many ways with love offerings, gift cards, taken us out to eat, etc. Also, the church is going to hire him, and part of his responsibility will be to fix up the house on Southwood! We will live there free of charge until we go back to Northern Asia! God is amazing!

~

June 14, 2004—Tonight at WMs, Darcy spoke about overcoming bondages. No one went forward. God gave Mom a tongue and interpretation that said, "What are you waiting for?"

I went forward once again for my thoughts. I didn't tell anyone what I was praying for. Darcy prayed powerfully over me. In the prayer, she said, "You have called her from her mother's womb. Set her free. You have destined her to have children that will touch the world." I knew God was telling me I would have children! Then Charlotte told me, "God wants me to tell you that your answer is on the way." I knew that applied to my thoughts. God wants me to look to Jesus, not my struggles, or my fear of falling. Just look to Jesus.

After I sat down, Debbie came over to me and said, "May I talk with you? While you were praying, God showed me something. You were sitting on a bench that was around a tree. All around you, sitting on the ground were children of many races. You were teaching them the Bible. And God said, 'I will give you children to many nations.'" She said she didn't know if it meant they would be from my womb or if they are spiritual children.

~

"So then, those who suffer according to God's will should commit themselves to their faithful Creator and continue to do good" (1 Pe. 4:19). "The righteous person may have many troubles, but the Lord delivers him from them all" (Ps. 34:19).

~

June 26, 2004—This morning at three thirty, God woke me and called me to Himself, wanting everything—my thoughts, will, time, and future. I gave myself to Jesus (again). He took me for who I am, weaknesses and all. He reminded me of 2 Corinthians 10:4. "The weapons we fight with are not the weapons of the world. On the contrary, they have divine power to demolish strongholds." Before I woke up, I was praying in the Spirit in my dream.

~

June 30, 2004—Jamie received three good doctor reports yesterday. Praise the Lord! Two doctors released her; the third wants to see her in four months. One minor problem must heal—a tear caused by the laser surgery. Otherwise she is doing great. All praise and glory go to our Lord!

~

July 6, 2004—Jamie spoke at our ladies meeting last night and gave her very personal testimony of the pain and suffering she has endured since her wedding night including her experience with HPV.

"My flesh and my heart may fail, but God is the strength of my heart and my portion forever" (Ps. 73:26).

"But he said to me, 'My grace is sufficient for you, for my power is made perfect in weakness.' Therefore I will boast all the more gladly about my weaknesses, so that Christ's power may rest on me" (2 Cor. 12:9).

September 8, 2004—Dear Jamie: Hi, beautiful. Happy eighteen month anniversary! I've been thinking about you all day today and realize just how much I love you and miss you when we are apart. If you're a little taste of heaven, then heaven must be pretty awesome! You're the rainbow in my sky, the colors in my sunset, the roses in my garden, the skip in my step, the beat in my heart, the consuming thoughts on my mind, and the love of my life!

These verses summarize you pretty well: "She is clothed with strength and dignity; she can laugh at the days to come. She speaks with wisdom, and faithful instruction is on her tongue. Charm is deceptive, and beauty is fleeting; but a woman who fears the Lord is to be praised" (Prov. 31:25–26, 30).

July 17, 2005—He and Jamie were in an accident yesterday on the interstate between Joplin and Springfield. A piece of black debris (perhaps a piece of tire) came through (bounced off) their windshield. It crumpled the hood and broke the windshield. They are okay except for cuts and scrapes. They are still picking out glass. God protected them. Jamie had just read Isaiah 54:17, "No weapon forged against you will prevail," the day before. We are so thankful to God for His protection. I have a feeling the enemy does not want Jamie to return to her city. Our God is greater still!

~

October 21, 2005—Today we will take them to Dallas to board the plane in the morning. They are ready to sew their lives into Northern Asia. God has blessed them in every way. He is faithful to Gene and me too. I know He is in control and He will bless. They will live in a larger city for the first three years and attend language school.

~

October 23, 2005—We said our good-byes at the DFW gate at 6:00 a.m. yesterday to our precious children. Yesterday was an emotional day. I'm still teary, but it will get better.

~

February 7, 2006—Jamie called yesterday morning from Thailand, and we talked for over an hour. She has been to a doctor, and they think they have nailed her problem—a problem she has had since seventh grade when she first sensed God's call on her life. I thought she was over it because she has not mentioned it to me in several years.

Jamie has wrestled for seventeen years with her mind—not being able to control her thoughts, mind racing, thoughts of sin, unworthiness, repenting over and over when there is no sin. This is something people are born with; it is how their brain is wired from birth; a condition seen in highly intelligent individuals, highly religious, and very conscientious people. She finds it difficult to sit still for twenty minutes and listen to God. It involves the brain and how it produces glucose and usually means a deficiency in serotonin. It is a chemical imbalance in the brain. It is Obsessive Compulsive Disorder (OCD) or sometimes called the doubting disease.

She has done a lot of reading and study on the subject. It all makes sense to her. She must learn to balance eating, rest, stress, and work in her life and remove caffeine and sugar from her diet. The doctors have prescribed Prozac 20mg/daily. "Dear God, please help my baby."

~

March and April, 2006—He has been sick for several weeks with what the doctors thought was pneumonia, then possibly typhoid. Both were ruled out, but they did find liver damage and a heart problem.

~

October 4, 2006—Jamie called me yesterday morning at work. They are in Thailand for a few weeks and doing well. They are beginning the adoption process. They are very excited! May God bless them and that little one God has for them.

~

November 19, 2006—We talked to Jamie last night. She told us they are going to name their Chinese daughter Karen Vi after both grandmothers! I'm thrilled!

"May you live to see your children's children" (Ps. 128:6).

~

February 10, 2007—Jamie called and told us she is pregnant! And they will continue the adoption process as planned. We will soon have two little ones! We are thrilled beyond words!

~

March 14, 2007—Gene left for Austin at four this morning to go pick up their criminal background checks at the DPS and take it to the Secretary of State's office for authentification. Hopefully this will speed things up in the adoption process.

As their power of attorney, Gene and I have taken care of all of their business stateside while they are oversees. I also type and mail all of their newsletters and help them stay in touch with their many prayer and financial supporters.

~

March 22, 2007—Yesterday, Gene and I went to Austin again to do more paperwork for their adoption. Gene talked to her last night. She is doing better (she has been spotting). There is still much to be done by the May 1 adoption paperwork deadline.

~

June 9, 2007—e-mail from Jamie:

Happy 35th anniversary! I am so thankful you guys have a great marriage, a successful and strong marriage that has helped make me and Janet strong, has helped us feel secure our whole lives, and has modeled for us how to have the best Father has for us!

I know that there are many ways to "evaluate" a marriage, but I think that one thing you can do is look and see who your daughters chose for spouses, and how happy we are as wives. You guys have given us such a precious gift! Thank you!

But of course, your anniversary is your day. We hope you have a very special day today. You deserve it. We are so happy for you! It was such a treat to talk to you last night on the phone. Your encouragement was just what we needed. You always have a way of brightening our day! Thanks. We are getting so excited to see you soon! I better go. I have another e-mail coming your way with "business" items. I wanted to send this one first. I love you!

July 22, 2007—The church gave Jamie a baby shower yesterday and it was wonderful! She received so many things she needed and people even helped with shipping! We will box and ship everything this week.

July 28, 2007—Jamie called yesterday morning to let us know it's a boy! We are so excited to have Caleb Daniel Lund on the way! Jamie and Caleb are doing fine.

August 10, 2007—We shipped eight boxes to them today, full of baby things.

# Chapter 20

## *Prayers for My Children*

Children are a heritage from the Lord, offspring a reward from him.

—Ps. 127:3

May 14, 2007—Today as I prayed for our children and us, I realized that Father has a destiny for our family as a whole, not only a destiny for each member. There is a reason why our adoption process met the May 1 deadline, a reason why the two babies will be so close in age, a reason why we had to wait two and a half years to get pregnant, even a reason why the baby in my womb is either a boy or a girl. He has a plan—a destiny—for us as a family.

"What the righteous desire will be granted" (Prov. 10:24). What I desire for my family is that our home will be a place of love and a safe haven. That we and our children will love Jesus and the world He created. That our children will surrender their lives to Jesus at an early age and never turn back. That they will see in me and their daddy unconditional love and thus know and understand the Father's love better. That we would all be healthy and live long and productive lives for Father's kingdom. That my children will marry godly mates and serve God with their mates in the capacity He calls them. That our little family will fulfill the destiny for which God has created us.

May 17, 2007—My biggest prayer for us during this pregnancy has been for wisdom to raise these children right. On the eve of becoming king, Solomon asked God for this one thing, and God was pleased with His request and gave him much more. I believe the Lord will also be pleased with my request for wisdom. I need wisdom, not just to be a good mom, but to be Karen and Caleb/ Katie's mom.

May 18, 2007—"A friend loves at all times, and a brother is born for a time of adversity" (Prov. 17:17). We believe that this is why Caleb is being born right now, so close to us getting Karen. Why, in other words, did I suddenly get pregnant after two and a half years of trying, and finally pursuing, adoption? He and I believe one reason is that Caleb will help Karen.

When we get Karen, she might not know how to cry, because orphans here usually don't cry. They don't cry because it does no good; no one helps them. But when Karen comes into our home, she will have a brother that, though small, can teach her by his example. When he cries, we will be there for him. Karen will thus learn it is okay to cry and that she is in a place of love and care where her needs will be met. What a beautiful reason for Caleb to be born right now at this point in history. Even before he knows what he is doing, he will be used by the Lord to bless his sister. Thank You, Lord Jesus!

June 22, 2007—The Lord is showing me things about His love. Right now, I have never seen my babies. I don't know if they are going to be plump or thin, extroverts or introverts, strong-willed or mild, even if they will be boy or girl. But I love them! Their personalities don't matter. I love them! They are mine. That is like

Father's love. He loves us unconditionally—period. Not because of who or how we are, but because He loves us.

~

June 30, 2007—My prayer for Karen Vi today is that she will not be defined by others as being "the Chinese orphan who was raised by foreigners," but as a girl/woman who is full of Christ's character—His fruit of the Spirit and gifts of the Spirit in operation—full operation in her life.

~

July 7, 2007—I am so thankful to be a woman. I love having this little baby in my womb. It is so beautiful to carry this life inside of mine. I have been told before how wonderful it is to be a woman and to have the privilege of childbirth, but I have never quite understood it until now. It truly is a miracle that God puts a life—a soul—into my womb, nurtures it, and then sends it into the world for me to nurture! What a special gift from Father it is to be a woman! To be a wife! To be a mom! Thank you, Jesus.

~

July 29, 2007—Dearest Caleb: Two days ago we found out you are a boy! Your daddy and I are so happy to welcome a boy into our home! We had to call your Memaw and Papa Norton and your Mimi and PopPops immediately! Everyone is so excited at the news! Before you are even born, you are giving many people so much joy!

We are naming you Caleb after the Caleb in the Bible, because we want you to be faithful to the Lord even when that is the unpopular thing to do. We want you to be faithful all the years of your life, even when you are old and to be used by God, as was Caleb in the Bible. The Daniel in your name is, of course, after your daddy and PopPops. I want you to continue following the heritage of both sides of your family to love and serve the Lord.

Oh, sweet Caleb, I want you to love Jesus, and to know Him for yourself. This is my biggest prayer for you. I pray that your daddy and I will be the kind of parents who model a love for Jesus and a devotion to Him that you will choose to follow.

My mom and dad have always been my biggest fans. When I was an elementary spelling bee queen, they spent countless hours calling out words to me so I could practice. Every time my heart was broken as a teenager, they listened to me. As a band student playing the French horn—which is still one of the best and happiest memories of my life—they went to as many games as they could, even out-of-town ones, to watch me march. They supported my decision where to go to college. When I started telling them within the first two months of studying at Bible College that Father might be speaking to me about living overseas, they listened respectfully and prayed that He would make His way clear. When I got on the plane five years later as a single twenty-four-year-old woman going to a place where people lived in caves and where there were only three foreigners in a large city, they were there. They took care of so much stuff for me stateside, including my finances, newsletters, etc. And when your daddy and I answered the call to live across the ocean for as long as we are allowed to, they stood behind us again, knowing we would only see each other every few years for the rest of our lives. Caleb, they are my biggest fans and always have been. I want to, along with your daddy, be your biggest fan here on earth.

We love you Sweetie Pie. We can't wait to see you. You couldn't have two parents who are more thrilled to welcome you and Karen Vi into our home. We thank God for you today and every day. I love you.

Mommy

August 6, 2007—Today, when I was praying, my cup overflowed with joy because of my two babies on the way! I never knew I would grow up to be a mom of a beautiful Asian girl and a handsome little boy. God has swept me off my feet in joy and gratitude! I'm going to be a mom! There is no more challenging and fulfilling duty on earth than lovingly raising children. God is smiling down on me!

August 28, 2007—Dear Karen: Last week I had a dream that a man took in an orphan and raised him, giving him a new life, including an education and all the necessities of life. I woke up thinking, "Wow! This is a great way to impact a life for the Lord!" Then I realized that is exactly what your daddy and I are doing by adopting you into our family! We hope to give you everything you need, to help you grow into a healthy young lady, to give you a great education and all the love we can. Most of all, our heart's desire for you is that you love Jesus from a very early age and all through your life.

We want you to know that, in our eyes, you are *not* an orphan we are bringing into our home. You are our daughter, even though right now we don't know where you are, how old you are, what makes you smile, or what you like. I told someone the other day that I have a son in my tummy and a daughter in my heart. That's where you are—in my heart and in the Lord's hands. I long to hold you and play with you. I long to show you off to everyone.

You are going to be a beautiful girl, and I will always love you. Nothing can ever take away your daddy's and my love for you. You are our very special gift from heaven. You are especially designed to fit into our family. God also called and designed us to be your mommy and daddy. Come to us soon, my little one! Your mommy loves you!

September 6, 2007—This year has been one of the best years of my life, even better than my nine-month engagement period when I was also walking through return-culture shock at the time. It has been better than our first year of marriage, which, although sweet, was hard due to physical problems. This year has been full of hope, joy, and anticipation! From the day the doctor in Thailand told me I was "weakly pregnant," I have been so happy and felt so blessed. I can't wait to be a mom!

October 5, 2007—We are in Beijing awaiting the arrival of our Caleb. I really want him to come soon. I have been walking more; the doctor said that could speed things up, and I have been asking the Lord to help him be born soon. But today, the Lord reminded me that His ways are higher than our ways. "As the heavens are higher than the earth, so are my ways higher than your ways and my thoughts than your thoughts" (Isa. 55:9).

# Chapter 21

## *A Grandson!*

October 9—November 6, 2007

October 9—It is 11:30 a.m., and Gene and I are currently at O'Hare Airport in Chicago waiting to board for Beijing. Our grandson was born approximately seventeen hours ago! Jamie endured thirty hours of labor and then a C-section after her water broke about 12:30 a.m. Monday morning (Oct. 8). Gene and I played the waiting game (not fun), waiting to hear from them. Finally, we heard at seven last night—eight pounds three ounces and twenty inches long, light brown hair and hungry! We woke at two thirty this morning, and Jeremy drove us to Houston at three. If our first grandson had been born in America, he would have the same birthday as great-grandmother Helen Waldron (Gene's mother). We are excited to see our Jamie, son-in-law, and grandson! God is so good to make a way for us to go. The bills are paid and the house is clean!

October 11—We arrived at the hospital about 4:30 p.m. yesterday. Jamie was radiant with that precious smile. We hugged and kissed and then I spotted that beautiful baby in the hospital basinet. O how precious he is! I immediately thought he looked so much like his daddy except for that cute little turned-up nose which definitely came from Jamie. The four of us were so proud and grateful to God for this precious gift to our family.

Monday, October 15, 8:00 a.m.—Yesterday, Jamie and baby were dismissed from the hospital and they all came to our hotel. We then took two taxis and all our luggage to the apartment they had been staying in while waiting for delivery. The people here believe a new mother and baby should remain indoors for at least thirty days, so we have been gently scolded by men and women for being out so soon. A five-day-old baby is never seen on these streets.

6:30 p.m.—He and Gene went to the Forbidden City, Tiananmen Square, and the Great Wall. Street sweepers with straw brooms can be seen everywhere earning a living for their families.

Tuesday, October 16, 10:00 p.m.—We are on the night train to Jamie's home. At the train station, we saw the "sea of heads" as far as the eye could see. Jamie has done remarkably well for having just had a C-section. I carried the baby. He went first as he was taller and bigger than everyone else and cleared a path for Jamie behind him, myself, and Gene bringing up the rear. All he had to do was raise his hand and people stopped so his family could stay together and get through the crowd safely.

Thursday, October 18, 7:40 a.m.—I did not sleep any on the train (maybe thirty minutes all night). Too much noise (grinding, rattling metal) and shaking going on! What an experience! Train-lag! But around five thirty this morning, I could see the countryside, mountain, snow-covered peaks, hills, a multitude of small gardens, and large fields. We saw a few people, including women, working in the fields, oxen plowing, and farmers slinging seed. We passed numerous shanty houses (very poor) and beautiful countryside, hills and valleys. The sleepless night was worth it.

Their apartment and nursery are beautiful. I see so many of the baby items I shipped to her that LFA blessed her with at the baby shower back home. God has given them much favor and rich blessings. They live on the seventh floor of a fairly new building. The language school is across the street.

Friday, October 19, 11:00 a.m.—We all went to a huge outdoor market. It was such a great experience. Jamie has made so many good friends who were delighted to see the new baby. However, we were still on the receiving end of the familiar scolding from perfect strangers on the streets telling us in their own language what a travesty it is to have such a tiny baby outside. We knew what they were saying. Jamie tried explaining, to no avail, that this is what we do in America. Also, everyone would tell Jamie that she doesn't have enough clothes on the baby. They overdress their babies to the max! It's all a cultural thing and I understand that, but still we explained ourselves numerous times, Jamie always smiling sweetly at the people, taking it all in very gracefully.

~

October 20, 8:30 p.m.—This morning I went with him up on the wall around the city to walk and quietly pray. I witnessed many unfamiliar and amazing sights which are difficult for me to describe—smells of food cooking, noise, poverty, so many people, so many tiny shops selling unidentifiable food, hanging raw meat, children playing and peeing in street drains, a man washing clothes on a washboard, alleys leading to shanties where people lived behind their shops where anything and everything is sold. I did not see many smiling or foreign faces but many beggars and old people with withered faces. Jesus loves each one.

~

Sunday, October 21, 11:45 a.m.—A friend took Gene and I sightseeing. I had already seen some of these attractions back in 2001, but we loved every minute of it. We took the bus back to the apartment. That was an experience in itself! Very overcrowded, but whenever a policeman was spotted, everyone standing squatted so that the bus didn't appear to exceed its passenger limit.

He and Jamie are so sweet and treat us with so much kindness. He cooks great pancakes and omelets. Team members are serving us a meal every day. It is good to know the team loves and cares for each other so well. Our grandson will definitely not lack love and attention here.

I made a list of things to send Jamie as soon as Gene and I return home: freezer Ziploc baggies, baby food, Dr. Pepper, Clorox wipes, Zone bars, stuffing, and other ingredients to make Christmas dinner.

~

Monday, October 22, 9:00 p.m.—At this moment, he and Gene are on the train to Beijing. Gene is on his way home. I get to stay two more weeks with Jamie and my new grandson. At thirteen days old, his newborn clothes are already getting snug, his eyes are focusing on our faces, and we are seeing more smiles.

Side note: In the wintertime, it is common for people to hang dog meat out of their apartment windows to keep it frozen. It gives new meaning to the song "How Much Is That Doggie in the Window?"

True story: A family friend went to a pet store to pick out a kitten. There were several kittens to choose from, so they decided on which one they wanted and told the owner. He promptly chopped off the kitten's head! He was in the business of selling meat for dinner!

Wednesday, October 24, 10:00 p.m.—About eleven this morning, Jamie and I took a taxi to the market, an outdoor market with fresh vegetables, fruit, hanging meats, fish, eels, snakes, whole chickens, etc. We bought cauliflower, carrots, cucumbers, potatoes, squash, and tangerines. We were told today that a new Walmart opens at seven in the morning. We will have to go! Gene called and said everything is fine at home and that he lost six pounds the last two weeks!

Thursday, October 25, 7:00 p.m.—He and I left about nine fifteen this morning for the wall. It is a seven-mile-long wall built around the city some 1,300 years ago. Of course, the city has expanded tremendously outside those walls in every direction. The walls were built to protect against invaders. I'm guessing the wall is about thirty feet high and thirty feet across. We rented bicycles and rode the entire wall in one and a half hours. It was a bumpy ride, but I loved it! We stopped and took pictures several times. He took a lot of video. It was a fantastic adventure. I saw a Buddhist temple and enclosure where they were burning incense and bowing down to an idol.

~

Friday, October 26, 2:20 p.m.—The four of us left the apartment around nine this morning for Walmart. Today was their second day of business. There were so many people we could barely walk through the store. It was busier than a USA Walmart on a Black Friday! The only thing I bought was fresh ostrich meat right beside the nine-foot stuffed ostrich. (The meat was very red and lean and it made a delicious vegetable stew which cooked all day in the crock pot.) He then took me to a very nice tea shop where I purchased a very beautiful tea set and several kinds of tea. The owner gave me chrysanthemum and rosebud teas. We went to a friend's scroll shop and purchased a very beautiful scroll inscribed with Micah 6:8. Everywhere we go, everybody is so curious about the baby in the stroller. We went to a Muslim restaurant and ate lamb with bread, vegetables, and rice noodles.

~

Saturday, October 27, 5:15 p.m.—It is so nice to see many of Jamie's friends and former students whom I met in 2001 come by to see the new baby. One of them gave our baby a traditional child's suit her mother had made for him—split pants and all! Why the split, you ask? So babies can squat and use the bathroom, of course! One doesn't see many diapers here. We had another interesting ride in a taxi today. Taxi rides have definitely increased my prayer life, and I've seen God do miracles—like get us safely to our destination time and again! Today we were almost broadsided by a bus. I gripped my grandson's carrier, closed my eyes, and said, "Jesus," over and over. The bus stopped inches away from us. Jamie just rolled her eyes. That was not close in her book!

My beautiful grandson is getting stronger every day, holding his head up, focusing his eyes, smiling more, and he is growing so fast. I enjoy holding him and looking into his precious face, praying over him, and kissing him. This has been a beautiful time for me here in their city. Jamie is such a good little mommy. She is nursing him (which she continued to do until he was twelve months old).

~

Sunday, October 28, 9:15 a.m.—Jamie experienced some back pain last night and a little "new mom anxiety," but she is okay this morning. I am so thankful I have this time with her. She is a good mommy and he is a good daddy.

A few minutes ago, we heard a lot of firecrackers going off. I looked out of our seven-story window and saw some people at the gate, a man walking around holding a long string of exploding firecrackers, a black car with flowers on the trunk, and young men holding gifts. Jamie explained that it was a wedding. Traditionally, the groom must take his groomsmen and everyone takes gifts to the bride's family and persuades them to give him their daughter. It's a fun celebration. The groom just came out carrying his bride dressed in white. They got in the car followed by many friends and family in cars and will go to a nice restaurant for a big meal. Caleb needs a diaper change! He is not interested in the wedding below.

6:15 p.m.—After lunch we took a taxi to the team meeting. I admire these team members so much, beyond words. May God bless each one as they invest their lives into others for the sake of the greatest story ever told. Today, the leaders talked about taking steps for greater protection and security. Apparently, one of the team member's apartments was entered while she was away and her computer tapped into. Jamie is sure their apartment has also been entered and that they are being watched. It doesn't bother them.

Monday, October 29, 10:00 p.m.—Today Jamie and I ventured out to a few little shops close by. It was a cool morning. She placed her son in a baby carrier on her chest. We went to see her tailor friend who was very friendly but told Jamie she shouldn't be out with the baby for thirty days and they both needed more clothes. How many times have we heard that? In walked a few of her friends who proceeded to scold me soundly. I didn't understand a word but knew they were telling me the same thing. How could I as a mother and grandmother allow them out of the house before thirty days with so few clothes on? I know these ladies are just trying to be helpful, but I was about ready to run! This same scenario repeats itself every time we go outside.

Friday, November 2, 1:45 p.m.—Since the water is off again (happens a lot around here), we can't wash lunch dishes, so we're just relaxing. I have a few observations about this city. It is full of tiny storefront shops, approximately ten feet wide and twelve feet deep, side by side for miles. Everything under the sun is sold. Alleys have still many more crowded fruit stands, veggie stands, etc. I even saw one shop that sells western toilets. Small businesses such as tailors, shoe repair, etc. practice their trade on sidewalks in front of their shops. There are many brothels everywhere. Countryside people peddle into the city on their three or four-wheel carts to sell their produce and wares. Many just come into the city looking for work, bringing their own paint brush. Their bikes have signs on the front that tell what their skill is. It's very cheap labor.

Saturday, November 3, 7:30 a.m.—I have to mention the several storefront dentist offices I've seen. The dental chair and patient are right in the front, just behind a large window. A crowd will gather on the sidewalk to watch the dentist work on his patient. Nothing is personal here. Everything is everybody's business. He and Jamie are always asked very personal questions—their age, how much money they make, how much their apartment cost. They always give ambiguous answers when it comes to money.

2:40 p.m.—Jamie received an e-mail this morning from the adoption agency which said it will probably be July or August before they get their baby daughter.

After our meal, we entered a nice department store to look for Ziploc bags of all things. We didn't find any, but we did find tomato sauce!

He and Jamie have treated me like a queen here.

9:30 p.m.—It's been a very good day. We spent the rest of the day in the apartment. We played Phase Ten, and I beat both of them.

While rocking my grandson, I began to cry tears of thankfulness to God for His many blessings to me and our family. I'm truly thankful for His grace, mercy, loving kindness, and faithfulness. I'm so grateful to Him for making a way for me to spend these four weeks with Jamie and her beautiful family. I praise Him that my children are living and giving their lives for Him.

"Always give yourselves fully to the work of the Lord, because you know that your labor in the Lord is not in vain" (1 Cor. 15:58). Jamie came into the nursery with me, and we both cried tears of appreciation to our Lord.

Sunday, November 4, 5:30 p.m.—About eleven thirty we took a taxi to the team meeting. Again, meeting with these people was such a blessing. The Spirit of the Lord was in the room as people worshiped. During the service, God used me in tongues and interpretation. The message was to not fear or doubt the task

God has called you to do because His grace is always sufficient. He is walking with you.

God has allowed me to see many of Jamie's students whom I met in 2001. What a joy to see and visit with them again. Many of us went to a local restaurant and enjoyed "Hot Pot," one of their favorites.

~

Tuesday, November 6, 5:00 a.m.—This morning, he will take me to the airport. A driver from the travel agency will pick us up. I have had the best four weeks ever! I praise God for this time. What a blessing it has been!

10:40 a.m. San Francisco time—I'm sitting on the plane waiting to fly to Houston. A prayer is in my heart continuously for the family I left behind and the family awaiting my return. We were just notified that some maintenance is being done on the plane's tail section. Oh great! I mean, "Great is the Lord and greatly to be praised" (Ps. 48:1, KJV).

~

Gene had a few contributions to the pages of this journal, but the following is his most memorable. It took place on October 22.

I didn't feel well this particular day. Although I am now at home (November 8, 10 p.m. as I write), I have a most vivid recollection of that day! Let me first say that I will put a disclaimer on the following because while attempting to not be overly graphic, I may tell you that this day will go down in infamy. It's not for the weak stomachs to read further. Curiosity may be your worst enemy.

Okay. Here goes. As I said, I woke up with a stomachache—not really serious, but I was uncomfortable. Then, it hit! I desperately needed some Imodium. Man, it was quick to make my tummy do handstands! Never before (and I hope never again) have I had such a problem.

Around 11:00 a.m., I started feeling better and agreed to go to a local McDonald's. Really, I felt okay and thought the worst was over. I could not have been further from the truth. After a good meal, we went to the nicest store I have ever seen, especially in that part of the world. This was a five-story department store that would have made Macy's look cheap. Seriously, it was a very nice store. Escalators took us to the fifth floor.

While we were talking to the lady that sold Jamie their crib, that old familiar pain hit. I told Jamie, "I really need to find a bathroom—soon." We found one and when I opened the door, it was a huge restroom, very clean with only two stalls. They were squatty potties, I might add. I had no experience with these and still don't. I didn't make it. I was about two steps away.

What happened in there is only for family and close friends to know, and they must give me their oath they will never repeat it. I got out of there as soon as I could, found my family, and said, "We need to go—now." I had to tell them again, "We need to go—now."

We went down the escalators as fast as they would take us. At the bottom floor, I thought, *Oh, I hope security hasn't been in there. I know they have cameras throughout the store. I may be arrested.* I pulled a Jack Bauer for you *24* fans. I really did this. I took off my hat and pulled my hoodie up over my head for a disguise.

I know there are some janitors who quit their job that very hour. At the apartment, I took off my clothes. Karen washed them and I took a shower. Yes, it was that bad. Okay, I have been totally transparent here and now. I do not feel any better, but I will never forget my first experience with a squatty potty. And now you know the rest of the story. Good day.

# Chapter 22

## *More Mom Journal*

November 2, 2007—Wow! I finally get a chance to write in my Mom Journal! Caleb, you have changed our lives forever, and you are only twenty-four days old! I have been holding things in my heart, just as Mary did about Jesus, and I have to write them down now.

When Dr. Farhad took you out of my tummy, you came out whimpering, "Waa Waa Waa Waa!" It was so cute. As I lay on the operating table, the nurses cleaned you up. You teeteed! I couldn't take my eyes off of you. You looked like I thought you would, only more beautiful. Your skin was a perfect creamy-white and your face wrinkled like a little old man's when you cried or stared at someone. Your eyes were dark blue, even the whites were bluish. Your hair was blond in front and light brown in the back. The nape of your neck's hairline was perfectly straight as if God had just given you a haircut. Your eyebrows were so light that I could hardly see them; your eyelashes short and light too. The crown of your head came together like a star. Your nose is mine! Your lips are beautiful like Aunt Janet's, but bigger. Your neck was wrinkled, your shoulders and back were scrawny and red. Your baby skin peeled off your back after several days. Your chest seemed broad like an athlete's. Your little legs reminded me of a chicken's legs—scrawny, but beautiful. Your fingers were precious and your little toes were long. You were eight pounds, three ounces, and twenty inches long at birth.

You are twenty-four days old now and about to outgrow your first newborn outfit. We think you are over ten pounds, and when you try to stand up in our arms, you seem so strong. I don't ever want to forget how you look, or how you make me feel. My cup overflows with love for you and gratitude to the Lord for giving me a perfect son.

Delivering you took so long. My water broke at 12:30 a.m. on October 8. We checked into the hospital at 3:00 a.m. I was so excited that I couldn't sleep. By 11:00 a.m. that day, I still wasn't having labor pains, so they induced labor. My body didn't respond well to the Pitocin. Around 5:00 p.m. the pain got harder, but I was still only dilated to a two. I got an epidural to help the pain. Labor progressed very slowly, and the epidural didn't block all the pain. The anesthesiologist said it was because your head wasn't turned the right way. They told me to get some sleep and that the next day you'd be born. Yea right! Who could sleep at a time like that! I was too excited and the pain kept me awake. By 5:00 a.m. the next morning, October 9, I felt such a strong urge to push, but I was only dilated to a six. It was so frustrating; I couldn't push because it was too early. The nurse told me I'd probably be to a ten in three hours, and then I could start pushing. But I knew I could not hold off for three more hours; the pressure to push was too great. At that point, my strength was so low, and I hadn't slept for three days. I knew that even if I could hold off pushing for three hours, I didn't have the strength left to push for two hours after that. I started begging the doctor and nurses for a C-section. They wanted me to keep trying to have you naturally, but I knew my limit—and I was there!

So they wheeled me into an operating room. Your daddy was right there, dressed like a doctor, holding my hand. Music in the background was playing about you being born with angel dust in your hair. The operation didn't take long, and there you were—my pride and joy! I love you!

~

November 8, 2007—Since Mom left two days ago, it has been difficult. I am going through so many emotions. I also had some unrealistic expectations of myself, wanting to be Supermom from the beginning. There is so much I want to do—continue my language studies, have a nice lunch for your daddy every day, entertain, and of course, take care of you. But yesterday, the Lord reminded me that I am called to three people—first to Him, then to your daddy, and then to you. Everything else—having a perfect house, cooking perfect meals, leading the TESOL Committee, studying the language, reaching out to others—comes after that.

~

December 6, 2007—From Jamie in a Christmas card she mailed to us:

Addendum to Will: In the event of both of our deaths, we want Jeremy Yancey and Janet Yancey (the brother-in-law and sister of Jamie) to raise Caleb Daniel Lund and any other minors we have at that time. We want them to have full guardianship of our children until they are legal adults. We believe that Jeremy and Janet are the best "parents" (guardians) for our children in case of our untimely deaths. We trust that they will love and raise our children as we would. Signed by both on 12/06/07

~

December 10, 2007—You laughed yesterday for the first time! You did it twice. My favorite time was when I came and picked you up from a nap. You looked up at me from your crib and just laughed! It made me so happy! I have been singing "Amazing Grace" to you. When I get to the last verse about "when we've been there ten thousand years," it has a deeper meaning for me now. What I want more than anything else is for you and Karen and your daddy and me to all be in heaven together one day.

~

December 30, 2007—Sweet Karen, it's now been over fourteen months since we started the adoption process to bring you into our home. I want you here with us! We have a happy family, but it won't be complete until you join us.

~

January 3, 2008—"But from everlasting to everlasting the Lord's love is with those who fear him, and his righteousness with their children's children" (Ps. 103:17). Last night I read Psalm 103 about the blessings of being saved. I love verse 17. This is the life I have always known. I am so blessed. Every day, I not only walk in His blessings for me, but I am blessed because of my mom and dad, grandparents, and great-grandparents, who loved Him! I live the good life, what Jesus calls, "the abundant life." And I want your life and Karen's life to be the abundant life too. I want to pass down His blessings to you and Karen. You will grow up knowing His presence and blessing! Amen! Thank you, Jesus!

~

January 9, 2008—Happy three month birthday, Caleb! You are getting so big. We have had some special moments with you this past week. A few days ago, I was leaning over you as you laid on your back, and you grabbed my hair with both fists, holding on tightly so I couldn't leave and looking up at me with eyes of love. You took my breath away as we had those few moments together gazing into each other's eyes. You were saying, "I love you, Mommy," and I will never forget that moment.

~

January 10, 2008—Dear Karen: Are you warm? Do you have enough to eat? Is someone tickling your feet? Is someone kissing your nose? Is someone making funny noises on your belly? We pray that you are getting all the love you need. We know God will take care of you. We "miss" you, even though we haven't even seen you. We need you to join our family fast. We'll be ready for you when you get here, and we'll make up for lost time together. We gave you the name Karen Vi because we want you to love and serve God like your grandmothers. We will do our best to help you know and love Jesus. And we know Jesus will help us raise you and Caleb. We love you, our beautiful China pearl! Love, Mommy.

March 24, 2008—Today you were in your walker with your back to me as I sat at the table. You kept turning your head to look at me and make sure I was still there. It reminded me of me and God. Sometimes I must reassure myself that He watches over me. He always does, just like I will always watch over you as long as there is breath in me.

April 2, 2008—Dear Caleb: Two days ago the Lord reminded me of how much He loves me and you. You don't know it, but Mommy used to be on some medicine. After I got pregnant with you, I stopped taking it because I didn't want the medicine to harm you. I am still not taking it because now I am nursing you. I told some friends that I need to take the medicine, but don't want to stop nursing. The next day, a friend prayed for my healing so I wouldn't need the medicine. Although I don't feel healed yet, the Lord has given me hope again. He really loves me and you. He wants what is best for both of us. God is good.

April 18, 2008—Dear Caleb: Your mommy isn't a rich lady. I don't have a car, a house, beautiful clothes, or expensive jewelry. I can't travel for fun and spend money like it grows on trees. But do you know what? Mommy is rich in moments—special moments looking you in the eye, listening to your chuckle, imitating your little sounds, watching you wave your arms in delight, feeling you lying against my chest as I rock you. These moments make me rich. God has given us beautiful, priceless moments together. You won't remember them, but I will always treasure them in my heart. I look forward to a lifetime of moments with you and Karen. I love you, Sweet Pea!

May 11, 2008—My first Mother's Day. A card created by him with beautiful pictures of Caleb and these words: Dear Jamie, Happy Mother's Day! You are an amazing mother to Caleb. He absolutely adores you! I know Karen will adore you too. Thank you for the way you take care of Caleb. While nursing, you're giving him all the nutrition he needs and a whole lot of love, which is a huge factor in his healthy self-worth. The time you spend reading to him and playing with him helps him develop and learn. Your choice to stay home with him and not have a nanny because you want to spend that time with him is so special. Caleb is definitely a momma's boy, and he will always be one. I am so blessed to have a wife who loves me and my son the way you do. There are no words to describe how much I love you, my Jamie. I'm so glad that you have chosen to spend this special time with Caleb because I know you will look back one day and have no regrets. Caleb is so blessed to have a virtuous Mom who is a beautiful example. Watching you take care of Caleb has made me love you even more and has made me more aware of how special a gift from God you are to Karen, Caleb, and me. I love you, my rose.

May 14, 2008—Monday was a day we will never forget. At two thirty in the afternoon, I was at the hospital chatting with some friends in their father's hospital room because he had an operation a few days before. Suddenly we all began to shake, but we kept talking because we didn't realize what was happening. When we saw the water in the glass shaking, we knew it was an earthquake.

We heard yelling in the hallway telling everyone to get out of the building. I helped my friend get his father out of the hospital along with his IV pole. The floor was shaking; we were on the second floor. The entire hospital evacuated, so we stood outside under some trees for a long time, surrounded by mommies who had just given birth, people on hospital beds, etc.

Meanwhile, Caleb and Daddy were at the international school. When the earthquake hit, Caleb was playing in the living room with his toys on his blanket. Daddy was sitting on the couch nearby. He could see the building swaying as well as the building next to ours. He grabbed Caleb and ran down all seven flights of stairs, forgetting to put on his shoes. Caleb thought it was pretty fun!

We all had to stay outside several hours. People were finally allowed back in their buildings around 7:30 p.m., but thousands of people slept outside near our apartment because of fear. We slept in a friend's second floor apartment. There were several smaller quakes. The first quake was a 7.9 on the Richter scale. So far, twelve thousand are confirmed dead.

God kept us safe. That morning He reminded me that when the enemy comes in like a flood, His Spirit raises up a standard (i.e., people pray). People must have been praying, because he and I had such peace and courage, while being terrified at the same time. We knew we were okay. There is a hedge of protection around us, and if our time comes, we will be in heaven! What a great way to live life—unafraid to die!

Karen, I pray you were safe and warm during the quake. I know you are okay, because Father told me last year that He holds you in His hands. I love you two little ones so much.

~

May 20, 2008—People are still camping outside, afraid to go into their buildings, and sleeping in cars, tents, and on the open ground. It's crazy. People are everywhere. The guards evacuated our building again last night for fear of another quake. I pushed Caleb in his stroller outside of our gate and then was trying to strap him in when someone almost backed into him with their car. Once again, God kept you safe.

~

May 25, 2008—There was another tremor today, a 5.7 or 5.8. Evacuation again, but we are safe. Fifteen million people are homeless because of the earthquake two weeks ago.

~

June 1, 2008—I answered the phone, "Hello."

"Mom, it's Jamie."

She is crying and obviously very upset. "We're coming home! I can't take it anymore! Our marriage is in trouble! We've got to get help! I just want to let you know that I'm getting tickets for us all to come home as soon as possible. Can we stay with you while we try to get counseling?"

"Of course, y'all can stay with us. Calm down, honey. Can you tell me what is going on?"

"I can't talk about it right now, Mom. I love you. Just pray for us."

~

June 3, 2008—Dear Caleb: Mommy and Daddy are going through a hard time right now. But last night Papa gave us a verse from the Bible to encourage us. "All your children will be taught by the Lord, and great will be their peace" (Isa. 54:13). We will fly back to Texas this week and stay for six weeks to get some help, and we will stay with your Memaw and Papa in Lufkin. They will love spending time with you.

~

June 8, 2008—We are in America! Today at church, Pastor Andy talked about our words, how they can give or destroy life. He said that often the people who love us the most hurt us without meaning to with their words. Caleb loves the church nursery and being with the other babies.

Karen, we have to redo some of our paperwork for your adoption. We are doing a lot of it here in the States. You are worth every piece of paper we have to fill out and worth every day we have to wait. We love you, little one.

~

July 3, 2008—The professional counselor prescribed a light medication for him to help with his depression, which he has a history of along with obesity. Jamie is battling depression and mild OCD but does not want to get back on medication until she has weaned Caleb.

~

July 17, 2008—Card from Jamie:

Dear Mom and Dad: I love you both so much. I wish I had the words to say what you guys mean to me. This time home has been so wonderful. I am so blessed to be your daughter. Thanks for being available to us and for your encouragement this summer. God really used both of you to bless us.

~

July 18, 2008—Gene and I drove our kids to the airport early this morning. It was hard to see them go. God has blessed all of us with an extremely good six weeks. Jamie believes God accomplished much in their lives during this time.

~

The apostle Paul was a brilliant man and used by God in such a mighty way that God permitted difficult circumstances to invade his life, a thorn in the flesh that kept him on his knees and living in a state of forced dependence upon God. After praying repeatedly for God to take his weakness away, God said this: "'My grace is sufficient for you, for my power is made perfect in weakness.' Therefore I will boast all the more gladly about my weaknesses, so that Christ's power may rest on me" (2 Cor. 12:9).

Was OCD Jamie's thorn in the flesh? I know for a fact it kept her on her knees seeking hard after God all those years.

Jamie confided in me shortly before her death that the counselor seemed to ignore a much bigger issue in their marriage and his life in particular that he had struggled with for a long time and focus more on her OCD. I had suspected that as a problem in his life for some time but never shared my intuition with Jamie. We prayed for God's deliverance.

~

July 21, 2008—We are back home, and it is 2:30 a.m. Caleb is sitting on the living room floor playing with a plastic bat, wide awake. It will take a few days to get over jet lag again, but we'll do it together. He had such a good time in Texas with grandparents, aunts, uncles, cousins, and friends. Everyone loves Caleb!

Dear Caleb: While we were in Texas last week, you got even better at communicating. One day you crawled on the floor and called, "Mama," and then looked to see if I was coming to chase you. You would crawl a little and I would be right behind you. Then you would turn around to see if I was chasing you and kept crawling. It was so sweet. On July 18, in the wee hours of the morning, as we drove to the airport to go home, you said, "Mama," and took my fingers, holding my hand as we rode in the car. It was so beautiful. I've never seen anything more beautiful than you. Your smile is so sweet and cute, and when you sleep, I can see your pretty eyelashes, and you look like an angel lying there as still as can be, not a care in the world. I told your daddy yesterday, "I've never seen anything as beautiful as him!"

July 23, 2008—Sweet Karen, while we were in the States, we took care of more processing for your adoption. And then, just before we left the States, we found out it might be a much longer wait until we can hold you in our arms. It is so disappointing. We are still waiting for you, though. Hang in there, my love. You don't know it yet, but you have a mommy and daddy who love you very much!

July 28, 2008—Hi, baby boy and girl. Today I read the story of Moses's mommy having to cast him into the Nile River. He was only three months old when she had to give him up and trust the Lord to take care of him. Now that I'm a mommy, I see this story differently. I can't imagine giving up my babies. When she put her little one into the water, she had to trust the Lord to guard him. In putting Moses into the Nile, she was really giving him to the Lord. She had nursed him and cared for him for three months, made the little waterproof basket with her own hands, gently placed her baby in it, and set the basket in the shade of the Nile reeds. God, in return, allowed her to take care of Moses longer, until she presented him to the princess. In my life, I will trust the Lord to take care of both of you, regardless what circumstances come our way. May the Lord help me with this. I love you both.

~

August 2, 2008—Hi, baby. I want to share with you a testimony of how the Lord takes care of us. While we were all in America, Mommy and Daddy decided it was time for us to get a nanny to help take care of you part-time. Mommy needs some help so she can study more and do other things that she needs to do. We prayed about this. You see, not just any old nanny will do. She has to be very special—someone who will take great care of you. Guess what? When we returned home, we weren't here twenty-four hours when we learned some of our friends will soon go back to the States, and their nanny will need another family. Yesterday, she started keeping you. She did a great job. And guess what else? She found a group of local believers who meet nearby and will meet with them before working in the mornings. God answered her prayer for a job and fellowship and our prayer for a nanny. He sure does love all of us!

~

August 7, 2008—Caleb and Karen, the Lord reminded me today of how I am only your temporary caretaker. God is your eternal Father. He has simply entrusted you two to me and Daddy for a while. He is the One you can ultimately trust regardless of what the future holds for Mommy and Daddy. I love you, little ones.

~

August 12, 2008—Hey, baby, you tried to sing again while nursing today. I had been singing, "You Are So Beautiful to Me," our special song, and after I finished, you took a break from nursing and made little sweet sounds. My big ten-month-old! I love you. And by the way, you like rice! Today I fed you rice at the little village restaurant where Mommy and Daddy like to eat, and you loved it!

~

August 15, 2008—We took Caleb back to the Muslim Quarters yesterday and his face lit up when he saw one of our good friends and her family. They *ooh*ed and *aw*ed over you and passed you around. You enjoyed every minute! Mommy even left you there with them about an hour while she ate. You were so happy. I am glad you love people so much. You just make everyone's day!

~

August 17, 2008—Today was another unforgettable day. Around eight this morning, you pulled over a hot water thermos, which spilled over onto you. We were in the home of some friends and had spent the night. Mommy and Daddy were in the living room with you, but it happened so fast. You screamed terribly, as your right leg blistered. You had second-degree burns according to the doctor. We are so thankful that after we let you sit in lukewarm water about thirty minutes, you didn't cry so much. The doctor was impressed that you didn't cry in the hospital either. I know the Lord was watching over you again. And he has taken away your pain. I love you, baby. Just as Psalm 121 says, the Lord continues to watch over you. That is the promise we have, and He showed us today just how good He is.

~

August 26, 2008—Hi, baby love. Guess what? The Lord healed your leg! The doctor told us last week you might need a skin graft. But today we were amazed when his wife, who is a pediatric physician's assistant, looked at your wound and said it was remarkable how fast you had healed. We thank the Lord and give Him all the glory. Wow! Praise the Lord!

~

September 11, 2008—Hi, Karen. Yesterday the Department of Homeland Security called us. They received our reapplication to adopt you! I hope we can get you before you have to spend another winter in an orphanage. I want you to be warm in my arms.

~

September 26, 2008—Today is the last day I will nurse you, because you bite with all your new teeth! I did it for almost one full year. I will always treasure this special time.

~

October 2, 2008—On September 30, we were walking down the street. Daddy was holding you, and Mommy saw a manhole uncovered with just two boards lying across it. I tried to warn your daddy, but it was too late. He fell all the way to his crotch with one leg in and one leg out. He tried to hold onto you as long as he could, but he dropped you, and you were thrown to the ground, landing on the back of your head, falling with a thud I will never forget. You cried so loudly. I picked you up while some friends helped your daddy. You were screaming and your eyes were not focusing. We all prayed for you. You fell asleep at dinner, but then you woke up suddenly and started vomiting. We took you to a clinic down the road and they said you needed a CT scan, so we took you to the hospital. After a lengthy delay, they finally were able to do the scan. Everything was normal. Praise the Lord! Once again, God kept our baby boy safe.

October 11, 2008—Caleb took his first step today! I'm so proud of you!

October 27, 2008—Karen Sweetheart, Mommy is sad because your adoption still hasn't been finalized. We thought we would have you in our arms so long ago, and now we're going back to America without you. We will come back to get you sometime next year. But I trust the Lord that His timing is perfect. He still has you in the palm of His hand, and He has everything under His control.

November 23, 2008—I just read about passing down memorials to our children and their children—memorials of our faith. I think this book is a precious memorial I'm giving to Caleb and Karen. Not only does it chronicle you guys as you grow up, but it reminds you over and over of our God. He loves you so much. Mommy and Daddy pray every night that you will serve Him all the days of your lives and use your gifts and talents for His purposes. I love you, Caleb and Karen.

November 26, 2008—Hi, Caleb. Today I want to tell you and Karen about a new person I admire. His name is Manoah, the father of Samson in the Bible. Today when I was reading in Judges about Samson's birth, I noticed something special about Manoah. After the angel appeared to his wife and said she would have a special child, Manoah prayed and asked the Lord to please send the messenger back to tell him how to raise the child. Now that I'm a mommy, I admire Manoah for this prayer. He was a childless man, but as soon as he found out they would have a special child, he asked the Lord to show him how to raise Samson. Mommy and Daddy ask the Lord for wisdom every day to raise our kids. We always ask for wisdom when we tuck in Caleb at night, and we will do the same for Karen. You are both special children with special calls on your lives that only God knows. And Mommy will do her best to raise you to love and serve God. I love you, my babies. Good night.

December 7, 2008—Hi, baby, we're home in America! All of our family was waiting for us at the airport. We already have a fully furnished duplex to live in while in the States. What a blessing!

On Wednesday, December 3, I read something wonderful in my Bible. It is in 1 Samuel 1:11, where Hannah said of her son, "I will give him to the Lord for all the days of his life." The study notes say that "Christian parents may express their commitment to God and His kingdom by giving their sons and daughters to the ministry or to the work of missions in other lands. Those parents who support, encourage, and pray for their children will find great favor with God." Caleb and Karen, this is the gift my parents gave me. They have always been supportive of me as I followed God's call on my life. I am so thankful for that! And this is the gift I want to give both of you. No matter where God calls you and no matter what He calls you to do, your Mom and Dad will be your biggest fans and supporters. Amen.

Then the next day, I read another awesome verse about Samuel, who grew up in the tabernacle. 1 Samuel 2:21 says, "The boy Samuel grew up in the presence of the Lord." Wow! This is what I want for the two of you! For you to grow up knowing His love, talking to Him and listening to Him, and serving Him wholeheartedly. This is my prayer: "Lord, do it! Lord, help me know how to raise these babies in 'the presence of the Lord.' Help me walk in your presence daily. I love you, Lord."

# Chapter 23

## *2009–2010*

I am the Lord, who heals you.

—Ex. 15:26

Praise the Lord, my soul; all my inmost being,
praise his holy name.

—Ps. 103:1

January 4, 2009—Gene and I bought a Hyundai Santa Fe on Friday. We will let Jamie and him use our car this year so they don't have to buy another one.

February 28, 2009—Jamie called about 12:45 yesterday and Caleb is very sick and having a difficult time breathing. The doctor sent him to the hospital, Children's Medical Center, which gave him breathing treatments, cleaned out his airway, etc. That hospital did not have an available room so they sent him to Legacy Hospital in Plano. Jamie called about 10:00 p.m. and they were finally in a room. The doctor said he has "bronchiolitis."

~

April 5, 2009—This evening, Jamie and he will speak at our service. Jamie will preach. God is so good. He has blessed us with a precious family.

~

April 8, 2009—Jamie called last night and said they heard from the adoption agency, and they should get their picture and info on Karen Vi this week!

~

April 10, 2009—They received e-mail pictures from the adoption agency last night of their baby, and they forwarded them to us. Karen Vi is beautiful. She is nine months old, born on July 22, 2008, abandoned at a bar, found the next day, and has lived in an orphanage her entire life. She was less than five pounds when found, a preemie. Caleb is nine months older. He is a big brother! God is so good. She looks healthy. It will probably be around June 1 before they can go get her. "God, please watch over her, keep her safe, healthy and growing. Thank you, Lord."

~

May 7, 2009—Jamie and Caleb went back on Saturday, but they are all coming back tomorrow and will stay a couple of weeks with us.

~

May 20, 2009—He and Jamie went to Dorothy's Place for three nights on a prayer retreat. We have Caleb until we take him home on Friday.

~

June 2, 2009—He and Jamie will leave Friday, June 5, to go get Karen Vi; they will return on Father's Day.

~

June 5, 2009—Gene drove to DeSoto last night so he could take them to the airport. Their flight leaves around seven this morning. "Dear God, give them a safe flight. Bring them home safely with our precious Karen Vi."

~

June 23, 2009—We picked up he and Jamie and Karen Vi from DFW around midnight Saturday. Karen Vi is tiny. She cries a lot and wants to be held.

~

July 16, 2009—Yesterday he took Karen for a checkup with Dr. Huggins. She found a serious problem with Karen's blood and recommended they take her to Texas Children's in Dallas immediately. So they left yesterday for Dallas, and Karen was admitted. We have Caleb. So I'm still spending nights with Mother (she had knee replacement surgery), taking care of Caleb, and working too. God is my strength each day. We are trusting God to take care of our precious little Karen Vi.

~

July 20, 2009—Karen was released from the hospital yesterday but still a very sick little baby. She will need a lot of therapy (physical, occupational, speech, hearing, cranial-facial), and more tests on her blood and possible blood transfusions.

~

July 24, 2009—Karen Vi had a wonderful first birthday party on Wednesday. Yesterday she received a blood transfusion.

~

August 4, 2009—We talk to Jamie every day about Karen. She had more tests and exploratory on Sunday morning, including bone marrow. She had complete bone scan on Monday. Possible diagnosis is histiocytosis.

~

August 11, 2009—Wow! A lot has happened. Karen was readmitted to the hospital on Wednesday. She was positively diagnosed on Thursday night with Langerhans Cell Histiocytosis (LCH). The disease has involved her spleen, skin, and intestines and is treatable with chemotherapy. A port was installed in her chest on Sunday, and she should have received her first chemotherapy treatment last night. He is staying with her. I spent Thursday night and Friday with her in the hospital and the rest of the time at Desoto with Caleb. I cleaned their duplex good on Sunday, my birthday.

~

September 11, 2009—Jamie called last night to update us on Karen's fifth chemo yesterday. The doctors are not pleased with the results. Her skin is getting worse, not better. They will give her two more weeks. If she does not make substantial improvement, they will begin a stronger chemo that could produce more severe side effects. "Dear God, please have mercy and give us a miracle in Karen Vi's life."

~

October 17, 2009—He experienced chest pain and light-headedness yesterday, so they all drove to Lufkin to see his heart doctor. He must lose weight, exercise, and restrict his caffeine intake. Karen has her helmet now. She had tubes put in on Wednesday. She is doing well.

~

November 4, 2009—Jamie called yesterday after taking Karen Vi in for ultrasounds. The doctors said her spleen and liver are normal. Praise the Lord! She is well! After twelve weeks of chemo, there is no trace of the disease. We are praising God. They will take her in on Thursday to see what precautionary measures she should have. God has answered many prayers for our precious Mei Mei (little sister in Chinese).

~

November 6, 2009—I talked to Jamie last night. The doctors say Karen Vi is in remission. Praise God! As precaution, they are prescribing nine months of one chemo treatment every three weeks along with a daily medication by mouth. She is also flat-footed, so she will begin wearing special shoes which will help build arches in her feet. She is having a complete makeover!

~

November 23, 2009—Jamie called last night to tell us what God has done. At Living Word Church in Alvord, Texas last night, the people prayed for Karen Vi, two by two. They specifically prayed for each need. The peace of God came over Karen and Jamie! After all the prayer, Jamie felt Karen's head and there was shape where it had been flat! There were arches in her feet where there was very little arch! God has done miracles for our children. "Thank you, Lord! I praise you!"

~

May 1, 2010—Yesterday Karen Vi had three procedures at Dallas Children's Medical Center to determine if the LCH had returned. The doctors did not see any evidence of the disease; however, several biopsies were taken and it will be seven days before those come back.

~

May 6, 2010—Jamie called last night and Karen's biopsies all came back negative! Praise God! He is so good.

~

May 25, 2010—Gene and I are meeting our children and grandchildren in San Antonio today to spend three nights and go to Fiesta Texas, and SeaWorld. We ask God's blessings on our trip and our time together.

~

June 4, 2010—This morning Gene and I will go to DeSoto to spend a little time helping them get ready to leave. We will stay at their duplex Friday through Sunday nights. They depart DFW at six thirty Sunday morning. God has blessed us these past eighteen months with him and Jamie, Caleb, and Karen Vi. I will miss them so much. "God, please help us this week."

~

June 10, 2010—We said our good-byes at 5:30 a.m. Sunday at DFW. Gene and I stayed in the duplex Sunday night, so we could clean it all day on Sunday. He left Monday morning; I continued to clean until noon.

~

August 1, 2010—Yesterday morning, Jamie Skyped us. She told us God woke her up at 4:00 a.m. Saturday (our 3:00 p.m. Friday) and said, "Let me take care of it myself, and I will save you and your family." She wondered what He meant. Thirty minutes later, there was a loud knock at the door and someone telling them to leave the building. The apartment next door, the one being remodeled for them, was on fire. God took care of them. Jamie had a profound peace through it all. "Thank you, Lord."

~

August 11, 2010—Jamie called yesterday morning about one of her students. The girl's father is paralyzed from an accident on August 1, and she is unable to attend her junior year of college because he supports her. I sent this need out on e-mail and raised the $1,200 she needs to attend school next year. Thank you church family and thank you God!

~

August 14, 2010—Gene sold his and Jamie's car yesterday. Praise God! They can use that $4,700 now!

~

November 19, 2010—Our little Karen Vi is in a Beijing hospital. She got very ill while they were all there for routine checkups—vomiting and diarrhea. Her immune system is weakened because of chemo. Yesterday Jamie said she was better.

November 22, 2010—I received an e-mail yesterday from Jamie. Karen Vi is well; they are all back home. We also received a sweet e-mail about Caleb praying and asking Jesus into his heart. God is so good.

December 15, 2010—He called yesterday and said Jamie was in a lot of pain. When they found someone to watch the children, he took her to the hospital. A urinalysis and ultrasound revealed an inflamed left kidney. She called us last night; she is on medication and feeling better. "Thank you, Lord."

December 16, 2010—He called again about 12:30 a.m. He had Jamie back at the hospital; she is very ill and in extreme pain. Possibly, the pain is coming from a kidney stone in the kidney. She called at 4:15 a.m. They leave for BJ hospital at 10:30 a.m. Friday. Friends will stay with the children. Daddy and I spent several hours in prayer. In my desperation, I heard the Lord ask, "Do you trust me?" "Yes, I trust you!" Jamie could not administer final exams, and he has closed the coffee shop. There will be no Christmas production like they planned. But God! I know the Lord is with them. Jamie started getting sick about a week ago while they were in another city; she thought it was a urinary tract infection.

December 17, 2010—Jamie called. She is feeling better. They are in a hotel. Tests are showing a kidney stone that they think has left the kidney and is making its way down. The kidney is very infected for which she is taking antibiotics. They will go in again on their Saturday morning for another CAT scan and determine if they need to do laparoscopic surgery. We are praising the Lord for His goodness to us again. The children are doing fine. "Thank you, Jesus, for your mercy and healing power."

~

December 24, 2010—Jamie called and Caleb has been very sick. He has strep throat.

# Chapter 24

## The Ultimate Attack

> With this in mind, since I myself have carefully investigated everything from the beginning, I too decided to write an orderly account for you...so that you may know the certainty of the things you have been taught.
>
> —Lk. 1:3–4

This is God's and Jamie's story. All other characters are minor in comparison.

Jamie discovered that insidious lump while showering. She couldn't help but notice it because it was so large. It wasn't there a few days before when she took her last shower. (Daily showers are unheard of in her city.)

She wasted no time and went to the extremely limited medical facility nearby. The doctor wanted to remove both breasts promptly. No way, Jose! She wanted a second opinion, so she went to the next largest city. Tests revealed the malignancy. Preparations were made immediately for a trip to the international hospital in Beijing. Surgery was scheduled.

Here's where I enter this part of Jamie's story—me and my trusty journal(s). I recorded every detail of Jamie's and my journeys from this point to the present. Why? Because I was sure God would miraculously heal our Jamie, and all of my notes would make a great book, a testimony to the divine healing power of the mighty God we serve.

And so this leg of the journey begins. To God be the glory!

I, by chance, noticed my passport would expire in 2011, so I decided to reapply just in case. You never know. But God knew I would need that, and I received it just in time.

It's Mother's Day 2011. I've already said it, but I'll say it again: we have the best church family in the whole world! They have prayed for Jamie so many times over the years, and now with their help—prayerfully and financially—I am able to fly to the other side of the world to be with her during this surgery. "Thank you, God."

The surgery lasted eight hours. The tumor was larger than expected. The doctor removed a large portion of the upper right breast and all of level one and two lymph nodes because they were hard and probably cancerous. He put in drains and a port for chemotherapy.

It's a week later and Jamie has done so well. We have shared some good laughs and many good conversations this week. She loves the people here. She loves her city and her students; her heart is here. She wants to raise her children in her city, but she knows she must go back to Texas for a season. This country does not have the advanced treatment she needs. Her oncologist here has been in communication with M. D. Anderson Hospital in Houston, and we will take her medical records with us.

Wednesday, May 18, 6:30 a.m.—We're in our hotel room and Jamie is still asleep. I'm thankful she is resting well. I'm on my knees at the window again, looking down into the busy street, reading my Bible and praying. I see and hear God all around me—such a sweet presence and peace and even joy from Him. Am I just needier and more receptive now? God supplies what we need moment by moment. He is a good God, and I love Him so much. I'm so thankful for His Living Word. Every page drips honey into my soul. "Lord, this day is yours; we are yours."

I must tell you what I see as I look into this very interesting street below. There are bicycles, cars, buses, and motorcycles everywhere, people walking dogs, and street cleaners wearing orange suits and breathing masks as they sweep trash from the street with straw brooms and dump the debris into the carts attached to their bicycles. There are motorized bicycles, portable bicycles that can be folded and taken into businesses, and parents pedaling their children to school. Still more bicycles pull small wagons loaded with who knows what and covered with burlap (UPS and FedEx wannabes). And the continuous horn-honking night and day—it never stops! This morning I even saw a lady pedaling a bicycle with an enclosed glass restaurant on wheels (a street vendor). It had a big pot of something in it with produce and food around it.

May 19, 2011—Jamie cried today. She is worried about his reaction when he sees her. He and Karen Vi will fly here tomorrow. We'll all spend tomorrow night and then leave the hotel at 5:00 a.m. for the airport. Karen Vi will fly back with Jamie and me. He and Caleb will fly to Texas soon. "Dear Lord, please strengthen my Jamie and pour your abundant peace and joy into her. Please heal her and give her a long life. I love you, Lord."

It was Sunday, July 3, and Jamie didn't go to church because she wasn't feeling well. Since coming back to Texas, she and her family lived with us. Gene and I took care of the children whenever he took her to Houston for treatments. It was a busy household with a three and two-year-old running around. Overall, Jamie tolerated the chemotherapy treatments pretty well. But today her hair came out in clumps. Most of that beautiful thick wavy hair was in the bathroom sink. She noticed it starting to come out a couple of days before.

I called Whitney, my hairdresser. She told us to meet her at her shop at three. It was Sunday afternoon on a holiday weekend. Jamie called Janet to let her know, and she met us there. Whitney gently cut off the remaining hair. I cried silently. Jamie had a wonderful attitude and a beautiful head, and Janet was a great support to her sister.

At home, Caleb and Karen laughed out loud. "Mommy, you are the most beautiful mommy in the wide world!" Caleb exclaimed. I vacuumed up hair from everywhere. It was the first time I ever vacuumed a bed! After we put the kids down for the night, the four of us played trash train until almost midnight. We still know how to have fun.

~

That July 4 was a great day—grilled hot dogs, home-made chili, watermelon, ice cream, and a patriotic cake. That afternoon, the six of us went to Lake Tejas. The kids loved the water! We all swam except Jamie who waded around the water's edge and wore a wide-brimmed hat. She felt good and enjoyed the day.

That evening after the kids were asleep, Jamie asked me a question, "If I don't make it through this cancer, will you and Daddy be intentional about being an important and big part of Caleb and Karen's lives?" I assured her we would, but I also reinforced to her that she will make it through this cancer. "My God, help us! Thank you for this day."

After three months of living with us, Jamie and her family moved out of our house and into their own apartment. I really did not want that to happen, but tension was rising in the home and things were becoming increasingly difficult. Gene and I did everything we could possibly do to help them—take care of the children, cook, clean, wash clothes, everything, and all while working full-time jobs. Perhaps we did too much. Jamie was unable to help with much housework; she did what she could. They did give us a little financial help for extra expenses. While he has many wonderful qualities, we found it almost impossible to have an adult conversation with him, because he would get very defensive and leave the room. You learn a lot about someone through observation when you live in close quarters with them. He seemed self-absorbed, spending much of his time in front of his laptop, eating, and sleeping.

The day came when I asked them for one long weekend a month, just enough time to relax and catch up on things around the house—a breather if you will. That didn't go over very well. I didn't want them to move out; I only wanted a break now and then. His family in Dallas never seemed to have much time for them.

Jamie and I had a long heart-to-heart private conversation. It was obvious she loved him despite his insecurities and other unresolved issues. She had learned over the years to pick her battles cautiously and wisely. I understand every one of us has personal struggles, imperfections, and weaknesses—but I digress; this story is about Jamie. Nevertheless, our church family came through again for them big time by giving them all the furniture they needed for their upstairs apartment.

Through it all, I knew I had to keep my early morning time with the Lord. I had to protect that time, often praying and reading my Bible on the closet floor. His Word has always been the anchor of my soul—the difference between surviving and being swept away. I must work hard at keeping the mind of Christ while emotions explode in my heart. Even now as I write her life's story, painful emotions surface. If it were not for God's grace and strength, this would not get done, but "I can do all this through him who gives me strength" (Phil. 4:13).

God always gives cause for celebration! Since her return to Texas, Jamie received e-mails from two of her beloved students saying they had crossed over and become part of the family. What joy this brought to Jamie's heart!

Jamie is taking a graduate class in Greek. What can I say? She loves school and enjoys studying. She will soon complete twelve weeks of chemo and will begin the next twelve weeks shortly thereafter, which will include an even stronger chemo, followed by six weeks of daily radiation. He and Gene and I take turns driving her to Houston for treatments and doctor visits. The Greek gives her something to do while she is at the hospital. I still keep the children often which I want to do.

Friday, October 21, 2011, 10:30 p.m.—Jamie and I are at a ladies retreat. Tonight following the message, Jamie went forward for prayer. Ladies gathered around her and prayed. One lady told her, "Buddhist priests have put a curse on you." It all began to make sense to Jamie. This past year in her city, she experienced much persecution—the fire, the kidney stone, incidents involving Caleb's care, and the sexual assault on her. Yes, Jamie was attacked in her apartment by a repairman, all this following the news about the tumor and while she was preparing to fly to Beijing for surgery. She screamed and fought off her attacker, and he finally released her and fled. The five Buddhist priests from Bangladesh with their bald heads and long flowing orange robes lived above their apartment and could be heard chanting constantly.

I had a problem believing that a curse was leveled against Jamie. What about these Scriptures? "Like a fluttering sparrow or a darting swallow, an undeserved curse does not come to rest" (Prov. 26:2) and "You, dear children, are from God and have overcome them, because the one who is in you is greater than the one who is in the world" (1 Jn. 4:4).

~

Monday, November 21, 2011—Today is day three of radiation. Jamie will begin staying at a Catholic nursing home near the hospital in Houston to keep from having her family drive her back and forth every day. She is okay with it. She will come home for Thanksgiving and on weekends.

~

Christmas Eve 2011—We had a wonderful time with family today. The highlight for me was Jamie's gift to me. She had found her first baby album in the top of my closet; it was ragged and falling apart. She carefully removed every precious picture and carefully inserted each one into two beautifully decorated pink albums, writing beside each picture all of my notes I had scribbled on the backs of the pictures. I know it took her many hours to accomplish this act of love. This gift brought tears to my eyes—and still does.

~

Saturday, December 31, 2011—Jamie is thirty-six today. She received a good doctor's report today from a liver test. That was a good birthday present! He and Jamie are spending three nights in The Woodlands for her birthday and to celebrate the end of treatment. Caleb and Karen are with us and are very good. What a year it has been! God has poured His grace, peace, and healing abundantly upon all of us. We are so thankful to Him for His truth, mercy, and faithfulness. It has been a good year, and I praise God for every prayer that has gone up for our Jamie.

~

Monday, January 9, 2012—Jamie is tired and her back hurts a lot. It is also getting more difficult for her to walk up the stairs to their apartment. She is unable to get the rest she needs, so she is moving in with us today. They have talked about it, and they feel it is the best thing so Jamie can heal quickly. She spends time with him whenever the kids are in their playschool, and they all come over often and have meals with us. His family is helping more with the children too.

~

Monday, March 12, 2012—Jamie has been doing well. Several tests and x-rays haven't revealed anything new. They are busily preparing for departure and are anxious to return to their home in Northern Asia.

~

Thursday, March 15, 2012—Yesterday after work, they brought the children to us for the night. We flew kites, ate popsicles, jumped on the trampoline (that trampoline is a godsend!) and watched *Happy Feet Two* until 10:00 p.m. We love our four grandchildren! Our front bedroom has been turned into a playroom; so on those occasions when we have all four, they will sleep on pallets on the playroom floor. It's the perfect place for lots of bedtime stories and laughter.

~

March 20, 2012—Jamie is still having pain and not sleeping well.

~

March 22, 2012—He has been moving everything over here as they're packing. I'm starting to get sad; they are excited.

~

March 27, 2012—Today, Jamie will have tests all day at MDA.

~

March 29, 2012—We did not receive the good report we wanted yesterday. Jamie has a bad infection that will require an IV every day for one week starting today. A home healthcare nurse will administer it in Lufkin. And a blood test was high for a cancer possibility in her body. They will not be able to return to Northern Asia for at least another month. She will receive the antibiotic through her port because her veins are collapsed. She asked if they can move in with us because they have boxed and packed almost everything. She is very sad, weak, and running fever. The wound looks bad. They are disappointed and frustrated and don't understand. But God understands, and He's still in control and we will never stop trusting him.

~

*April 2012—I knew there would be a book about Jamie's life and healing. She did receive her healing but not in the way we prayed and expected. Her life's story had a much different ending, one that only God could have designed for His purpose. Over the next few years, I would start and stop this book several times, unable to continue, paralyzed by the memory of her agony. However, I continued making notes as God spoke to my heart and as I processed everything that happened—and it has been a slow process.*

~

Jamie did not come home but was admitted into the hospital for a biopsy. She was unable to walk because of weakness. Caleb was sad that his mommy and daddy did not come home, but he was okay.

She has two serious infections—staff and live bacteria. She stayed five days in the hospital, and Caleb and Karen stayed with us while he was with Jamie.

~

April 2, 2012—Jamie was dismissed from the hospital. The biopsy showed cancer. We all cried and prayed. She is tired, sad, discouraged, and disappointed that leaving for overseas will be postponed again.

# Chapter 25

## *The Fight for Survival*

April 5, 2012—He took Jamie back to MDA yesterday to talk with her doctor and then back to our house. The news was not good. It has reoccurred as inflammatory cancer. It will be a fight for survival now. The infections had masked the cancer. Chemo starts again tomorrow and surgery is imminent. Basically the chemo and radiation she had accomplished nothing; the cancer resisted it. What we see now on her skin is more cancer than infection. We dare not mention Northern Asia to her because it makes her cry. She must concentrate on getting well and living to see her children grow up. I will take her to MDA tomorrow for her first new chemo treatment.

~

April 19, 2012—Jamie has been staying some with us and some at the apartment. When she needs peace and quiet, she calls us to come get her. He will take her to MDA again today to see the surgeon. Our church family is awesome. People are giving them money, meals, and gift cards; they are babysitting, calling us, praying for us, and giving lots of hugs. Mothers of Preschoolers (MOPS) have been a tremendous blessing to them. "Oh God, please heal our little girl. We need you desperately. We worship you. We trust you. Please help us."

~

April 27, 2012—The pain is increasing and so is the pain medication. However, she tries to spend as much time with Caleb and Karen as she can. A few days ago, we all went to a small parade downtown. She sat in a lawn chair as much as possible. The children enjoyed riding ponies. Last night, we went to the rodeo. She had a good time watching the children have a good time. He will take her to MDA today for her third round of chemo, and I will stay home with the children.

~

Saturday, April 28, 2012—He and Jamie called several times from MDA yesterday with not-so-good reports and then came in about 8:30 p.m. Jamie did not take chemo because it's not working and her blood count was low. Her oncologist said the cancer had grown since Monday. They scheduled her for surgery on Thursday to remove that breast and all affected tissue. The surgeon will have to take skin from her back to do skin grafts. She will be in the hospital three to five days. They increased her morphine dosage to help with the pain.

Dear God, is it wrong to ask why? Please forgive me if it is. Why are you allowing Jamie to endure such suffering? She willingly goes to your harvest field and you call her back. "The harvest is plentiful, but the workers are few. Ask the Lord of the harvest, therefore, to send out workers into his harvest field" (Lk. 10:2). God, I don't understand. Help me, Lord. Please, God, help our Jamie.

~

Monday, April 30, 2012—Yesterday, Jamie and he were at Sunday school and church. She did not feel well but she was there. She hadn't slept the night before. Her pain increased today and medication was not helping. He took her to the emergency room at MDA and she was admitted.

Thursday, May 3, 2012—Jamie had surgery today. The surgeon was confident that she removed all the cancerous tissue leaving a wide margin. She had to go deeper into the muscle in the chest than expected. She said not "if" but "when" the cancer comes back that it could show up anywhere in her body. She said Jamie's cancer is extremely aggressive and that concerns her. She knows she did not get all the cancer in her body, only what she could see and feel. She may have a few months or a few years to live. She said MDA has exhausted everything they can do for her. They have nothing left to offer. She encouraged him to check into alternative treatments. She said that she will remain her surgeon and take care of her as needed. When she walked out of the waiting room, Gene and I broke down.

Gene, Janet, and I went to the hotel around 5:00 p.m. thinking we had time before Jamie went to recovery, but she came out earlier than expected and was saying, "I want my sister!" She gave her nurse Janet's cell number and he called her. He was impressed that she could remember the number while coming out of anesthesia! Janet turned her car around and went back to the hospital.

May 10, 2012—And so he begins the all-natural cancer treatment. He is desperate; he wants to help Jamie any way he can; he wants her to live. I understand and appreciate that. Application has been made to Camelot Cancer Care in Tulsa, and generous friends and churches have already given $12,000 to go toward expenses.

May 11, 2012—Jamie walked around the block early yesterday in her pajamas! She had a good day. On Wednesday, the surgeon removed a stitch and left a hole for drainage.

Today, I watched him as he pushed packing in the hole to absorb some of the liquid—with his bare hands using my all purpose scissors that were not sterilized. He patched and taped her. This has to be done twice daily. It made my skin crawl, especially watching him not take precautions.

May 14, 2012—While I changed her dressing about nine o'clock last night, she made the comment that he spends money like there's no end to it. She said he has to buy something every day. She wanted to go back to the apartment about ten o'clock because he was crying, and he hardly ever cries. She said he's tired of caregiving. In our conversation, I encouraged her to get their finances organized legally to protect the children's future. Yes, we're all tired of this trial and want normalcy. But we're not there yet. "Dear God, please help all of us today and this week."

June 2012—While Jamie and her family were in Tulsa for her treatment, Gene and I took an Alaskan cruise and vacation to celebrate our forty years of marriage, a trip for which we had planned and saved a very long time—a dream come true. God gave us such a great time together.

July 3, 2012—Jamie lay on our sofa this morning in pain. I knelt beside her, crying softly. This mother's heart was broken at seeing her daughter suffer. She touched my face tenderly and smiled. "Mom, God's got this. Don't worry."

~

July 5, 2012—Jamie stayed with us yesterday. She can't walk very far now; it hurts to breathe; her neck, right shoulder, and back always hurt. She can no longer stand up straight and can't be in one position very long. She must take pain medication every few hours. He and Jamie left at 7:00 p.m. for Houston; she has a 7:30 a.m. PET scan appointment tomorrow. They will spend the night at Margaret and Lawrence's home. These good friends have allowed them to stay in their home and use one of their vehicles as often as needed. Caleb and Karen are with us. I will miss work again tomorrow while I stay home with my precious grandchildren.

~

July 7, 2012—The report is not good—stage four cancer. It's in her lymph glands under both arms, in her neck, lungs, and skin. They got home about 6:45 p.m. She rested in my bed while he knelt beside the bed and I sat on the bed. She is disappointed and angry with God. She cried briefly and questioned why God is allowing her to suffer. I assured her God is big enough to handle her anger, questions, and discouragement. She was very tired. Her oncologist told her she would not live to raise her children.

I assured Jamie that God still has this. We will fight; we will continue seeking God, believing, and trusting Him for a miracle. We will live each day to the fullest, loving God, serving Him, receiving His encouragement and strength from His Word. God has not dropped Jamie. He will pull her closer to Himself. God's got this! She went back to her apartment while the kids stayed another night with Memaw and Papa.

~

July 8, 2012—Jamie said she is not mad at God anymore. I wasn't worried about that. God has been dealing with me about reading the Bible completely through in August. I've read the Bible through many times but never in just thirty-one days. I'm not sure that is even possible. I work full-time and take care of grandchildren all the time and try to help Jamie as much as possible. When would I have the time?

~

July 19, 2012—I just e-mailed him after I read through pages of "all-natural" mumbo-jumbo he posted on his Facebook. He probably won't take it well, but the reality is Jamie is not getting better from all these natural "cancer-fighting" remedies.

"I have read about all I can stand of your display of all knowledge of natural treatments. What a joke! The truth is none of it is working. You're making it sound like she is getting better. She is not. Who are you trying to impress? If you would spend your time seeking God and His Word, His truth, maybe we would get somewhere. She's not drinking that water or juicing at my house. Yes, I am all for eating healthy and using wisdom, but your ramblings irk me. Get a reality check! Fall on your knees more often; read the Word more than all this natural garbage; fast more. Her healing will come from God and nothing else. I love you, but your eyes are only glancing God's way, whereas they should be glued there."

And everything—everything—changed. "And Jacob noticed that Laban's attitude toward him was not what it had been" (Gen. 31:2). God works to accomplish His ultimate purpose in spite of weaknesses, struggles, and blemishes in our family.

Dear Mom:

If I hear that you've been talking to Jamie this way or if you mention another word like in your e-mail about this all being a joke, I will post your judgmental reaction for everyone to see. "Before you judge the speck in another person, look at the plank in your eye." That's Scripture too. I'm deeply hurt by what you wrote. I have forgiven you already, but don't expect to see me in any of your Sunday school classes ever again!

I trust God above everything else, and you know that! He also gives us wisdom to do the right things. I believe the cancer is dying inside of Jamie. And I think it's better that it's coming out of her than going the other way into her liver, spleen, pancreas, heart, and bones. You can speak negatively over her and choose to look at the symptoms on the outside that will not kill her; that's your choice. I have an incredible peace that God is touching her from the inside out. Why do you think the cancer is coming out? Something good is happening inside of her. We praise God for that!

July 20, 2012—Yesterday was a horrible day. He was furious when he read my e-mail. He e-mailed me back three times. Then I received three hateful texts from a near relative. So my day was filled with crying and regret. I admit that my wording in the e-mail was wrong; I could have reworded it. My message would have remained the same, but the wording should have been different. Sometimes I feel stuck between a rock and a hard place. Do I tell him what he wants to hear, or do I tell him the truth? So Gene called a meeting between the three of us from 5:30–6:30 in my office. Jamie dictated to Gene what she wanted to say and he read it to us. In the end, forgiveness was given and received, Satan was recognized and disarmed, and hopefully this incident will make us all seek God more and guard against Satan's attacks.

"I have forgiven in the sight of Christ for your sake, in order that Satan might not outwit us. For we are not unaware of his schemes" (2 Cor. 2:10–11).

Jamie is awake (4:30 a.m.) now and hurting badly; she only slept a couple hours. I write this through tears. I feel so helpless. I pray. I ask her constantly, "Is there anything I can do for you?" "There's nothing you can do, Momma." That is hard to hear. "Oh my God, please hear our cries for mercy."

Gene took her to occupational therapy yesterday. They recommend wound therapy.

~

July 21, 2012—I packed all of Jamie's things, and she went back to their apartment.

~

July 22, 2012—Today is our Karen Vi's fourth birthday. We had a party for her yesterday at Chamber's Park at 3:30 p.m. She loved it! Jamie was there and did her best to push through the pain, but I could tell she was very uncomfortable.

The Lord reminded me that people, for the most part, don't like the truth and don't receive it well when it's directed right at them. He does not receive truth well. A lot of people didn't receive truth well in the Bible either. The truth can hurt, and we lash out in defense of ourselves. The Word tells us to examine the fruit of people's lives. I hope people will look at my life overall and see Jesus and not only focus on my mistakes. I hope people will remember Jesus in me over my lifetime. I hope there's plenty of fruit and very few bugs. I pray for him that his eyes will be open to the truth about himself, and he will allow God to uproot the deep-seated insecurities, pain, and lies buried in his heart.

~

July 23, 2012—Jamie is taking the higher dosage of morphine. She seems easily agitated and unable to focus. She did attend early service, Sunday school, and the evening service yesterday.

Our church family gathered around Jamie again and prayed for her.

~

July 24, 2012—Jamie called about 7:00 a.m. yesterday, talking in a hushed voice, saying that he is not allowing her to take Karen for her four-year-old shots because of something he read on the Internet. She asked us to pray; we did. I called back about nine o'clock, and she had to cancel her doctor's appointment because of his stink. He would not listen to her. I talked to her later and she was crying, saying that he wants her to stay at the apartment. He doesn't want a family meeting because he's outnumbered. He wants to talk to a financial advisor about her life insurance money. If she sets it up and he's not agreeable, he will change it after she dies. She told me she was sorry she ever brought him into our family. Basically, he does not want to honor her last wishes.

Jeremy and Janet came over and we talked for several hours. Jeremy believes Jamie should be able to carry out her wishes for the $500,000 life insurance. Jamie also told me (when I asked her if there is anything I can do to help her) just to love him. She is very much afraid that if she passes away, he will never let us see Caleb and Karen. She wants the children to know us and for us to have access to them. It is not right for Jamie to have to deal with all this dissension on top of her illness. So Jeremy will talk to a lawyer friend today. He and Gene will have a conversation encouraging her to have all her wishes drawn up with an attorney as soon as possible. We can't allow his threats to stop her from legalizing her final wishes.

Gene and I prayed again so hard that God will intervene and work all this out for Jamie's good. We still pray all the time for her healing, but wisdom compels us to protect Jamie and to protect him from himself.

July 25, 2012—E-mail from Jamie: Hi, Mom and Dad. First I want to say that I believe I will live for many more years to come, and I also believe that your and his relationship will improve as time goes by. So this e-mail is probably irrelevant. But here it is anyway.

It is so important to me that the kids know my side of the family as they grow up. I cannot use enough words to express the importance their relationship with you is to me. Of course, if he lives with them in Northern Asia, you (and his side of the family) won't have a lot of chances to see them. But when they are in the States, I don't want you to miss opportunities to be with them.

I hope that in order to spend time with the kids, you will never need to invoke grandparents' rights. But I easily and quickly found the right for grandparent visitation below. The first sentence would apply to you guys:

Texas Grandparent Rights

> Grandparent Rights to Possession and/or Access to Grandchildren:
>
> - Visitation may be granted if the grandparent's child has been incarcerated in jail or prison during the three month period preceding the application, has been determined to be legally incompetent, or is dead;

I don't want to get into a big discussion about this. Like I said, I don't think it will be necessary. Although he has been stretched this past year, he loves you both very much. He also knows how important it is to me that the kids continue to have a relationship with you all. Just please save this email in case you ever need it.

I love you!
Jamie

July 28, 2012—Jamie called her Daddy yesterday to come get her for the night. She just wanted a little quiet away from the kids so maybe she could sleep better. She is resting in her Daddy's chair now.

August 1, 2012—Today I begin a thirty-one day partial fast and will read the entire Bible during this time, reading at least fifty-three pages per day. I will also continue my usual Bible reading, prayer time, two devotionals, and journaling every morning from four to seven. I want to hear from God and not someone else telling me what God is saying, and I will write down each day the truths I see. It will be very challenging, but I want to learn, grow, die to flesh and self, and seek God for Jamie's healing. "He must become greater; I must become less" (Jn. 3:30).

(Since that time, every August has been a month of deeper prayer and fasting, denying myself so that I may have more of Jesus Christ. Little did I know in August of 2012 that I would need that intense time with Christ and His Word to survive the next few months.)

Jamie found another lump and red place on her lower back.

# Chapter 26

## *The Ultimate Attack Intensifies*

Yet I have written you quite boldly on some points.

—Rom. 15:15

August 3, 2012—Jamie called, extremely upset. He left in the middle of their argument. He wants to control everything about Jamie—every penny of life insurance. He is being so hateful to her; she does not need this conflict. He should be honoring her more now than ever. She wanted her Daddy, so Gene went to see her. Gene said some things that needed to be said with no regrets. At the end, they prayed together. Last night, Jamie called to talk to her daddy. She sounded better. He got on the phone and told Gene he didn't want us interfering. He told Gene he would take his family and move to Dallas. Gene said, "Don't threaten me."

Jamie needs healing in her body, but he needs healing in his heart. At times, the latter produces more pain for Jamie than the former. Only God can touch both.

Abigail spoke the truth about the situation to Nabal and his heart became like a stone (1 Sam. 25:37). The prophet Nathan confronted David with the truth (2 Sam. 12:7) and he repented and received forgiveness. He didn't sugarcoat anything. David made the choice to repent.

Some may argue that Nathan should have "spoken the truth in love" more. The truth is the truth. It's our individual responsibility to respond to God in the right way. Jesus spoke the truth to the Pharisees when he called them "whitewashed tombs and a brood of vipers" (Mt. 23:27–33). Some may argue that wasn't very loving. The Pharisees, unlike David, rejected the truth and did not repent.

~

August 6, 2012—Gene and Jeremy met him at Starbucks yesterday at 6:30 p.m. for about forty-five minutes. Then they went to see Batman. When Gene got home about 11:00 p.m., he told me of their visit. He said it was great. The old son-in-law is back! Gene cried while telling me everything he said. He is sorry for the way he has been acting for the past few weeks. He will honor Jamie's wishes in every way. He will not take the grandchildren away from us. He loves us. We praised God while sitting in our bed! Thank you, Jesus!

I called Jamie and talked to her yesterday. Caleb and Karen were spending the night with Janet. Jamie had a rough day. She can't bathe herself now because of the pain. He must do everything for her. She is losing strength in her right hand and arm. She dropped a cup of water because it was too heavy. "Dear God, thank you for healing his heart. Please heal Jamie's body. I love you, Lord, and I worship you."

~

September 1, 2012—I completed the thirty-one-day fast and reading the entire Bible through in August and taking notes of everyday's reading highlights. God helped me accomplish this and it has been a blessing to me. Jamie continues to grow weaker and the pain continues to increase. She is losing weight. Melissa, my niece, is coming to help Jamie this week.

~

September 8, 2012—I took lunch to them and stayed a few hours. Jamie was completely out of it. She would only take a few bites. I washed her face. He stripped her, picked her up, and put her in the bath tub on her hands and knees. He was not gentle. I could not believe what I was witnessing but was afraid to interfere. He poured water over her head and called it a bath. She was totally helpless. He and I wiped her down with baby wipes while she lay in the bed, and he changed her dressing. He was so rough with her. My heart broke for my little girl.

She was hallucinating. She hasn't slept for several nights. Her muscles were tense. A little later, Jamie sang old church songs and quoted whole passages of scripture—loudly. He refuses to consider hospice care. I don't see Jamie getting better. To my eyes, she has gotten worse this week. I see my baby frightened and scared. The only time she seems to relax a little is when I read the Bible to her or she sings or quotes Bible verses. A friend went over there last night; she left a message on my phone:

You won't believe what I saw last night. I hesitate to tell you because I know it will upset you. Jamie was sitting in the big overstuffed La-Z-Boy chair that you and Mawmaw bought her, and I was sitting beside her. She was not herself—so weak, hurting so badly, and saying crazy things. I think she was over-medicated. He came over to us and I suggested the possibility of hospice to help take care of Jamie. He became furious. He grabbed Jamie around the shoulders and neck and shook her until her head flopped around like a rag doll. He screamed in her face. "They don't love you! Tell her you don't want hospice! They kill people! Hospice starved my mother to death! Tell her! Hospice will kill you!"

"Stop it! Please stop shaking her!" I just stood there. I couldn't move. I could not believe what I was seeing.

Jamie came to long enough to say, "I want hospice to help take care of me."

~

September 9, 2012—What a day yesterday was! So thankful for friends like Liz who help with the children so much; Caleb and Karen have stayed with her several times while Jamie was so ill. I went to see Jamie about 10:30 a.m. He asked me to call our friend, Eric, who is a PA, to come over and examine Jamie. Janet came over as well. Eric was concerned with her muscle movement in her legs, feet, left arm, and hand.

He agreed to take Jamie to the hospital. It was difficult for her to go down the stairs. She stayed in the emergency room until being admitted about 6:00 p.m. The CAT scan on her head came back clear. Then the doctor ordered a chest x-ray. He went home to shower and was not in the room when the doctor came in with the report. The doctor told us the cancer was all over both lungs. He would admit her for the neurologist to determine if she needed an MRI on her spine that might explain the involuntary muscle movement. I followed the doctor out of the room and asked him about length of life. He said the cancer is growing fast, and since a PET scan two months ago showed one little spot in her lung, he gave her possibly a couple of months to six months at the most.

He finally came back to the hospital while the admitting doctor was in Jamie's room. He is so against any medication even to help her sleep. He argued with the doctor about the x-ray results. He insists on natural treatments. Before the doctor left, I asked him to please tell the family what he told me outside her door in the emergency room. He said six months is generous. I wanted him to hear it. After he left, we all talked around Jamie's bed. He said we will not discuss how long the doctors think she has left around Jamie. Jeremy was good in talking to him, trying to help him understand we are not the enemy. We love him. Jamie talked to all of us, reassuring us that she wants God to get the glory no matter the outcome, which will be good no matter how it goes. She is concerned that people not lose faith in God should He take her home. She knows Sage and her Sunday school class are praying for a miracle. She wants those little girls to know that she is okay. She is amazing. I think we all left him on good terms. His sister is coming to get the children today to take them to her home for a few days.

September 10, 2012—Karen Vi did not want to go; she wanted to stay with Memaw and Papa, but she settled down. Gene and I led the way to the hospital. The children saw their mother. She saw them and smiled and acknowledged them. They stayed about ten minutes. I was standing right beside him by Jamie's bed when he told his sister that the chest x-ray only showed about four small places in her right lung and her left lung looked good. A blatant lie! I did not say anything. He saw the x-ray just like Janet and I did. It showed Jamie's right lung was full of cancer and the left lung had some, just not as much. Is he in denial?

Jamie was unable to tolerate the MRI, so the doctor released her to our home where she could get the rest she needed, and he could bring the children over whenever she was able to visit. He needed a good night's rest. He was exhausted from trying to take care of Jamie as well as two four-year-olds. Humanly impossible!

We settled Jamie into her bed in our home at 4:30 p.m. She ate a few bites. Then she sat in Gene's chair for about an hour and talked intelligently to Gene, Janet, and I about how he tries to control what she says to doctors, nurses, and family and that she doesn't agree with that.

September 11, 2012—I am taking a leave of absence from the church office now to take care of Jamie full-time. He was here most of the day and spent the night to be with Jamie.

~

September 12, 2012—Last night, she was in so much pain after he changed her dressing. Her wounds look much worse to me. Janet was here. The four of us gathered around her on the bed and literally prayed her to sleep. Gene anointed her with oil. We prayed in English and in the Spirit. She prayed in the Spirit. God touched her, and she went to sleep.

~

September 14, 2012—He and I took Jamie to the wound care center yesterday morning. The nurse changed her dressing and showed me how to do it. This whole experience was extremely tiring and painful for Jamie. Afterward, he stayed gone most of the day and came in around 9:00 p.m. Jamie was in Gene's chair, so Gene and I went to bed. A few minutes later, I walked to the kitchen to get a drink of water, and he was standing over her trying to convince her to go back to the apartment. She was upset, crying, begging, and pleading with him to let her stay here, saying she wants to see the children every day but cannot live under the same room with them 24/7. After a few minutes of listening to this, I had to step in and come to Jamie's defense. He would not take no for an answer. He is trying once again to manipulate and control her and the situation. Gene had to intervene. We helped Jamie to bed, and I tried to help her relax so she could go to sleep. After several minutes, he came into the room and apologized to me, spent a few minutes with Jamie, and then left. Jamie and I never slept all night. We talked, prayed, cried, read Scripture, and I massaged her right arm.

I know he's struggling with Jamie's illness, but Jamie is struggling too, and the patient's wishes should be honored. True love is unconditional; anything less is manipulation.

~

September 15, 2012—Jamie hurt so much yesterday, crying out to God for mercy and healing. She asked me to call the MDA Breast Center and ask someone if she can have something else for pain. I found the number and called. A doctor returned my call. I filled him in on the situation and told him what she was currently taking for pain. He said that wasn't nearly enough and she did not need to be in so much pain. He increased her morphine.

I want to say again how much our church family has blessed us all during this time with so many good meals. And so many people are praying all over the world for Jamie. Our hearts are grateful.

~

September 17, 2012—Good friends Andrea and Eric have helped me several times change Jamie's dressing, but I did it by myself yesterday; God was with me. I am not a nurse, so God definitely helps me do what I need to do for my child.

~

September 18, 2012—Yesterday was a horribly painful day for Jamie, for all of us. He came over briefly about 8:30 a.m.; the kids stayed in the car. He brought supplies for Jamie. He went to her bedside and totally upset her again saying he would not bring the kids in to see her here because she has made her choice. He won't be coming to see her either. She cried and begged him. He walked out. I followed, begging him to bring the children in to see their mother. "Please don't do this to Jamie. You're punishing her. This is wrong." He would not listen to Gene or me.

Jamie wailed, prayed, cried, questioned—broken hearted. She and I prayed throughout the day. The emotional pain she is suffering now (that which morphine can't touch) exceeds the physical pain. She cried sporadically all day over the mean things he said to her. She opened up to me about their relationship. This emotional abuse—control, threats, punishment when he doesn't get his way, manipulation, selfishness, lying, and never listening to the truth—has been going on for some time in their marriage, escalating exponentially since her illness began. The pain he is inflicting is unholy and evil. He has abandoned her in her hour of deepest need. He is not honoring her in sickness and in health. He is trying to force her to go back to the apartment by keeping the children away from her.

He called her on the phone about 6:00 p.m. "Caleb and Karen have asked, 'Where is Mommy?' I told them that even though Mommy is better and symptom-free, she doesn't want to come home." That statement broke her heart—again.

"The doctor wants to start you back on antibiotics through your port, but I won't show your mother how it's done. You have to come home first." She was crushed again by his words and could not believe her ears. "You've made your choice. You're turning your parents against me by all your whining and crying." What? Absurd!

"Oh God, judge him for what he is doing to me! Oh God! Oh God, I forgive him," she said while I readjusted her oxygen and attempted to calm her so she could breathe more easily. I'm wondering what symptoms he is talking about. Yes, the hallucinations and involuntary muscle movements have stopped because she is not over medicated as before. "Lord, you have seen the wrong done to me. Uphold my cause!" (Lam. 3:59).

"The Lord is close to the brokenhearted and saves those who are crushed in spirit" (Ps. 34:18).

"I the Lord search the heart and examine the mind, to reward each person according to their conduct, according to what their deeds deserve" (Jer. 17:10).

The physical pain coupled with the emotional pain inflicted on her by someone she deeply loved was almost more than any human could bear, and except for God's grace given us in abundant measure, she, Gene, and I would have been sucked under by the whirlpool of grief, bitterness, and unforgiveness—never to breathe again. But God—God rescued us time and time again, buoying us to the surface to breathe in His faithfulness.

September 19, 2012—It's 5:30 a.m. It has been my habit for many years to rise early and spend those first few hours of each day in prayer, reading my Bible, and journaling. And this is no time to stop now. I need God more now than ever. Jamie did not sleep well last night. I woke Gene up at 2:00 a.m. to take over so I could sleep a few hours. Yesterday was another extremely difficult day for all of us.

A home health nurse came over to get information and begin their services. He and the children walked in about that time. Jamie was sitting in Gene's chair while I went to the kitchen to fill out paper work.

He began trying to convince Jamie to move back to the apartment again. She grew increasingly upset. Gene tried to reason with him, but he would not listen. I finally had to ask him to leave because Jamie was struggling to breathe. He got up to leave, trailing hurtful comments about Jamie making her choice again. She asked to kiss her children. Karen was in the house at the time and she kissed her mommy. "I want to hug Caleb," she said. "Caleb doesn't have to hug you," and he walked out. She cries. The nurse is obviously shocked at what she is witnessing at that moment. Gene and I follow him out the door. It was a shouting match for a few minutes, but we were sick and tired of him ripping Jamie's heart apart. Gene talked to him a few minutes before he drove away while I tried to console Jamie. I apologized to the nurse. She showed me how to do wound care for Jamie. Exhausted, Jamie slept two hours.

Last evening, I sat beside her bed, listening, watching. She sang softly to the Lord. She prayed. "Oh Jesus, I love you. I forgive him for everything, Lord. I forgive him. Help him, Jesus. Heal me, Lord. Take care of my Caleb and Karen. Bless my students and colleagues back home in the city I love. They need you so much, Jesus. I love you, Lord. I worship you."

Like Stephen, Jamie forgave. She refused to allow unforgiveness to cloud her heart. "Then he fell on his knees and cried out, 'Lord, do not hold this sin against them.'" (Acts 7:60).

Jamie loved all those whom God gave her. Her desire for her husband, children, family, students, and friends can be found in John 17:24. "Father, I want those you have given me to be with me where I am, and to see my glory, the glory you have given me because you loved me before the creation of the world."

September 19, 2012—My Wishes—Jamie Norton Lund

To my husband,

I am of sound mind as I dictate this to Mom. Thank you for the good care you have provided me since the time of my diagnosis. You have labored many hours of love, and I know you are tired. Thank you for trying to keep our children in as normal routine as possible during this time of sickness. At this point, my body is very weak as the cancer has spread and the pain has increased. I have been bedridden for quite a while now and don't see when I will likely be up on my feet again. For some reason, when you were taking care of me, between the two of us, we managed to mess up my medications and I got very sick. Now that the effects of that incident are over, I want to be more careful so that we don't accidentally cause the problems with medication to return.

Therefore, these are my wishes: I want to stay in the home of my parents where I feel like I can get the best care. I want my mother to become my primary caregiver, which I feel is in the best interest of my health. This is also in the best interest of our family because it will allow you to give better attention to the children and will allow me the best possible chance of survival. I want you to continue to take care of our children. I also want you to be emotionally supportive of me by spending time conversing with me daily. I feel it is my right as a mother to see my children every day as I have not abandoned either them or you. I am not being selfish in making these demands; rather, I am trying to think about what is best for us and our children. I expect to see them at least thirty minutes every day as my limited health faculties allow. I expect you to stop threatening me as if you are dangling the children over my head. I have the right to see them regardless of where I choose to receive my treatment and care. Based on our marriage vows to each other, I expect you to walk through this time as an emotional support for me all from your love and understanding and unselfishness. I expect you to no longer threaten my parents, and I request that you recognize that you are an important and permanent member of our family whom we all love.

I will do the following things: I will continue to pursue God's healing for my body through intensive prayer and by taking good care of myself physically. As a patient, I will choose my medical treatment. I will keep you up to date on my progress and believe until the end for healing. I will always love you and honor our marriage commitment. And finally, my children, Caleb and Karen, I will always delight in being your mommy and be so thankful that God gave you to me, even if it might be only for a short time.

Jamie

~

September 20, 2012—Jamie's days and nights are now filled with constant and increasing pain, quietly crying out to God for His mercy and healing power, softly singing choruses learned long ago in church, songs Gene and I haven't heard in years. Worship, prayer, Scripture, singing—all emerge from deep within her soul. God's tender love and presence envelop her. She radiates the existence of a loving Father even in the deepest darkest valley. My heart continually cries out to God for our beautiful daughter. My God is a mighty healer. Nothing is impossible with Him. I reach deep within my soul for faith and trust. He provides.

A home health nurse came over yesterday for a couple of hours to help me do wound care and teach me how to administer antibiotics through her port. I'm still not very confident, but I'm learning.

He came over around 10:00 a.m. with roses and a card for Jamie. The card contained more hurtful words. He blames her for the current disconnect from him and the children and that she is being selfish and shirking her responsibilities as a wife and mother. He said God told him that Satan is telling her she is a bad mother. (Nothing could be further from the truth.)

She called and asked him to come over so she could talk to him about the card. He would come over only on one condition: that we all leave the house. So we all left. We walked back in the house about two thirty, the time he was supposed to pick up the children from preschool. He was still in Jamie's room but left two minutes later. His condition is, in order for him and the children to come see Jamie, Gene and I must leave our own home. It's not happening. We want him and the children to come over and we will give them privacy, but we will never leave our home or Jamie.

We have a pallet on the floor beside Jamie's bed where either Gene or I sleep at all times. I'm losing weight. I believe I eat a healthy diet. How could I not? So many friends keep us supplied with delicious meals on a regular basis. I attribute the weight loss to constantly being on the move 24/7 and sleeping only a couple hours at a time. I hear every sound Jamie makes. It reminds me of when our girls were babies; I heard everything. God gives me strength and grace every day. He is so faithful to all of us. I just want to take care of our daughter, comfort her, and help meet her needs.

Dear God, we ask again for your mercy and grace today. Please speak peace to Jamie. Please work all this out with her husband. We need you so much today, Lord. Forgive me when I fail and don't do things perfectly according to your Word. I ask for your help and wisdom. Bless our Jamie today.

Jamie has a rule. Everyone who comes to our home to see her or brings a meal must pray for her; then she prays for them (as she is able).

She wants her daddy to arrange her funeral, so she is telling him everything she wants. Don't get me wrong. We are all still praying for a divine miracle of healing and believing God with everything that is in us. At the same time, we are using wisdom. That's Jamie.

At times, the only way she can go to sleep is for Gene and I to pray over her until the pain subsides, she relaxes, and drifts off to sleep. The nurses are helping me gradually increase and adjust her pain medication as needed.

September 22, 2012—He came over about 9:10 a.m. yesterday after he took the children to preschool. Gene went to work. I began cleaning the kitchen. Then it started again. I heard Jamie getting upset.

"Just come back home and everything will be okay."

"I can't just go home. Don't you understand?"

He walked away from her and started packing up all his little "all-natural" pills that Jamie is not interested in taking any more. I helped him pack.

"I see that smile," he said to me.

"What? I can't smile in my own home?"

"It's more like a smirk."

"I feel sorry for you." And with that, he left again.

Jamie called one of our district church officials and had a long conversation with him and explained to him exactly how her husband was treating her. He prayed with Jamie and said he would contact him.

September 24, 2012—She called him twice yesterday and left messages saying 3:00–5:00 p.m. would be a good time for him to bring Caleb and Karen to see her. He never returned her calls. She called him again at four to see when he was coming over; he was on his way to Tyler to meet his sister and give her the children.

Jamie cried, "You just left and never talked it over with me? You didn't bring the children to kiss me bye? Where are you now?" He would not tell her.

"I will never take the children to see you again until your mother deals with her issues. She has an evil spirit of rage akin to witchcraft, and there is an evil spirit in that house."

"Are you praying about all of this?"

"I am praying and have other people praying for you that you will see what you are doing to our family.

"I almost had to go to the hospital Saturday night." Silence.

"I will take you to MDA for the PET scan on Tuesday."

"My parents have already made arrangements to take me."

"I want to take you so we can go stay a few days in a hotel for my birthday."

What? What is he thinking? She can barely walk. She can't do anything but lie down and receive care day and night. He has not spent any time to speak of with her in twelve days. She has not seen her children for more than ninety minutes in the past two weeks. Amazingly, after the initial shock of this conversation, she remained calm. She told me last night all she can do is walk by faith, not by sight.

~

September 25, 2012—Home health came yesterday and observed as I did Jamie's wound care and administered the antibiotics through her port. She said I did well! While the nurse was here, I heard the garage door open. I had removed the house key from the garage so he couldn't just barge in anytime he wanted. When the nurse came back in from going to her car to get supplies, he walked in the front door behind her and went directly to Jamie's room. I spent a few more minutes in the kitchen with the nurse before she left; then I went to check on Jamie.

His visit started pleasant enough with prayer and praise. He said God had confirmed to his spirit that Jamie would be healed today. She asked him to read Psalm 91. When he finished, he turned to me. "Do you want to be set free from the spirit of rage?" I was taken aback, but he would not allow me to address his question. "Just say yes or no. Do you want to be set free from the spirit of rage?"

"You are getting very close to blaspheming the Holy Spirit."

He did not appreciate that statement. He was angry. Jamie was becoming more troubled. I asked him to leave—again. He would not leave. I called Gene at work and asked him to come home. Finally, I followed him out the garage door as he continued to berate me and locked the door behind him. I looked out the window, and he was talking to a man standing beside his vehicle with another vehicle parked on the street with a woman inside. When Gene drove in the driveway, the man got in his vehicle, and both vehicles left. Gene talked to him in the driveway or should I say, listened to him as he loudly interrupted everything Gene had to say while pointing to our house. After about twenty minutes, he left and Gene walked inside.

There was a good part to this day. One of our district officials came over at 5:00 p.m. and spent time at Jamie's bedside, prayed with her, sang, worshipped, encouraged her, and listened to her while she explained the dilemma with her husband. "But now be so kind as to look at me. Would I lie to your face?" (Job 6:28).

He was very supportive. He advised us to set boundaries with her husband for Jamie's sake. He told us to not allow him in the house when I'm alone with Jamie and that someone else should always be with me when he comes around. And nothing unkind should be allowed to come from his mouth. Gene changed the code on the garage door keypad. Jamie was in total agreement with everything he said. He also said that her husband's reality is not the true reality and that he probably needs professional help.

Soon after this district official left our home, another district official and his wife came to visit Jamie. She was tired and in pain, but they went to her bedside and prayed a beautiful prayer and stayed a few minutes with her. I then visited with them in our living room for about thirty minutes before they left.

September 26, 2012—Gene and I took Jamie to MDA yesterday for the PET scan.

On the way I noticed a text on my phone:

> 9/25/12, 6:17am, There is absolutely no way under heaven that you can be a born again Christian and be treating my brother the way you are. Your behavior doesn't match up to the Biblical fruits of the Holy Spirit. There is something severely wrong with you! I haven't heard of such hate even coming from a non-Christian. I know because I felt it when I was there. My brother has literally thousands of people who deeply love him and in my entire life I have never known anyone to come up against his Godly spirit as you have. A true Christian has a heart of compassion and repentance, desiring to make things right. A true

> Christian has love which draws people to them and does not lock them out and hide the key. That instead is fear. I am especially surprised that Jamie is agreeing with this behavior and continues to split her family up by staying there. Weird. Not normal. Godly parents would take their daughter home to her husband and children. I know because I had Godly parents. I will continue to intercede for this whole situation. I am standing on the promises of the Word!

"Their venom is like the venom of a snake, like that of a cobra that has stopped its ears" (Ps. 58:4).

About forty friends gathered in a circle in our backyard last night and prayed. Thank you, Lord.

I received a text from him about 8:15 p.m. asking for Jamie to call him. She did. She talked to Caleb and Karen very briefly before he got on the phone and proceeded with his meanness again. Jamie said it was a bad connection, and she heard him say, "She hung up on me." She called him back but he would not answer. She left a message. "Honey, I did not hang up on you. I would never do that. I don't understand what is happening. I have never been unfaithful to you or our marriage vows. I love you."

September 27, 2012—Jamie called him three times yesterday to wish him a happy birthday. She left messages, but he never returned her calls. He has broken her heart, yet she maintains a sweet and forgiving spirit and prays for healing and restoration.

As I clean and dress her wounds daily, I notice the cancer spreading in her skin and feel lumps underneath. She is requiring more pain medication. We spend our days talking, praying, singing, and reading the Bible.

A couple nights ago, with tears in her eyes, she shared something with Gene and me. "Mom, Dad, I want to tell you something that I've never told anyone." She paused. I could tell this was going to be difficult for her but had no idea what she was about to reveal.

"I knew in my heart that I should not marry him. Even the night before the wedding, I knew."

"Oh, baby"—now I was crying—"why didn't you tell us?"

"Ya'll spent so much money on the wedding, I just couldn't tell you."

Now Gene spoke up, "Jamie, that would not have mattered to us. You matter to us." We're all crying by this time.

"I didn't want to be alone, and we really do love each other. He has so many good qualities, but I knew he had major issues in his life. I thought it would all work out. I'm so sorry. I thought I could make it work."

"It's okay, honey. Look what God did. He gave you Caleb and Karen. Caleb would have never been born, and Karen would have never survived if you had not adopted her," I said.

"I know. For that I'm thankful."

September 28, 2012—This morning, Jeremy will drive Jamie and I to MDA for a nine thirty appointment with her oncologist so she can give us the PET scan report. She had company yesterday as she does almost every day—friends brought flowers, other friends brought a meal, and a pastor of a neighboring church stopped by. They all prayed with Jamie, and she prays for her visitors as her strength will allow. The card from the pastor contained money. What blessings to Jamie and us!

She tried to call him in the evening—still no answer, only voice mail. She so wants to talk to him and the children. She wants to see them. She wants them to be with her. More tears.

My heart breaks for my daughter. She is not only experiencing severe physical pain, but the emotional pain is almost unbearable. Morphine doesn't touch that. Even though her heart is broken, her spirit gets stronger and more Christ-like with each passing day.

She finished reviewing the draft of her will yesterday morning. Jeremy brought over a video camera. Jamie wanted to make a video for him to explain her reasons for changing her will. She talked for about thirty minutes into the camera, using a sheet of notes she had written with her left hand because she could no longer use her right arm.

~

September 29, 2012—Now it is clear to me, so very clear, why the Lord prompted me to fast and pray and read the entire Bible through in the month of August—because September 2012 has been the most difficult month of my life.

Dr. K and I made eye contact as she walked into the examination room. I knew immediately that what Jamie and I were about to hear was not going to be good news. Her eyes offered me no hope.

She asked Jamie how she was feeling and where her husband was. Jamie explained to her briefly his behavior over the past three weeks. This news upset Dr. K greatly.

"The report from the PET scan is not good. The cancer has spread to your liver, bones (sternum, vertebrae, ribs), and left breast. The tumor markers are very high. However, there is no evidence that the cancer has spread to your brain."

Through flowing tears and difficulty in speaking, I asked her how long Jamie has to live.

"Maybe two months. Jamie has the most aggressive case of cancer I have ever seen."

This was a lot to hear and process. Jamie kept her composure; I tried, but unsuccessfully. I regained mine after a few minutes. Dr. K wept with us.

"I would like your permission, Jamie, to call your husband and talk to him." We gave her his numbers.

Before we left Dr. K's office, Jamie prayed and thanked God for Dr. K and the care she had received at MDA and for God to bless her in her work. She prayed for God's miracle working power to be evident.

Jeremy helped me get Jamie off the examination table into the wheelchair, and we all went to the hospital pharmacy. While there, several social and case workers came by to see her. They carried paperwork for me to be the medical power of attorney. Dr. K knew that had to happen since he was out of the picture. The case worker advised us to talk with hospice ASAP.

While we were still waiting for the pharmacy, Dr. K's nurse stopped by to check on Jamie. She said that Dr. K had called him and talked about thirty minutes with him. She came away from that conversation very upset.

We all prayed in the parking garage before we left the hospital for the last time. Her faith and resolve are so strong. On the way home, she called the district office and asked for their help to see her children.

Dr. K called last night to check on Jamie and give her an update on her conversation with him. Gene and I both talked to her as well. She urged reconciliation for the sake of the children. We assured her that is what we want more than anything.

Jeremy and Janet came over. We ended this very long day gathered around Jamie's bed praying, worshiping, and singing choruses to the Lord.

"Thank you, Lord, for your sweet presence. We know you're in control. We trust you. You give us everything we need. We love you."

September 30, 2012—He and the children got back in town late last evening, but he refused to bring the children to see Jamie because Gene and I would not leave the house. We can't do that. We want to see our grandchildren too. Jamie begged him on the phone to come see her and bring the children. She cried again. She just wants to spend time with her children while she can. Utterly heartbreaking.

~

October 1, 2012—He and the children came over yesterday for thirty minutes while Gene and I left, but Jeremy was here. Caleb and Karen Vi were happy to see their mommy, and she was so happy to see them. The children really can't get physically close to Jamie now because of her pain. He now wants a schedule of when we will be out of our home so he can see Jamie. It's not happening. We must take one day at a time.

Gene and I spend much time gently rubbing her right arm and hand. She is unable to do much for herself. It is my joy and honor to minister to and love my daughter in this way. Her spirit is sweet and her faith is strong.

~

October 2, 2012—Janet visited Jamie in her bedroom a few days ago. "Janet, I want you to do something for me. Please tell my attorney that I want twenty-five thousand dollars of my life insurance to go to Mom and Dad." She started to cry. "I won't be around to take care of them in their old age, and maybe this will help a little bit." So precious.

"There is something else I need to tell you. I want to apologize. I was so jealous of you when you got married before I did. I always thought I should get married first. I'm sorry. Will you please forgive me?"

"Of course, Jamie." Both girls are crying now.

"That is the second greatest regret of my life."

It is extremely hard on Janet to watch her sister suffer. However, she is doing a superb job taking care of much of Jamie's business. She is her go-between with her attorney in drawing up her will the way she wants it. We want more than anything to honor Jamie's last wishes. Jamie wants her sizeable life insurance to take care of her husband and children for years to come, but she also knows that it is not a good idea to give him total control of the money. Past experience has proven the fact that handling finances is not one of his strong points.

~

October 3, 2012—Yesterday, Jamie was resting in her daddy's recliner in the living room when she looked up at the ceiling fan and said, "Mom, you need to dust the tops of your fan blades." Now I'm a fairly decent housekeeper and often dust my ceiling fans. For the life of me, I could not see dust on that fan from where she was sitting. I have also noticed recently that Jamie's hearing is over the top. She can hear my hushed conversations with the hospice nurses all the way in the kitchen! What does this mean?

Pastor Andy and the entire deacon team came to see Jamie last evening as she reclined in Gene's chair. It was such a special time of prayer for our Jamie.

I want to say here that Jamie has taught us how to live and is teaching us how to die—with a heart of continuous prayer, praise, and forgiveness. I lay beside her in bed a long time last night as she agonized in excruciating pain, crying with her, praying with her. It is almost more than I can bear.

"Dear God, help our Jamie today. We love you, Lord, and are grateful for your presence, mercy, and so many wonderful friends who are praying."

~

October 4, 2012—I helped Jamie to Gene's chair, and Alissa came over with her guitar. She played and sang softly. Jamie enjoyed it so much and worshiped and sang along with her. She left at 6:45

when he and the children came in. He visited Jamie in the living room while I fed Caleb and Karen their dinner. Janet came over about 7:10 and Gene arrived home at 7:30. The children were so happy to see their Papa. He hugged and kissed them, and I saw Gene give him a big bear hug too.

~

October 6, 2012—Yesterday was a weepy day for Jamie. We are all still praying for a healing miracle. Our faith and trust are in God. At the same time, Jamie confessed she realizes she may miss seeing her children grow up, teaching them about the Lord and ministry, and seeing her grandchildren. We talked about God's ability to take care of her children should God take her to heaven. She is tired of being sick and not being able to do anything for herself.

She doesn't have an appetite and only eats a few bites a day with my help. She has fever every day. I hear her praying and talking to God during the night. One of her favorite verses during this dark time is Psalm 119:50: "My comfort in my suffering is this: Your promise preserves my life."

He is doing better around Jamie. However, as her primary caregiver, I will serve as a shield between them, protecting her as much as possible from any verbal or emotional attacks. He has never once apologized to Jamie or any of us for his horrible behavior this past month. We treat him as if nothing has happened. I choose to forgive him and love him. I believe Gene, Janet, and Jeremy are doing the same.

~

October 7, 2012—A close childhood friend came to see Jamie yesterday for about forty-five minutes. A few minutes into their conversation, Jamie looks at her and says, "I love you and you have been a good friend, but I have always wondered about your relationship with Jesus."

She gently patted Jamie's hand. "Don't worry about me. I'm okay."

"Jesus is the only way to God and heaven. I want to see you in heaven one day. All it takes is prayer and reading the Bible to have a relationship with Him."

She struggled to keep from crying, but a couple of tears fell from her eyes. I just sat on the floor beside Jamie's chair in total awe of what I was hearing and seeing. Jamie, in pain and in the battle of her life, reaches out to a friend, wanting to be sure of her friend's relationship with Jesus Christ. Beautiful.

Shortly after her friend's visit, Karli and her daughter Abby bring our family a delicious dinner. Jamie was in her bed, but she wanted them to come to her bedroom and pray for her. She spoke into Abby's life, quoting Scripture and telling her she is an elder among her peers. Jamie asked them to anoint her with oil and pray over her. They did. It was another precious moment.

October 8, 2012—We now have a hospital bed and bedside table. I hear her praying and crying out to God. "Dear God, I forgive him. Help him, Lord. Forgive me, O God, if I have failed you in any way. I want to know you better, Lord."

"Dear God, may today be the day of a divine miracle. She is suffering so much." Each time I cleanse her wounds and change her bandages, I see the cancer literally devouring her skin, creeping over her chest, up her neck, down her arm, exposing tissue down to the bone. It's as if I am looking into the face of the devil himself. If the cancer is this bad on the outside, I can only imagine what it is doing inside of her. Her strength is diminishing daily. She eats and drinks very little; she is extremely restless and not sleeping well. "And after my skin has been destroyed, yet in my flesh I will see God" (Job 19:26).

"The Lord will rescue me from every evil attack and will bring me safely to his heavenly kingdom. To him be glory for ever and ever. Amen" (2 Tim. 4:18).

I told Gene yesterday that we must look at this time with Jamie as a blessing. We prepared for her birth into this world. We walked through pregnancy and preparation together. Her birth came with pain. Now we are walking together preparing for her departure from this world should the Lord choose to take her to heaven and her ultimate healing. We watched Jamie enter the world, and we will watch her exit this world. We saw her come from the Father; we will see her return to Him. What a blessing! We will come full circle. God gives us His strength and grace every day.

October 11, 2012—Another friend, Avery, brought food two days. She also gave Jamie a memory foam mattress topper and pillow for her hospital bed. Later she brought over a coffee machine for us—just to bless us. This is just another example of love in action by so many friends and church family.

"Dear Lord, our Jamie (your Jamie) is in your hands today. Thank you for this new day. May we walk in your continued peace, strength and joy. Bless everyone who is praying for Jamie and expressing their love and kindness in so many ways."

October 21, 2012—We learned yesterday that the Jamie Norton Lund Scholarship has been created to assist students with callings similar to Jamie's—to teach English as a Second Language (ESL) in closed or restricted nations. What a noble and high honor! Jamie was very humbled when she heard the news.

~

October 27, 2012—Jamie is having a difficult time breathing, so yesterday hospice ordered oxygen for her. In times of agonizing pain, she cries out loud to God for His mercy, and Gene and I hit the floor crying and praying with her. She is suffering so much. This disease is ravishing her body. She often quotes these words from Psalm 138:8: "Do not abandon the works of your hands."

"Oh God, how I need your strength today! I don't know how to give her up. I don't know how to let her go. I can't bear the thought of not being able to see her, touch her, talk to her, or hear her voice. Oh God, we need your help today. Please comfort our Jamie."

A text from his sister:

> 10/27/12, 6:53 p.m., May you feel the Holy Spirit blanket you with peace and comfort. Thinking of you all and feeling for you with what you are going through and understanding how hard it is. Words are inadequate. Lots of prayers are going up for you all.

~

October 28, 2012—Jamie and I talked a few minutes yesterday after her time of loud praying for healing in the recliner. I asked her, "If God should take you to heaven, does that mean He didn't answer your prayers?"

"No."

"If God should take you to heaven, does that mean His Word is not true?"

"No."

"Maybe taking you to heaven is the answer to all of your prayers." She agreed. "When I get to heaven, I want to see Jesus first, but you better be standing right next to Him!"

"I'll try, Momma" and she smiled.

Before she went to sleep last night, Gene on one side of her bed and me on the other, we listened to her praying with all the strength she could gather. "Dear Lord, forgive me for any sin in my life or anything hidden or anything not pleasing to you. Purge me, Lord. Cleanse me. I love you, Jesus, so much. Thank you for everything you've done for me."

Gene and I wept as we listened. How precious she is to us! How much more precious she must be to God!

October 29, 2012—Janet came over yesterday around 3:00 p.m. He came over at 4:00 p.m. I asked him, "Where are the children?"

"They're with someone."

"Who?"

"They're in a safe place." He went to Jamie's room. She asked him the same question; he gave her the same answer. She asked again, "Where are my children?" He finally said, "They're at my sister's."

"But I didn't get to say bye to them."

I chimed in, "Jamie needs to see her children again to be able to say bye to them."

"They already have closure. They know Mommy is going to heaven soon."

Gene, Janet, Jamie, and I could not believe our ears. Jamie started to cry, "I want to see my children." I felt as if I had just witnessed the ultimate punishment and control!

"I made the decision. They're in Fort Worth by now."

We begged him to call her and ask her to turn around. Gene and Janet both offered to go get the children. "Just please allow Jamie to see her children one more time to say good-bye."

I hear Jamie quietly say to herself, "I forgive him. I can't allow myself to get upset or hold a grudge." But underneath the whisper, I heard a broken heart—again—broken by a totally self-centered and unloving husband in her dying moments.

Gene said to him, "I want to talk to you in the living room."

"No. You can talk to me here."

Gene pleaded with him. He said again, "You have not allowed me private time with my wife since she's been here" [not true]. "I thought she did not want to see the kids again since she refused their visit the last couple of days."

"That's because she was in so much pain and feeling so bad at the times you asked to bring them over. It did not mean forever. If we had known she was coming to get the children, we would have insisted they come over first," I said.

He finally agreed to talk to Gene in the living room; Janet and I followed. We begged him to call his sister and ask her to turn around. Janet started crying, "If I were dying and could not see my children to say good-bye, that would be the most heart-breaking thing ever. A mother has the right to see her children before she dies."

He stepped outside to call her. He came back in and said they would be here in about an hour.

Didn't he just tell us they were probably in Fort Worth by now which is a four-hour drive? Jamie asked him why he lied to her. He apologized. We were just all relieved that Jamie would see her children one more time, to tell them she loves them and say good-bye.

Soon Caleb and Karen were beside Jamie's bed. "I love you so much, Caleb and Karen Vi. I will soon go to heaven to live with Jesus. If you will always love Jesus and serve Him, lead others to Him, and always stay close to Him, then one day we will all see each other again."

At four years old, Karen was easier to talk to. Caleb had a harder time. Jamie asked her five year old, "How does this make you feel, Caleb?"

"Sad." Caleb cried quietly.

"I love you both so much." She talked to them, touched them, and kissed them one more time. Then the children went outside to jump on the trampoline and eat ice cream. We all sat on the swing outside while he and his sister had time with Jamie.

Soon the children had to put on their shoes and say good-bye again to Jamie and us. Karen began to cry.

"I prayed for this child, and the Lord has granted me what I asked of him. So now I give him to the Lord. For his whole life he will be given over to the Lord" (1 Sam. 27–28).

It's now 6:45 this morning. I hear Jamie in her room talking to Jesus and asking Him to hold her and telling Him how much she loves Him.

"Heal me, Lord, and I will be healed; save me and I will be saved, for you are the one I praise" (Jer. 17:14).

~

October 30, 2012—It's about 5:30 a.m. now. Jamie, unable to get out of bed now, is praying out loud. "Dear Jesus, please heal me or take me to heaven quickly, Lord. Your will and not mine be done. I know you will protect your reputation in the land I love and get glory if you take me to heaven instead of healing me on earth. I love you, Jesus."

She looked at me. "I love you, Momma."

"I love you, my darling."

~

October 31, 2012—He came over at 12:30 yesterday and stayed until 9:15 p.m.

~

November 1, 2012—Jeremy came to see her about an hour yesterday morning, the first time he has seen her in two weeks because he was out of town. She was glad to see him. She talked and responded so well to him, asking about his trip, how his parents are since the break-in, and if he ever found his suitcase. He talked to her. She said he is a good brother-in-law.

He came over at 11:00 a.m. and stayed until 9:00 p.m.

About 3:30 this morning, Jamie cried out in pain. Gene and I were at her bedside. I fed her a few bites of apple sauce and she drank a few sips of juice before I gave her more morphine.

She looked at us. "Mom and Dad, I love you. Are you sleeping well?" She is still concerned about us.

"Yes we are, honey. We love you, Jamie. You are and always have been such a beautiful and sweet daughter. You have brought us so much joy over the years, and we have always been so proud of you." She smiled. "No fear," she said.

November 2, 2012—He, Gene, and I were in Jamie's room yesterday when she looked at us and said, "It seems to me that you're all getting along better these last few days. I just want to make sure everything is good between you and that apologies and forgiveness have been given and received."

Gene then asked him to forgive him if he had ever said anything to offend him. We all acknowledged that things were difficult at times between us, but that we had all forgiven each other.

I told Jamie, "I choose to forgive him every day by a conscience decision, not because he has asked forgiveness from me, but because Jesus commands it. He then asked forgiveness from us, and we said we have forgiven him.

I then asked Jamie, "Has he ever apologized to you for the things he has said and done to you? I know you asked him one time if he wanted to say he was sorry for anything, and he told you he didn't have anything to apologize for."

"I apologized to you a few days ago."

"No, you haven't," she said.

"I apologized to you last night."

"No, you didn't."

"Maybe you forgot."

"No. I would have remembered that."

After some hesitation, he asked her to forgive him for anything he had said to hurt her. She quickly said, "I forgive you."

Looking at the three of us, she said, "Never go back." We promised we would honor her wishes. Again, she exhibited the classic peacemaker heart, a characteristic she has possessed since childhood.

"Blessed are the peacemakers, for they will be called children of God" (Mt. 5:9).

"Peacemakers who sow in peace reap a harvest of righteousness" (Ja. 3:18).

# Chapter 27

## *The Ultimate Victory*

As for us, we cannot help speaking about what
we have seen and heard.

—Acts 4:20

~

"Daddy, get paper and pen and write something down for me."

Gene quickly finds the items and said, "I'm ready."

"This is what I want inscribed on the back of my tombstone: His grace was sufficient for me."

"Got it," Gene said. Wanting to have a little fun with her, he asked her, "How many letters are in the word *sufficient*?

Without hesitation, she says, "Ten."

"And how do you spell sufficient?"

She quickly spells it with no problem. Always the spelling champion!

~

It was 7:00 p.m. She asked us to praise and worship the Lord together. Her voice was weak and her breath short, but she started out singing "In Your Presence Is Where I Want to Be." We all sang as best we could. Gene led off in several other older songs. She prayed quietly in the Spirit, sang softly, and then she prayed for the generations, starting with Caleb and Karen, going to her nieces and nephews, then to her husband, Janet and Jeremy, his family, going to Gene and I, then to her Mawmaw Allen. Gene and I prayed for her.

I knelt beside her bed, tears flowing, thanking God for her life, for Him giving her to us to love and raise for Him, for her lifelong love for God, for all she's done in her lifetime, for His blessings and faithfulness to her and her family, and for the exceedingly great joy, delight, and pride she has brought to Gene and I. He also prayed a sweet prayer over her.

~

November 4, 2012—He left yesterday at 3:45 and only came back to get a few things he left in the bedroom where he slept only two nights. He said he needed a good night's sleep.

"You're a good mother and a good friend to me. You will make it through this," she said. I thought my heart would burst within me as tears soaked my knees beside her bed. Gene knelt on the other side of her bed. She prayed for us and all of her family and friends.

"Oh, hi!" She looked steadfastly and smiled at someone we could not see standing beside her bed. "Mom, do you see her?"

"No, who is it?"

"A little girl with reddish hair wearing a dress with butterflies all over it. She is so pretty. Her name is Lucy. I will be so glad when I go to heaven!"

It's 6:00 a.m. now. She is whispering to the Lord, "I love you more today than yesterday." She just told me she wants me to stay close by. She is now singing "Come Holy Spirit, I Need Thee." I'm sitting by her bed now, and she is talking to the Lord about her students in Northern Asia. She is quietly praying, "Holy Spirit, help me trust you more. Holy Spirit, touch me." She raises her left hand at the elbow to praise the Lord. "Jesus, I will never let you go."

> "I will praise you as long as I live, and in your name I will lift up my hands" (Ps. 63:4).

~

November 5, 2012—Gene and I slept on the floor again beside Jamie's bed. She begged him again to spend the night with her last night, but he wouldn't. He got here yesterday around 2:00 p.m. and left at 8:00 p.m. and spent a chunk of that time talking on his phone outside. Even when he's sitting beside Jamie's bed, he spends a lot of time texting. Gene and I can't help but wonder what in the world is going on.

Her good friend, Josh, and his wife came to see Jamie. She talked to him about putting God first in his life.

~

November 6, 2012—He came over yesterday about 8:15 a.m. and sat by Jamie's bed until she woke up about 9:45. "I'm so glad you're here," she told him.

"Honey, I'm here and I'm not going anywhere."

The nurse was on her way to help me do wound care, so I went into the room to prepare. He began to argue with me that she didn't need wound care every day. I explained that we do what we can every day for Jamie because of drainage and smell. I didn't want to argue with him in front of Jamie.

"Please step out of the room while the nurse and I take care of Jamie."

He turns to Jamie and says, "Did you hear your mom just tell me to leave? I'm your husband and I can stay."

"I asked you to step out of the room. You can sit in the living room until we're done. It gets too crowded in here."

Jamie looked at him and put forth the effort to keep the peace. "Honey, you're attitude is not good…" He interrupts her like he always does. "It's okay. Your mother is the one with the attitude."

"You can leave the room now," I said. "I need to get by the window and prepare the table on that side." He leaves the house. Jamie is not allowing herself to get upset; she doesn't have the energy for that.

He never came back and he never called. She called him about 6:00 p.m. "Where are you and when are you coming back over?"

"I'm cleaning the apartment and I'm not going back over there until I get some respect!" She did not have strength to continue the conversation.

Jamie maintains the ultimate sweet and forgiving spirit. Her spirit grows stronger daily and her communion with the Lord sweeter as her body declines.

November 7, 2012—Yesterday morning, Jamie wanted her daddy and me to join her in praising and worshiping the Lord, so we started singing those old choruses again. Then the doorbell rang. It was Melissa R. What a blessing from the Lord and perfect timing too! Jamie was happy to see her. She stayed about twenty minutes and sang some of the old songs with us. Jamie kept her eyes closed most of the time, enjoying every minute. We prayed. She prayed for Jamie and Jamie prayed for her. Melissa commented on the presence of the Lord in the room. It was a precious time.

He came over in the afternoon. About 4:00 I offered Jamie some medicine. He objected. "She doesn't have to take that. Her bowels are already shut down and it won't help. You're not a nurse anyway."

"I am her medical power of attorney." I then called for Gene to come in the room.

"Please listen to Mom. I want to take the medicine." She drank it. He upset her again. When that happens, it affects her breathing, so I work with her and the oxygen to get her breathing regulated again.

She begged him to stay, but he refused. He said he had to go clean out the refrigerator.

Jamie is at peace. She does not allow herself to dwell on his cruelty but has given him to the Lord. I've given him to God too, but I don't yet have the peace she has about him.

Alissa brought her guitar and came over again and played softly for Jamie. The music is very soothing to her.

~

November 8, 2012—"Jamie, I have a bean burrito and chips and salsa for you. Do you feel like eating?" A big smile covered her face; she was so happy. Janet and I laughed at her reaction. She took only five small bites and one chip with salsa. She thought it tasted divine!

Gene asked her, "Would you like a Dr. Pepper?"

"Oh, yes," accompanied by another wide smile. "Awesome." Oops. We were out of Dr. Pepper, so Gene and Jeremy jump in the car and make a fast trip to a convenience store and purchase two. She took a few swallows, savoring the taste.

~

November 9, 2012—Jamie slept most of the night, waking me often with her soft mumbling and talking as I lay on the pallet on the floor beside her bed. She is not requiring as much pain medication now. Her eyes are closed more now as she lies very still on her bed. He came over yesterday and stayed three minutes. This would be his final visit.

"Daddy, what do heavenly beings have in their hands?"

"I don't know. What do you see?"

"They are holding something in their hands, ready to throw—perhaps darts or javelins."

"What do these heavenly beings look like, Jamie?" I asked.

"Beautiful."

"Can you describe them to me?"

She smiled and exhaled softly. "No."

"Was caught up to paradise and heard inexpressible things, things that no one is permitted to tell" (2 Cor. 12:4).

What a blessing she has been to us these two months she has been in our home. Thank you, Lord, for giving us this time with our Jamie.

~

November 10, 2012—"Hi, little guy. Thank you. You don't want your turtle?" She is dreaming.

While Mother was sitting with Jamie and me in my bedroom on the phone talking to Jamie's nurse, he rang the doorbell one time. Mother heard it and thought I had gone to the door; I never heard it. He left. Jamie asked me to call him, so I did, but he did not answer. I called back a few minutes later and left a message that I never heard the door bell and Jamie wanted him to come back. I called again and put the phone to her ear. She left a message: "Please come over. I want to see you. I love you." He never returned her call and he never came over. What unbelievable emotional pain and suffering he is inflicting on her.

~

November 11, 2012—She called him yesterday morning. "I want to see you. When are you coming over?"

"I tried to see you on Friday, but your mother wouldn't let me in the house."

"She didn't hear the doorbell."

"I'm going to Fort Worth to see the children."

"I'm sorry, but I don't have the strength to talk anymore." Upset and struggling to breathe, she handed me the phone. I thought the conversation was over and hung up, but she actually wanted me to talk to him. I called back immediately. He didn't answer, so I left a message explaining that she did not hang up on him; I did. I asked him to please call back and let us know his plans. He never called and he never came over. Unfathomable.

> Even my close friend, someone I trusted, one who shared my bread, has turned against me
>
> —Ps. 41:9

> If an enemy were insulting me, I could endure it; if a foe were rising against me, I could hide. But it is you, a man like myself, my companion, my close friend, with whom I once enjoyed sweet fellowship at the house of God, as we walked about among the worshipers
>
> —Ps. 55:12–14

> At my first defense, no one came to my support, but everyone deserted me. May it not be held against them. But the Lord stood at my side and gave me strength… The Lord will rescue me from every evil attack and will bring me safely to his heavenly kingdom. To him be glory for ever and ever. Amen.
>
> —2 Tim. 4:16–18

It's 6:10 a.m. I'm kneeling beside her bed, rubbing her hand and arm, listening to her sing and singing with her those old songs that continue to come to the forefront of her memory. She thinks she is talking to him on the phone. "Please come see me. I want to see you and the children. Please." She begins to pray in the Spirit.

Janet came over yesterday afternoon to sit with Jamie while I walked to Trout school and back. Whenever I can get away, I spend these thirty minutes talking to the Lord; it is my therapeutic and restorative time with God. Today I cried, reflected, recalled Scripture, and tried to process everything that was happening in our lives. I breathed in deeply the fresh air to help clear away the fog in my brain. I looked at the blue sky and the trees in their autumn blankets scattered among the tall, stately, and evergreen piney woods of East Texas. I felt the cool nip in the air on my face and heard the mockingbird's familiar melody while perched stoically on the high wire above the road. I was reminded once again that my God is faithful and He is in control.

It was 8:30 p.m. I told Gene I was tired and went to lie down beside her bed; I thought she was asleep. "I'm sorry, Momma, that you're so tired. I'm sorry."

"It's okay, honey. I'm doing exactly what I want to do and wouldn't change a thing." She's still thinking about others.

"Praise the Lord. Blessed are those who fear the Lord, who find great delight in his commands. Their children will be mighty in the land; the generation of the upright will be blessed" (Ps. 112:1–2). After reading Psalm 112 to her, I talked to her about putting him in God's hands and not to worry about him. "I have. I'm not worried."

November 12, 2012—Jamie talked and prayed out loud yesterday much of the day. "They're lost and alone. Who will help them? Who will tell them about Jesus? They have nothing. The women and children are hurting. Who will help them? Dear God, if more will come to Christ as a result of my death, then so be it." She interceded for her friends in the city she loved.

"Jesus loves them. He came to seek and save the lost," I told her. We prayed together that God would call more laborers to send into the harvest fields that are white, ready to harvest and that more people will obey the call and go to the nations and tell people who have never heard. She became calm.

You see, Jamie was a Josiah. She was saved and on her way to heaven, but she cared more for those who were not, especially those who have not been so privileged as to hear the salvation story more than once. Just like King Josiah, she went to work (2 Kings 23 and 24) so that others might know the One True God, unlike Josiah's great-grandfather King Hezekiah who cared only for his own salvation in response to Isaiah's word from the Lord. "'The word of the Lord you have spoken is good', Hezekiah replied. For he thought, 'Will there not be peace and security in my lifetime?'" (2 Kings 20:19).

Jamie's sacrifice wasn't leaving home and America to go to Northern Asia. That was easy for her. Her sacrifice was to leave Northern Asia and the people she loved to follow God through illness and eventual death of her dream to reach the lost. She did not want to take her hands off the plow, but one day Jesus put His hands on hers and lifted them off the plow, and He led her into heaven.

November 13, 2012—Our night was punctuated with Jamie waking up often—worried, stressed, and upset over him. I would have to calm her down again and again. She asked me to call him on the phone about 6:00 p.m. yesterday. I put the phone on her pillow beside her ear. She quietly asked when he was coming to see her and that she wanted to see him and the children. I could hear his voice from the receiver. He became angry with her, raising his voice, saying again that I would not let him in the house and that I lied to him, that she lied to him, that he and the children already had closure, and he wasn't coming to see her.

She said very weakly, "I don't understand. What about me?" Her eyes and expression were filled with pain again. He hung up on her. She let the phone slip off the pillow. Something changed in Jamie at that moment. I saw it in her face. I sensed it in the room. She released him; she released life on earth. She let it go.

She was surely on her way now. Jamie died of a crushed and trampled heart before she died of cancer.

Gene was furious. He dialed his number repeatedly. I tried to console Jamie, help her breathe and regain her composure, and prayed with her. We gave him to the Lord again.

About that time, Alissa came over with her guitar. We desperately tried to refocus as the praise and worship softly filled the room. Tears and frustration were in the way. Gene cried hard. We were all hemorrhaging emotionally. We talked about forgiving him once again. Jamie did, then I forgave, but Gene could not at that moment. A few minutes later, he said he chooses to forgive him too. This forgiveness is definitely a decision. Jamie remained frightened and upset, and we did not leave her side.

Jake, a long-time friend, came to see her yesterday, but she slept during most of his visit.

It's now 6:45 a.m. Jamie is singing to the Lord and praying in tongues. "Jesus, name above all names. Beautiful Savior, Glorious Lord. Emmanuel, God is with us. Blessed Redeemer, Living Word."

~

November 14, 2012—The only time she mentioned him yesterday was last evening. "Marriage is not supposed to be this way. He left me." She became visibly upset. I reassured her that she has done nothing wrong and that she has been a very good wife and mother. He is the one at fault here. She knows this is true and agrees, but it still hurts her when she thinks about everything that has transpired. "He will rescue them from oppression and violence, for precious is their blood in his sight" (Ps. 72:14).

Her strong thirty-six-year-old heart fought to keep her alive. The only other organ untouched by the cancer as far as we know was her brain. This is no coincidence. Jamie had a sharp mind, and she retained her mental faculties until the very end. She knew exactly everything that was happening. Her heart untouched by the cancer felt the pain of desertion. Her brilliant mind untouched by the cancer understood the ultimate rejection and abandonment by the one she loved on this earth. She felt the full impact of his decision to leave.

So we remember again God's promises and how we can trust God completely. "Let Us Have a Little Talk with Jesus" is another song that Gene and Jamie have fun singing together. We are trying to be more upbeat around her and make her smile more often.

"I praise you, O Lord, for your blessings in my life, not because of anything I have done but because of who you are!" Pure and holy praise flow freely from Jamie's heart and lips. Gene and I wept and prayed on our knees beside her bed, and a sweet and beautiful presence of the Lord settled over the room.

This night found Gene and me on our faces before God on the floor of our bedroom crying out to Him and soaking the carpet with our tears. We knew what we had to do. With gut-wrenching sobs and heavy hearts, we finally came to the place where we could give Jamie back to God. We could not hold onto her any longer. Her pain and suffering—physically and emotionally—were more than we could bear. We thanked God for giving Jamie to us for almost thirty seven years. What a joy and delight she has been to us! We praised Him for her life—a life that has touched so many in such a short time. We praised Him for the blessing of Jamie. God has been good to us. "Not our will, Lord, but your will be done. Praise your Holy Name!"

~

November 15, 2012—Annette came to see Jamie yesterday. "He's all I need. He's all I need. Jesus is all I need." She sang very softly. Annette sang with her and wept.

It's 6:00 a.m. I can hear Jamie praying and asking God to help her. She called for me and asked to have her family near her. I talked to her about heaven and submitting our will to Him.

"I am crucified with Christ. Jesus, forgive me for any sin in my life. I love you, Jesus. Momma, I love you." I see once again that very little girl who spoke those words to me so many times. I remember Gene and I would tell each other that those three little words from both our baby girls' lips were always the most beautiful words ever spoken—music to our ears—priceless.

~

November 16, 2012—What a day we had yesterday. There is so much to record; I know I will surely forget something, but here goes. Jamie was lucid most of the day. She woke about 8:30 a.m. and wanted to talk to him on the phone—very insistent—against our better judgment. So Gene called him and gave Jamie the phone. I helped her hold it to her ear while Gene listened on the kitchen phone. We were hoping he would be kind to her. She is so weak and helpless. She kept repeating, "I want to see you. But I want to see you."

"The children and I have closure. I'm not coming back to Lufkin. They would not let me in the house the last time. I need to spend time with the children." Jamie was visibly upset and she handed me the phone.

Gene told him he knew the truth why he didn't come in the house the last time. "I have nothing to say to you," and he hung up on Gene. I tried to help Jamie relax and steady her breathing.

She is very restless and not sleeping well. She saw people in her room and talked to them. She talked to a girl named Ashley. At one point, she looked up at me as I knelt beside her bed and put her hand in my hair and said, "You're beautiful." She wants her daddy to sing with her, but mostly she is too weak to sing.

I noticed Jamie with a fixed gaze and a slight smile on her face. She was staring at something or someone in her room. She and I were the only ones I could see. "Jamie, what are you looking at?"

"Shabacha. He's over there. Can you see him?"

"No, honey, I can't see him." My mind whirled. Was Shabacha an angel sent by God to usher Jamie into the presence of the living God? Possibly. We read in Luke 16:22 the parable of Jesus about the beggar who was carried into heaven by an angel. A seasoned preacher told me later that *shabach* is a Hebrew word that means to praise loudly. "He persevered because he saw him who is invisible." (Heb. 11:27).

The last passage of Scripture, 2 Corinthians 4:16–5:8, I read to Jamie was on this night.

"Therefore we do not lose heart. Though outwardly we are wasting away, yet inwardly we are being renewed day by day. For our light and momentary troubles are achieving for us an eternal glory that far outweighs them all. So we fix our eyes not on what is seen, but on what is unseen, since what is seen is temporary, but what is unseen is eternal" (2 Cor. 4:16–18).

Saturday, November 17, 2012, 1:30 a.m.—I'm writing this by flashlight on the pallet by Jamie's bed. What a horrendous fourteen hours it has been. She is so restless and she's bleeding through her bandages. Shanta, the nurse's aide with Hospice in the Pines[1], came over at 11:00 a.m. and immediately noticed how cold and clammy Jamie was. She could not hear a blood pressure from three different BP cups. She called the office, and Debbie, a registered nurse, came to the house. She finally picked up a 100/80 BP with very shallow breathing. We called Jeremy and Janet. They dropped everything and came over. Mother soon joined us. At one point, she struggled to open her eyes and mumble something to Janet about her power of attorney and about Caleb and Karen. Janet reassured her that we will take care of her children.

Her feet and knees turned purple, and her legs and arms became cold. At 5:30 p.m., her pulse was barely audible and very rapid. Her blood pressure dropped to 54/38.

There we were—the four of us around her bed—Debbie, Shanta, Gene and I. She labored to breathe in death's grip. We were debating if we should try to change her bloody bandages. Should we put her through that ordeal again? I looked intently at my baby's face. In the middle of our contemplating, the totally unexpected happened. Jamie suddenly opened wide her eyes. A huge smile engulfed her face. She flung her head over her right shoulder and looked intently at the corner of her bedroom. "It won't be long now!" she exclaimed in a strong voice. Then, just as quickly, she returned to her unconscious state.

We all looked at each other, speechless at what just happened. I leaned over to her face. "Jamie, who did you see?" There was no response, only the same labored breathing. Did she see Jesus standing there? Was it Shabacha that she saw standing in the corner? Perhaps God dispatched Shabacha from heaven's portals to receive another of His children into glory? "And if I go and prepare a place for you, I will come back and take you to be with me that you also may be where I am" (Jn. 14:3).

Gwen, another registered nurse, came and stayed several hours. I just sent her home because I want to be with Jamie now. It's just Jamie and I in her room (at least we're the only ones I see). Gene, Jeremy, and Janet are all asleep. It's 2:15 a.m. Jamie seems to be resting, but she is still moaning and her breathing is very shallow.

I think about what several of the hospice nurses have told me. It has been their experience that at times a patient will wait until it's quiet and no one is around to leave. But I want to be here when she goes to heaven. I look at her sweet, precious face. Have we really gone full circle? She came into this world as a helpless fragile baby placed in my arms. I fed her; I took care of her. Now she is ready to go back to heaven. I have fed her and taken care of her every need. "Am I ready for this, O God? Do I have the strength to let her go? Dear God, help me."

It's 2:40 a.m. I stay on my knees with my face inches from hers, caressing her face, telling her I love her over and over. Once yesterday, she answered me and said softly, "I love you too." We have all tried to assure her that we are okay and that it is okay for her to go to heaven now. "Oh, Jesus, please don't let her suffer anymore. What a terrible thing this cancer has been. Have mercy on us, oh God."

Jason, a friend of ours, was duck hunting early that clear, cool Saturday morning when he witnessed a meteor shower. I later learned that it was the Leonid Meteor Shower that appears in the sky around this same time every year. "Lord, our Lord, how majestic is your name in all the earth! You have set your glory in the heavens" (Ps. 8:1). As Jason reveled in the beauty of the moment, the thought occurred to him that the angels were coming to take Jamie to heaven. And so it was.

"If I rise on the wings of the dawn, if I settle on the far side of the sea, even there your hand will guide me, your right hand will hold me fast" (Ps. 139:9–10).

It was about five thirty in the morning, and I was extremely tired. I looked at my sweet Jamie's face, the only part of her body along with her torso that still had a little warmth, and said, "Jamie, I'm right here. I'm not going anywhere, but I'm going to lay down a few minutes here on the floor beside your bed. I'm right here if you need me. I love you, baby."

Was it the quiet in the room or Jeremy in the hallway that startled me to my knees once again? I looked at the clock—5:47. Suddenly, I found myself looking into Jamie's face. She was still, relaxed, no more fight for air. I was gazing into "lovely." "Whatsoever things are lovely" described her countenance. I knew she was in the presence of her beloved Savior and Lord Jesus Christ. Her face still warm, I imagined her stepping into heaven, healed and whole, bowing at the feet of Jesus, embracing

Him and others with both arms, laughing, filled with everlasting joy. And my tears streamed down my cheeks as I worshiped my God. She waited until I took my eyes off her, that little stinker!

"Jeremy, she's gone. She's with Jesus. Wake up Gene and Janet."

"Very truly I tell you, unless a kernel of wheat falls to the ground and dies, it remains only a single seed. But if it dies, it produces many seeds" (Jn. 12:24).

Sorry is a board game for young children. You may have played it as a child. Gene and I have become quite proficient as we have played with master game players, Sage and Graham. The objective is typical for a board game: move your colored pawns around the board and make it home before anyone else. Each player enters a safety zone as they get closer to home. Once in the safety zone, your pawn can no longer experience setbacks or be forced out by another player. There are no more obstacles in your path, no starting over.

Jamie entered her safety zone those last twenty-four hours. She was closer to her home in heaven than she was to this earthly life. Home was in clear view, just a short distance away. Nothing or nobody could take her out of her safety zone. She was almost home and closing in fast. She had finished her trip around the board. Some of our trips around this game board called life on earth are much longer than hers while some are shorter. God controls that time table, and it's not over until He says so.

As children of the living God and should the Lord tarry His return, we will one day enter that safety zone where our home in heaven is in clear view and more real than our earthly home. We yearn and groan for that day. When that moment came for Jamie, she stepped into heaven. She won! She is safe forever!

> For this God is our God for ever and ever; he will be our guide even to the end.
>
> —Ps. 48:14

> Those the Lord has rescued will return. They will enter Zion with singing; everlasting joy will crown their heads. Gladness and joy will overtake them, and sorrow and sighing will flee away.
>
> —Isa. 51:11

Jeremy called him many times that morning to let him know Jamie had passed, but he never answered. Finally, he returned the call at 8:00 a.m. We met with the funeral director and paid for the entire funeral, and we did it gladly. He never contributed the first nickel. How sad for him to have missed these special times with and for Jamie.

> Now this is our boast: Our conscience testifies that we have conducted ourselves in the world, and especially in our relations with you, with integrity and godly sincerity. We have done so, relying not on worldly wisdom but on God's grace.
>
> —2 Cor. 1:12

Hundreds of people attended the visitation at the funeral home on Sunday evening. We greeted people as they walked by the casket from 4:45 to 8:30 p.m. Then on Monday at 1:00 p.m. in the Lufkin First Assembly Worship Center, about six hundred people witnessed a beautiful tribute to an amazing young lady. Jamie had preplanned her service, and I think she would have been very pleased.

> I have fought the good fight, I have finished the race, I have kept the faith.
>
> —2 Tim. 4:7

> The righteous perish, and no one takes it to heart; the devout are taken away, and no one understands that the righteous are taken away to be spared from evil."
>
> —Isa. 57:1

"For the Lord will vindicate his people and have compassion on his servants" (Ps. 135:14). The Lord proved His supreme compassion for Jamie in taking her to heaven, allowing her to safely and forever escape the pain she experienced in this life.

~

Janet spoke at Jamie's funeral as only a loving and adoring sister could do. Here's the abbreviated version: It's Thanksgiving week, and we are thankful for our sweet Jamie. She fought the good fight and won. Jamie was many things to many people. She was brilliant, dedicated, devoted, humble, selfless, and godly. I cannot adequately describe to you the depth of her life, but literally thousands have been, and will continue to be, impacted by her love for God. Today we give thanks for a teacher, mommy, big sister, daughter, wife, friend, and a woman who was willing to follow God no matter the cost. We give thanks today because many of our lives are better and more beautiful for having known Jamie, a woman who truly abandoned it all for the sake of the call.

Can grief and joy coexist? It does in me. I have joy knowing she is free from all physical and emotional pain and abuse. If God had divinely healed her on earth, she would still have had to return to earth's turmoil and anguish—but never again. I'm happy for her, and I know I will see her again. When sadness comes, I'm sad for me because I miss her so much, but I can rejoice because this life is not all there is. As a child of God, I have hope.

Heaven is never-ending. Think of a moment in your life—perhaps in the embrace of someone you love or on a quiet lake beholding the splendor of a sunset or that fleeting instant when all is tranquil and right in your world—and you exhale thankfulness and wish you could hold that moment forever. That is a very small taste of heaven, except in heaven the moment never fades; it is everlasting.

# Chapter 28

## *A Fitting Tribute*

December 5, 2012—The following tribute to Jamie was spoken by Dr. L at a memorial service on campus:

Early on the morning of November 17, in her parents' home in Lufkin, Texas, Jamie Norton Lund, a 1998 graduate of our beloved university, stepped into eternity after a long and painful battle with cancer. Today, in a brief time, we want to pay tribute to the warm and extraordinary woman we knew Jamie to be.

My purpose in speaking to you first is to recognize Jamie as a trailblazer. As the first student from our campus to graduate with the credentials to teach English as a means to share the gospel, Jamie was a trailblazer.

After earning her bachelor's degree, Jamie worked on a master's degree in linguistics from the University of Texas in Arlington to further equip herself to teach English to speakers of other languages.

And then she began her work in Northern Asia, where she taught first as a single lady for two years. When she returned to the States, she married him. He has said that while they were still engaged, he told Jamie, "You know that when we're married, we'll be living in Africa." As Janet, Jamie's sister, said at her funeral, "We all know how that turned out!"

Jamie's call to Northern Asia became his call as well. The couple returned to Jamie's second home together. Jamie taught

English at a small university while he opened a campus Internet café. And in both places, as they sowed the seeds of friendship and built lasting relationships, they shared the gospel. The couple would have stayed there with their children, Caleb and Karen, if not for Jamie's cancer.

One morning, as I was praying for Jamie, I felt an urgency. I wanted her to know how vitally important she has been to our English department here.

When Jamie was a student here in the mid to late 90s, there wasn't an English Department, per se, (that came in the fall of 2005), and there wasn't an English bachelor's degree. With students like Jamie in mind, we initiated an English bachelor's in 2003. Mainly because of Jamie, we made sure to include a linguistics component in that degree. In 2008 we revised the English degree, identifying separate fifteen-hour tracks in literature, writing, and linguistics, so that students could specialize in an area of their choice. By 2010 we initiated the TESOL Certification of Completion, the document which verifies that our students meet or exceed the international standard in TESOL teacher-training preparation. In 2011 the linguistics track in the English BA was renamed the TESOL track.

Since implementing the TESOL track and Certificate of Completion, we've seen a steady increase in the number of students like Jamie pursuing TESOL in order to teach English and share the gospel in other countries. This year in my creative writing class for the first time, the number of "Jamies" outnumbers other English or education majors. All of the above is why I felt an urgency to let Jamie know what we, Jamie's former teachers, know: she was the trailblazer for where our English department and degrees are today.

On that morning when I felt so strongly the need to let Jamie know how important she has been to our English program, I also had this thought: we need a scholarship to honor Jamie. Today all those who love Jamie are pleased to acknowledge the Jamie

Norton Lund Scholarship for students who share a similar calling—to study English for the purpose of teaching speakers of other languages and to share the gospel.

I'll close my portion of this tribute with a quick anecdote. This past weekend while grading short stories for my creative writing class, I read a story by a student who transferred here this fall whose call is like Jamie's. He could have written on any topic. His story was about a young man who went to visit his grandfather, a longtime missionary to Asia, now bedridden. The grandson asked if his grandfather was sad since his ministry was now over. The grandfather answered emphatically, "My ministry is not dead. You don't understand the power of fasting and praying. When I pray from this bed, all of Asia shakes!" As the grandson left his grandfather's side, he determined to fast and pray himself, and then go out to share the gospel with the persons God had laid on his heart.

When I read my student's story knowing of this tribute today, I thought about how God works. The story seems a confirmation to me of exactly what I've talked about. Jamie Norton Lund came to this university as a young lady intent on preparing herself to follow God's call. She earned a degree to teach English. And then she went to the foreign field and taught. I also know she fasted, prayed, and sowed seeds of the gospel that will bear fruit in those multitudes of dark-haired people for generations to come. My student in creative writing and his peers, following the trail that Jamie blazed, will also earn their degrees to teach English in a foreign land so they too can share the gospel.

~

Was her life a threat to Satan's stronghold in Northern Asia? A heavenly spiritual force to be reckoned with by the enemy of our souls? Was hell laughing when she was unable to return to the people she loved? No demon in hell or man-made border can stop God's Holy Spirit from pursuing those for whom His Son died.

God enabled Gene and I with the help of many friends and family to establish the perpetual and fully endowed Jamie Norton Lund Scholarship and were privileged to award the first scholarship in April of 2014. Each year a scholarship has been and will be awarded to a student exemplifying Jamie's same calling. The amount awarded has grown each year, and we trust will continue to grow in order to help send more laborers into God's harvest field.

God's comfort to me includes the promise that more souls will come into the Kingdom of God as a result of Jamie's death than if she had lived in her city alone until she was ninety years old. If Jamie could speak to us today, I believe her words would echo Philippians 1:12: "Now I want you to know, brothers and sisters, that what has happened to me has actually served to advance the gospel." In other words, everything Jamie went through in her life and death will serve God's purpose and result in many coming to Christ. Praise His Holy Name!

# Chapter 29

## *Nathalie's Chapter*

Jamie Norton Lund: A Profile in Commitment and Courage
by Nathalie Jeter

The great American revivalist Charles Finney, in writing his memoirs, began by stating, "My mind seems instinctively to recoil from saying as much of myself as I shall be obliged to do." Jamie would have expressed similar sentiments about writing about herself. But in God's sovereignty, that task has fallen to us, those she left behind, her loving family and friends.

In writing about Jamie now that she's gone, it's hard to avoid hagiography. In other words, it's hard not to make her sound like a saint, because in so many ways she was a saint.

*Hagiography*. That's the kind of big word Jamie would love to drop casually in conversation, with a little twinkle in her eye. She would have immediately told you it has eleven letters. She had the uncanny gift of knowing instinctively how many letters were in a word.

Jamie and I shared a love of words. In fact, it was in our college classes in advanced grammar and composition and introduction to linguistics that I really got to know Jamie. And were we ever competitive! Later, when we were roommates after college, we would engage in tournaments of the word game Boggle that would last for weeks and even months!

I first met Jamie Norton in her second year of college when she transferred from Steven F. Austin State University. We were both sophomores. At the time, I thought of her mostly as the sweet and soft-spoken Southern belle dating him. They were both universally loved and admired on our college campus.

At the end of the spring semester that year, I had my first chance to see Jamie in a leadership role. It was April 28, 1996—finals week. To relieve stress, several girls in the dorm where Jamie and I lived had gotten together to carry out a prank. Our dorm was co-ed in that there was a girls' dorm on one side of a large lobby area and a boys' dorm on the other side. At 4:00 a.m., a group of us got dressed all in black and put nylon stockings over our heads—as "ninjas"—with the intention of sneaking over to the boys' side of the dorm to pull pranks on them.

Needless to say, Jamie was *not* a participant in this planned raid. She was a hall captain at the time. We had nothing more mischievous in mind than to tie the boys' doors tightly across the hall with nylon stockings so they couldn't open them. If they tried to open their doors, we would spray them in the face with water bottles.

It was very daring as it was against the rules for girls to go over to the boys' side at any time. But we girls had assembled before the raid, talked about the risks and consequences of our actions, and even prayed that no one would get hurt and that, if found out, we wouldn't get in too much trouble.

All the girls were in position. Two by two, the girls ran through the unoccupied lobby to hide under the stairwell on the boys' side and wait for the rest of us. My roommate led the charge, and I was to bring up the rear. I got as far as the lobby reception desk when one of the girls yelled, "It's the security guard! Run!"

The campus security guard had been making his nightly rounds and noticed our unusual activity. Some of the girls had time to run back to our side of the dorm but others were stuck on the boys' side. The guard came into the lobby and called our dorm mother.

Frantic, all the girls ran back to their rooms, changed clothes, and tried to look like they were sleeping. Nothing doing. Soon we were all rounded up into one room and interrogated. I remember my resident assistant, Danae, standing bleary-eyed near the door. I can still see Jamie standing beside her looking tired and serious, but fighting back a little chuckle every once in a while at our ridiculousness.

After a good talking-to from the dorm mother, we were told that our punishment would be to go in shifts and clean the dorm mom's house and organize it. By then it was 5:30 a.m. She let us go off campus, exceptionally, for donuts and coffee.

This was my first glimpse of Jamie "on duty" in a leadership role. Leadership, I found out when I got to know her better, is something she took extremely seriously. However, I also discovered that she had a wonderful mischievous side, a fun-loving side, and a remarkable sense of humor.

Right after college, Jamie and I became roommates. She was working on her master's in linguistics and had accepted a teaching position at the University of Texas at Arlington. I taught German and English as a Second Language at a local high school.

Jamie and I soon discovered we had several things in common. We were both stubborn, opinionated, and obsessed with being right! And yet we got along great and had so much fun together.

Like a sister, I liked to pick on Jamie. I loved to tease her about her areas of vulnerability. She returned the favor.

Jamie had interesting eating habits. During the time we were roommates, she had an aversion to anything green. She told me her mother had tried to make her eat salad, but Jamie had put her foot down. Her favorite food was Mexican and her favorite beverage Dr. Pepper. Oh, how she missed her Dr. Pepper when she went overseas!

It amused me to hear about her food adventures when she wrote from Northern Asia. In May 2001 she wrote, "New items in my diet include lotus root (the root of a lily pad). It sounds gross, but it is one of my favorite 'veggies' here. I've eaten pig's stomach and drank cantaloupe-flavored cow's milk (yuck). Thus far, I have been able to gracefully decline donkey and camel meat."

Or this funny incident Jamie wrote about in May 2002: "My uncle has cooked for foreigners before. He insisted on helping the restaurant make dinner for you, because he knows what foreigners like to eat." When Lilly said this, I was quite curious to see what would be served. We dined on pig's ear, pig's stomach, three types of mushrooms, and dog! I don't know what foreigners he had cooked for, but they weren't Texans!

I remember standing on the stage in Jamie's home church in Lufkin, Texas, on March 8, 2003. I was wearing a long pink dress and carrying flowers. As I watched Jamie come down the aisle to marry the man of her dreams, I thought to myself that I'd never seen such a happier, more beautiful bride.

Who could have imagined on that day so full of joy and thanksgiving, that we would be assembled in that very place less than a decade later, saying good-bye to that same sweet bride?

*Jamie Norton Lund has been removed from your friends.* The impersonal Facebook message that popped up on my screen when I clicked on Jamie's profile hit me like a punch in the gut.

It was true. Just a few days before, we, Jamie's friends and family, had honored her life in an emotional, deeply moving ceremony. We had commended to heaven's care our sweet Jamie who had so courageously fought her battle with cancer.

Now her husband was closing down the various accounts in her name, including her Facebook account. Facebook had been the way Jamie and I kept in touch over the last few months of her life, when talking on the phone became too difficult. Our messages had all been deleted. I melted into a puddle of tears as I realized I had forever lost this last link with her.

I last spent time with Jamie during the weekend of October 7, 2012. She and I spent several hours together with her family, but a couple of those hours were spent talking to each other alone. Jamie was in a lot of pain, and when the pain became intolerable, she would pray out loud, quote Scripture, or sing hymns and choruses she had learned over the years.

Despite her excruciating pain and the medication she was on to alleviate it, there were times when she had surprising lucidity. She spoke words of encouragement to me that I'll remember as long as I live. That was so much like Jamie, encouraging others in her own time of pain and need.

Her memory, as always, was excellent—so much better than mine. She even helped me solve a riddle from over ten years before concerning an inside joke we had shared back when we were roommates.

We often hear that someone "lost their battle with cancer." Not Jamie. Anyone who knew Jamie knew she never lost at anything! Losing simply did not fit in with Jamie's philosophy of life. Nope, Jamie didn't lose. She gave her life to Jesus at a young age and knew from that point on that her life was not her own to do with as she pleased.

She had two overarching goals: serve God with all her heart—and marry him. She succeeded in both. And in her short thirty-six years of life, she lived more fully and left a greater impact than the vast majority of people who live to a "ripe old age."

Her life was filled with adventure, happy memories, trials, challenges, and tears but also with laughter, victories, and triumphs. She was dearly and deeply loved by so many people. Her life made a difference.

Jamie Norton Lund showed us how to do life right. She taught us by example that the only way to truly live is to abandon oneself completely to God's will.

# Chapter 30

## *Sorrow upon Sorrow*

How can I adequately put into words my heart for this book? It is an act of love and worship for my God, an act of praise to my God for His gift of Jamie. It is a sharing of extremely difficult personal times and the walk, process, and healing of my heart's pain and ultimate desire for complete relational healing and restoration.

I started and stopped writing this book many times. I had to wait until I could read her journals, as well as my own, without crying. During this time, God gave me the idea and the words for the daily devotional, so with His help, I was able to complete and publish it first.

At this juncture of Jamie's and my story, I ask the reader to hear the truth and hear the cry of my heart, for I strive to please God rather than man (Gal. 1:10 and 1 Thes. 2:4). I have something to say, and this book is it.

"I assure you before God that what I am writing you is no lie" (Gal. 1:20).

"Have I now become your enemy by telling you the truth?" (Gal. 4:16).

"For we are taking pains to do what is right, not only in the eyes of the Lord but also in the eyes of man" (2 Cor. 8:21).

~

The hospital bed was gone, so were the oxygen machine, bedside table, and medical supplies. Her room was empty except for personal belongings. I sat in the middle of that bedroom floor clutching her framed kindergarten picture to my breast. Job said it so well. "For sighing has become my daily food; my groans pour out like water" (Job 3:24). There were no words. I'm not sure how long I sat there, but then I heard the kitchen door open. "Mom?" It was Jeremy. He walked in; I couldn't move. He did the only thing he could do and I let him. He sat on the floor beside me with his arm around me and wept.

Yesterday morning, Gene crumbled and wept loudly while sitting in his recliner. His cry sounded a lot like mine at times; it came from deep within. Sobbing, I knelt by his chair and held him, weeping softly, a screenplay we would repeat multiple times. I'm glad we can cry. I'm thankful we have each other. We have both found crying to be therapeutic. We must walk through this valley of the shadow of death, so we embrace it. We don't suppress it, ignore it, or avoid it. We just cry.

Family issues following the death of a loved one compound the complexity and the intensity of grief. It has been my experience as an associate pastor and facilitator of GriefShare[2] groups for several years before and after Jamie's death that grief is seldom experienced alone. Most of the time it comes with baggage, and the wounds can be constantly reopened. This has been true for us.

Against Jamie's wishes and contrary to his promise to her, he has withheld our grandchildren from us and prevented us from having a healthy grandparent-grandchild relationship with Caleb and Karen.

Regardless of the fact that he began a relationship one month after Jamie died and remarried less than ten months after her passing, Caleb and Karen are still our grandchildren whom we love very much. We are trying very hard to keep our promise to

Jamie and remain a vital part of her children's lives. It has been a treacherous journey on rough and uncertain seas, one that we feel has prolonged the healing process in our lives. However, one thing remains true: our God is faithful and His Word is true. We have clung to Him like never before. He walks with us, comforts and strengthens us, and pours His grace upon us in generous quantities. Without Him, we would not be standing today. "God is our refuge and strength, an ever-present help in trouble" (Ps. 46:1).

You see, we lost more than a daughter. We lost a son-in-law whom we loved and considered a son, and we lost a normal relationship with our grandchildren. "Children's children are a crown to the aged" (Prov. 17:6). Don't remove my crown!

However, the ones who have lost the most are Caleb and Karen. They not only lost their mother, but their Memaw and Papa Norton, Aunt Janet, Uncle Jeremy, cousins Sage and Graham, and great-grandmother MawMaw Allen have been ripped from them.

February 12, 2013—I just looked at his FB page. He is calling Karen Viola now! Her name is Karen Vi. Why? Is it just another way to hurt me? Oh my God, help me! I give it to you. How long, oh God, must I endure such heartache? I would never make it through the day if God did not give me His strength each morning when I meet with Him. "I thank Christ Jesus our Lord, who has given me strength" (1 Tim. 1:12). "He gives strength to the weary and increases the power of the weak" (Isa. 40:29).

I may not know everything the enemy is doing, saying, or planning; but I do know what God's Word says. His truth always wins, and God fights for the righteous. It's not because of who I am; it is because of who He is—and who Jamie was. "For there is nothing hidden that will not be disclosed, and nothing concealed that will not be known or brought out into the open" (Lk. 8:17).

February 23, 2013—According to his FB page, he is legally changing Karen's name to Viola Mei. Words cannot express my heartbreak. What would Jamie think about all this? I'm grieved by his defiant heart, but I will not allow his words or actions affect my day. I will bury my heart in God's Word and receive His comfort and peace. "I lift up my eyes to the mountains—where does my help come from? My help comes from the Lord, the Maker of heaven and earth" (Ps.121:1–2).

Oh, how I miss Jamie and my grandchildren. My precious granddaughter will always be Karen Vi to me. Besides, she will have another name one day! "I will also give that person a white stone with a new name written on it, known only to the one who receives it" (Rev. 2:17).

March 6, 2013—There was a knock at our door yesterday at 7:15 a.m. We opened the door to find a sheriff's officer with court summons in hand for Gene and I. He is suing us for fraud, forgery of Jamie's signatures, stating Jamie was not in her right mind when the will was made, and that the will is invalid. Heartbreaking—again. All lies. "My tears have been my food day and night" (Ps. 42:3).

I left the house at one thirty to drive several hours to a prayer and Bible conference that I had planned to attend weeks earlier.

March 7, 2013—Yesterday was an awesome day of teaching, preaching, praise, and worship. I did not realize how very emotional attending this conference would be for me; I have many years of memories in that place.

Something amazing happened! Was it my imagination? A vision? Or deep calling to deep? I was standing in a praise and worship service with about two thousand others. Tears were literally gushing from my eyes as if someone had turned on a water faucet. My face, neck, and shirt became soaked. I had hit rock bottom in my grief and felt as if I would surely die at any moment. It was then that I opened my eyes, and I saw my Jamie very clearly standing in front of me just a few steps away, smiling, with a beautiful complexion and her shoulder-length thick and wavy hair; she was radiant and glowing. My first thought was that the Lord allowed her, for just a moment, to enter my dimension. She stepped forward and kissed my cheek. No, I didn't feel a physical kiss; I felt it much deeper within my soul. Then she spoke. "Mom, if you only knew how wonderful heaven is! I'm okay. Everything is okay."

I suddenly became aware of someone standing beside her whose face I could not see clearly. Was it Jesus? I looked again at Jamie. I must remember this moment forever. They turned and slowly walked away. Jamie threw her head over her right shoulder and smiled at me. They were gone. At that instant, I felt God's comfort, peace, and pure joy overflow my soul. Gone were the pain and grief. I will never forget what my God did for me in that moment of time. Praise His Holy Name!

On this very same day back home, God also ministered to Gene as he woke from a restless night's sleep. He opened his eyes, sat up on the side of the bed, and heard very distinctly these words. "God knows about this. He will take care of it. He will take care of it." It was confirmation to him that God was still in control. "Praise be to the God and Father of our Lord Jesus Christ, the Father of compassion and the God of all comfort" (2 Cor. 1:3).

~

Throughout this journey since Jamie's death, Janet has been the one to meet with attorneys, take care of all legal paperwork, and act as our liaison between him and us—all to the neglect of her own personal grief work. It is what she promised Jamie, and it is because she loves her mom and dad. Gene and I don't know what we would have done without our youngest daughter stepping in and working so hard, non-stop, for many months. Thank you, Janet.

~

March 18, 2013—Yesterday was an especially difficult day for me at church. It was the four-month mark of Jamie's passing. While standing during praise and worship, I was suddenly ambushed with sadness and grief. I could no longer stand but sat down with my head in my hands, creating a puddle of tears on the floor. "Oh God, it hurts so much." Then I felt someone, Jesus with skin on, sit beside me and grab my hand and quietly pray. My other hand enfolded hers. She cried with me. I began to feel His love and peace creep into my soul. I was okay; I would make it another day. Thank you, Karen F.

~

May 29, 2013—It's six months out, and we're still struggling. Some days are so sad I feel as though my insides are crying. He refuses to give us visitation rights. Janet told me yesterday that he is getting married in September. To top it all off, I could not get on his FB to see pictures of Caleb and Karen. I guess he finally realized he had not blocked me. So now I am blocked as are many of our friends. My heart is broken, not only over the loss of Jamie and my grandchildren, but over the state of his heart as well.

"Dear God, my sadness can only be touched by your hand. No human hand can mend my broken heart. Oh Lord, help me today."

~

June 4, 2013—My heart is broken. My world has been ripped apart again. I've been plunged into deep grief again. I have many questions. Where is God? Doesn't He even care that I'm dying inside? How much more must I endure? When will this horrible pain end? What about Jamie? Has God completely forgotten her and her last wishes for her children? How many more tears can these eyes cry? Why do the wicked continue to win? Where are you, God? What about the children? Do our district and national officials even care? Have you forgotten us, God? How do I go on living? Oh God, hear my heart and help me. I can't do this anymore. Will the tear-well ever run dry? I'm dying, God. Don't you even care? Have you forgotten me? How do I live through this day? I do not have the strength to live. If I am bereaved of my child and grandchildren, I am truly bereaved. I am in the bottom of the pit again. It's a long journey back up. I cannot make it alone. I will die here.

Yesterday about one thirty, Janet and Jeremy came into my office to tell me that the summary judgment was granted in his favor. He gets a check for $250,000. Apparently, community property is a big deal in Texas. The children's share of Jamie's life insurance must pay for their mother's funeral and expenses from her last days. Something is terribly wrong here. It's over. By all indications, we will never see our grandchildren again. I immediately plummeted into deep grief again and could not stop the river of tears. I went to Jamie's grave for the second time yesterday and sat in the hot sun.

My eyes are swollen this morning—again—but that doesn't stop the tears. Just how much pain and grief must I walk through? What have I done to deserve this devastation to my heart? God, I'm drowning. Please help me. I feel like I'm dying a slow death.

June 7, 2013—I've come to realize that God is my center of gravity, my sun, in which my life revolves; and when this world pulls me out of orbit, God pulls me back in with His great love. I let Him. Otherwise, I would become a renegade planet lost in obscurity, plunging into outer darkness with no direction, far from God's Son with no path or purpose, lost and far away from His warmth and stability. He is the core of my existence. I bow before Him today and praise His Holy Name.

I'm so thankful for Janet, my son-in-law Jeremy (whom we consider our son), and our beautiful Sage and handsome Graham. I'm glad we live in the same town, that they come over and eat meals with us, that Gene and I get to watch our grandchildren play basketball and baseball games and participate in other school events. I enjoy picking up Sage and Graham from school and have them spend nights with us, play board games, ride bikes, watch movies, and tell stories. They love their Memaw and Papa, and we love them. I am truly blessed in many ways. Today, I will think on those things I have, not what I don't have, and be thankful.

June 25, 2013—God is dealing with me about writing two books. One will be Jamie's story and the other a daily devotional using the One Year Chronological Bible. The fire in my heart and bones continues to grow! I'm writing down my thoughts and God's thoughts daily. But how do I accomplish this? I work full-time, and when one works full-time at a church, it is really more like overtime in high gear! Perhaps I should retire the end of this year after thirty years on staff at LFA. Would we be able to make it financially? Gene and I will pray about this.

~

July 5, 2013—In the past week, I played a part in leading a good friend of Jamie's to Christ. She planted many seeds in his life over the years. It was such a tremendous blessing to literally watch those seeds bear fruit.

Then yesterday, a friend told us of a group of college students who went to Jamie's city and university on a short-term missions trip. Since they were Americans, many people on and off campus, students and others, would stop and ask them, "Do you know Jamie Lund?" A bus driver was one of those people. He told them she had a great influence on many people in his city. What an indelible impression she left on many lives! To top it all off, this group of young Americans had the privilege of leading ten students to salvation in Jesus Christ! Jamie had invested love and time into some of those lives.

It's already happening! People with whom Jamie connected are entering the Kingdom of God after her death! God is faithful—again and always! God's promise to me is coming to pass! Now, instead of one plow in that area of the world, more plows with laborers are working in that harvest field. Thank you, Jesus!

~

July 24, 2013—We called several times to talk to Karen Vi on her birthday and left messages and e-mailed—no response. We mailed a large box of gifts from Christmas that we were never able to give them and for her birthday—no acknowledgement. I'm so weary from missing Jamie and yearning for my grandchildren.

I've come to realize that I'm still in the fire, and more is being burned off my life—things that don't belong there. But I'm so ready to get out of this fire; however, God is saying, "Not yet." It is so uncomfortable and painful in here. It's hot and I cry a lot, but God knows what He is doing. I trust Him. I will emerge from this furnace a vessel prepared for the Master's table. Only

God knows how long this process will take. He controls the furnace and He controls the temperature. He won't let it destroy me. He is watching over the process. Only He knows when the process will be complete, and all the gunk is burned off and this vessel is ready to bring Him glory.

"Thank you, Lord. Thank you for teaching me things much bigger than me."

~

August 2, 2013—I turned in my resignation at work this week, and it was made known to the staff today. I am retiring at the end of December after thirty years on staff. After much prayer, it feels right. I know God wants me to write two books—Jamie's story and a daily devotional. 2014! Here I come!

~

August 30, 2013—Nobody knows the extreme pain I feel right now—no one except God. I cry as I write this. I just want this pain to be over. "Oh God, if you're not going to do anything about this pain, please let me die and get out of this. I hate where I am today. Help me. I'm sick to death of pretending and going through the motions of life."

~

September 19, 2013—Yesterday morning, while standing in my kitchen waiting on a cup of hot tea, I was crying and missing Jamie. Then I sensed the Lord standing beside me with His arm around me reminding me of His blessing in giving Jamie to us in our home the last ten weeks of her life. Thank you, Lord. Thank you for loving me and never giving up on me. You are so good to me.

Then I noticed it again—the little plaque on my kitchen bar Jamie had given us years before. "Mom and Dad, for all you've done, my love and thanks…"

~

October 11, 2013—Caleb turned six years old on the ninth. We mailed gifts to him and Karen Vi several days ago. We don't have his number so we call his sister's number and mail gifts to her address. No return calls and no acknowledgement of gifts. All we wanted to do was talk to our grandson on his birthday. We know they received the package because we received a signed verification. We later learned that he never gave the children anything we sent them.

~

October 14, 2013—Janet ran a full marathon yesterday in Wichita. She said it was a hard race for her physically. She thought about Jamie the entire race, and then just a few minutes before the finish line a man ran past her and said, "It won't be long now!" Those were Jamie's last words. She pushed even harder and completed the race.

~

October 20, 2013—The toy box still sits on the back porch for the day when Caleb comes back to us. I remember how he loved to play in the dirt, and I can still see Caleb and Karen jumping on the trampoline. I'm hesitant to change anything in the house or yard because I want them to remember their Memaw and Papa's house. Oh, how my heart aches and longs for my grandchildren.

"Dear God, please work this out so we can have a relationship with Jamie's children, the grandchildren you gave us. Take special care of them. Remember Jamie and her love and prayers for her children."

Yesterday, during praise and worship at church, with my mind on the words of the song, my arms sideways and slightly lifted, not thinking about Jamie, but in one fleeting moment in time I sensed her put her hand in mine and say, "Let's dance!" She was in the aisle in glowing white and so beautiful. Then a smile hit my face and joy filled my heart, and I knew Jamie was dancing and praising the Lord in His literal presence!

November 28, 2013—Today is Thanksgiving. I'm thankful it is one year later. I'm thankful Jamie is in heaven. I'm thankful to the Lord for His grace, faithfulness, healing, strength, peace, His Word, His presence, provision, compassion, mercy, comfort, joy, my husband, children, grandchildren, church, good health, family, friends, and so many other blessings in my life. God is still in control. I can and do trust Him every day. He is good.

January 1, 2014—Yesterday was a day I don't want to relive. The pain of loss and crying were substantial. I cried most of the morning. Gene and I went to the cemetery early and took a little Happy Birthday balloon on a stick and stuck it in her flowers.

There was one highlight to our day. FedEx delivered a box of beautiful flowers from Michael and Laura in memory of Jamie's birthday. I called her to say thank you. It was so sweet of them.

I am now officially retired. It feels good, and I am filled with anticipation about what God has next for me. Two things I know for sure: He wants me to write a daily devotional to assist people in reading the Bible through in one year, and He wants me to write the true story of Jamie's life and death.

~

August 13, 2015—"God, I miss Jamie." "I'm still here."

~

March 16, 2016—Today he and his family leave for the field. "Take care of them, Jesus. Take care of my grandchildren." I'm so thankful there is no distance in prayer.

~

> But what does it matter? The important thing is that in every way, whether from false motives or true, Christ is preached. And because of this I rejoice. Yes, and I will continue to rejoice.
>
> —Phil. 1:18

> Yet now I am happy, not because you were made sorry, but because your sorrow led you to repentance. For you became sorrowful as God intended and so were not harmed in any way by us. Godly sorrow brings repentance that leads to salvation and leaves no regret, but worldly sorrow brings death.
>
> —2 Cor. 7:9-10

# Chapter 31

## *Making Sense of It All*

As the heavens are higher than the earth, so are my ways higher than your ways and my thoughts than your thoughts.

—Isa. 55:9

God has an eternal purpose in everything He permits to happen to His faithful followers, and in all things He works for their good.

And we know that in all things God works for the good of those who love him, who have been called according to his purpose.

—Rom. 8:28

I have not lived this life perfectly. I am a sinner saved by grace and faith in Jesus Christ. He is the potter and I am the clay. He is continually molding and shaping me, smoothing out many rough places, and teaching me things I need to know. I will forever be a student of His Word and a clay pot in His hands. He forgives me when I get it wrong and teaches me from each of life's experiences. I desire to learn and grow in Him every day. In other words, I'm still learning. Allow me to share a few of the lessons I am learning in my journey from mourning to joy.

"But grow in the grace and knowledge of our Lord and Savior Jesus Christ. To him be glory both now and forever! Amen" (2 Pe. 3:18).

There are many things in this world I do not understand. I don't fully understand my iPhone I can hold in the palm of my hand. Do I seriously think I can fully understand Almighty God, the One who flung the galaxies into the unknown from His fingertips (Ps. 8:3)? Do I really want a God I can wholly understand? He would not be very big if my peanut brain could understand Him. But I do want a God I completely trust. And I can trust Him in *all* things. He is true to His Word and proves Himself to this child of His every day. I rest in Him. He is the faithful and true God, and His Son, Jesus Christ, is my Savior and Lord forever.

Here is another lesson I'm learning: If something in my life doesn't seem to line up with Scripture, the fault does not lie in God or His infallible Word. The fault lies in me. I must humble myself before God, examine the Scriptures, ask God to show me what I don't see and teach me what I don't know, and ultimately trust Him and His Word—no matter the circumstances surrounding my current situation.

What do I do now? I can tell you one thing I won't be doing, and that is sitting around wailing, "Oh poor me." Jesus Christ is coming soon and people need to get ready to meet God. I will continue walking through God's open doors of speaking, teaching, preaching, helping others know Jesus Christ as Savior and Lord, and assisting His children to become self-feeders and lifelong learners and lovers of God's Word.

God has been good to me. I want Him to continue using my life experiences for His glory as He is doing now and even more so for as long as He allows me to walk His earth. I've learned God doesn't waste a thing—good or bad—if we give everything to Him.

> Praise be to the God and Father of our Lord Jesus Christ, the Father of compassion and the God of all comfort, who comforts us in all our troubles, so that we can comfort those in any trouble with the comfort we ourselves receive from God. For just as we share abundantly in the sufferings of Christ, so also our comfort abounds through Christ.
>
> —2 Cor. 1:3–5

> Rejoice with those who rejoice; mourn with those who mourn.
>
> —Rom. 12:15

> Even when I am old and gray, do not forsake me, my God, till I declare your power to the next generation, your mighty acts to all who are to come.
>
> —Ps. 71:18

## Forgiveness

The story of God's Word is the story of a God who loves His creation, especially those created in His image, whom He pursues relentlessly in order to have relationship. What do we do? We tend to play an eternal game of hide and seek. He finds us and we hide again. We are like the two-year-old child who covers his eyes with his hands and thinks God can't see Him, or the child behind the drape with his feet sticking out from underneath. When will we stop playing deadly games with God? When will we stop and say, "Here I am God. No more hiding. I've sinned against you. I'm sorry, Lord. Please forgive me. Hold me. I'm yours."

If we don't want to be found, He won't "find" us. However, one day the game will be over, and we will remain lost forever. "For he says, 'In the time of my favor I heard you, and in the day of salvation I helped you.' I tell you, now is the time of God's favor, now is the day of salvation" (2 Cor. 6:2).

> Am I only a God nearby," declares the Lord, "and not a God far away? Who can hide in secret places so that I cannot see them?" declares the Lord. "Do not I fill heaven and earth?" declares the Lord.
>
> —Jer. 23:23–24

Jamie never allowed unforgiveness to creep in and take root. She understood that unforgiveness is a deadly cancer of the spirit. Left alone, it grows and consumes and eventually destroys the one who carries it. She forgave him on her deathbed just like Jesus and Stephen forgave as they were dying. "Father, forgive them, for they do not know what they are doing" (Lk. 23:34). "Lord, do not hold this sin against them" (Acts 7:60). True forgiveness is the medicine that heals the deepest emotional wounds. Jamie knew this and forgave.

Her philosophy all her life was, "He forgives me; I forgive others." This is how she lived and died. She was gracious and noble; I'm still striving to learn how to do that.

May I be totally transparent and gut-honest with you? "Noble" has been the toughest characteristic in Philippians 4:8 for me to achieve in writing this book. In order to be "noble" or "honorable," I haven't said everything my carnal nature would love the world to know in Jamie's story. I know what you're thinking: "That statement alone wasn't very noble." And you would be right. See? I told you. I still have some growing in Christ-likeness to do.

My daily prayer is, "Lord, forgive me when I fail you, and help me to truly forgive others." When forgiveness doesn't come easily, I make it a choice. I choose to forgive—every day. Obeying God overrides obeying my feelings. I understand that it's only by releasing my offender that I set myself free.

True forgiveness, the kind that's taught in Scripture, is a commitment I must practice every day of my life. People need loving the most when they deserve it the least. So I forgive and release him every day. Do I really forgive him every day, or am I just reminding myself that I've already forgiven him? I think it's both.

"Then Peter came to Jesus and asked, 'Lord, how many times shall I forgive my brother or sister who sins against me? Up to seven times?' Jesus answered, 'I tell you, not seven times, but seventy-seven times'" (Mt. 18:21–22).

"Is not Ephraim my dear son, the child in whom I delight? Though I often speak against him, I still remember him. Therefore my heart yearns for him; I have great compassion for him," declares the Lord" (Jer. 31:20). This verse in the Old Testament reminds me of the parable of the prodigal son in Luke 15:11–24.

The son, whose name is not mentioned in the text, would have never experienced true and deep healing had he never recognized his sin against God and man (v. 18) and gone back home to the place where he lost out with God *and* his earthly father. He could have wandered around to the uttermost parts of the earth for years, and the pigpen would have remained in his heart. It took facing what he had done and going back home. Only then was the pigpen removed from his deepest heart and true healing received. We can walk ourselves out of the pigpens of life, but healing is not complete until we go back home.

When the lost son finally realized he could no longer control or manipulate his life or the lives of others, he walked out of the pigpen and began the walk home where he truly humbled himself, deeply repented, and sincerely reconciled with his father. His father loved him and gladly received him back. I picture myself in this story as the prodigal's mother (KFN version!) where I hear my husband gasp, "My son!" I look out the kitchen window and see him running to a figure in the distance. I throw the dishtowel in the sink, slam the screen door behind me, and outrun my husband just like John outran Peter at the tomb of Christ. I get the first hug!

Do you remember the story of the floating ax head in 2 Kings 6:1–7? The company of prophets was busy building a church when one of them suddenly lost an ax head. "Where did it fall?" Elisha asked. In order for the ax head to rise to the surface (a feat only the power of God could accomplish) and be restored to its rightful position, the one who lost it had to go back to the place where it was lost. God's Word gives us a road map to complete spiritual and emotional healing. Then it's up to us.

God is a god of mercy, grace, and compassion. Praise Him! If He were not, not one of us would make it to heaven. But, at the same time, He is also a god of justice. He gives you and me the choice which receiving end we want to be on. "Choose for yourselves this day whom you will serve" (Jos. 24:15). "I will punish you as your deeds deserve, declares the Lord" (Jer. 21:14). God always has the last word.

## GRIEF

In my younger days, I always loved a good roller coaster, but rarely could I persuade Gene to ride with me. "Someone has to hold the purses and souvenirs!" That was always his excuse. So Jamie, more often than not, helped her daddy hold our purses and souvenirs, while Janet and I screamed and laughed our heads off with mouths wide open and hair flying in the wind! It was great!

At the beginning of a heart-throbbing roller coaster ride, the highs are really high and the lows are really low. The twists and turns are fast and furious. The rider is jerked around, plunged into darkness, and unable to gain a steady composure even for a few seconds before the next cliff-hanger. But eventually it does begin to slow down. The highs and lows become less extreme and farther apart. The trip becomes a little less painful. A roller coaster ride is not meant to last forever.

Who wants to be stuck on a roller coaster forever anyway? Nobody. But sometimes we get stuck in grief—something God never intended. There are some things in life that only God can do. Only Jesus Christ can save us from our sins and give us new life, and only He can rescue us from the roller coaster of emotions following the death of a loved one. I'm thankful God heals our hearts as we give Him all the broken pieces. "Come near to God and he will come near to you" (Jas. 4:8).

We must not ignore, stuff, put off, avoid, cover up, or pretend grief isn't there. We must embrace it, face the pain head on, and weep bitterly in order to be set free. Walking through grief is not easy. It requires hard work, determination, and keeping our eyes on Jesus. Like any crisis, grief can be a journey toward greater wholeness or greater brokenness. We must walk through grief in order to be healed, and He will be with us every step of the way. "Even though I walk through the darkest valley, I will fear no evil, for you are with me" (Ps. 23:4). He keeps His promise to me.

During my grief journey when I was exhausted from sorrow, I knew I had to continue spending time in prayer and His Word. "When he rose from prayer and went back to the disciples, he found them asleep, exhausted from sorrow. 'Why are you sleeping?' he asked them. 'Get up and pray so that you will not fall into temptation'" (Lk. 22:45–46).

Along the way, I stopped asking God, "Why?" and started asking other questions. "How will all of Jamie's pain and suffering turn out for good? How will you get glory from her life? What are you trying to teach me, Lord? Who are you, God—really? I want to know you better. The answers to these questions and more are in the Bible.

"Why, my soul, are you downcast? Why so disturbed within me? Put your hope in God, for I will yet praise him, my Savior and my God" (Ps. 42:5).

## Moving Forward

Two and a half years after Jamie's passing, we had a landscaper come in and do some work in our front yard. We have a young oak tree beside our driveway that needed several lower limbs cut off because they would brush against my car as I drove into the garage. When the limbs were removed, I noticed it—a piece of electrical wire, wrapped around the tree. I tried pulling it off to no avail; it was securely imbedded in the trunk, the tree having grown around it in several places.

It was then I saw clearly in my memory a three or four-year-old Caleb tying that wire around everything he could—toys, car doors, furniture—a tree—creating "traps" and obstacle courses. Somehow that piece of wire escaped our untying, now permanently connected to the tree, enveloped within the tree.

My children and grandchildren live within my heart. They are a part of my life, never to be removed by separation of death or distance. My love surrounds and encloses them, much like our Heavenly Father's love for His children. No one can snatch them out of my heart.

He has never allowed Caleb and Karen Vi to come back into our home since before Jamie's death, and he has never come even though we've invited them and would welcome all four of them. He has only given us a few visits in a neutral public place for a couple hours at a time and always under his watchful eye. Yes, Gene and I are thankful for every minute we get to spend with the children, but at the same time, we are extremely saddened that we are not allowed a normal grandparent relationship with Jamie's children. This is not what she wanted.

"Finally, brothers and sisters, rejoice! Strive for full restoration, encourage one another, be of one mind, live in peace. And the God of love and peace will be with you" (2 Cor. 13:11).

I pray this prayer over Caleb and Karen every day: "Dear God, I ask you to take care of Jamie's children today. Watch over them and protect them. Guard their hearts, minds, spirits, and emotions today. May they grow up spiritually healthy and balanced and love you with all their hearts. May they always remember their Mommy, and may they know how much their Memaw and Papa love them."

God reminds me of how He protected and watched over the children, Moses and Samuel, as they were growing up and how both became mighty men of God. He is the same God today, and I trust Him to watch over Caleb and Karen as they grow.

This is my prayer for all four of my grandchildren—Sage, Graham, Caleb, and Karen—every day: "Dear God, thank you for my four grandchildren. Take care of them today. Place your seal upon their lives and your call deep within their hearts. May they love you, follow you, obey you, and serve you all the days of their lives. Use their lives to further your kingdom in the earth. May they lead others to Jesus Christ. May their lives make a difference in this world, and may I see them in heaven one day. Thank You, Lord."

My prayers have changed since Jamie went to heaven. I no longer pray, "God, bless Jamie," because it's impossible for her to be any more blessed than she is at this very moment. I no longer pray, "God, heal Jamie," because she is perfectly healthy today and forever. I don't pray for her to have peace and strength, because she now has everything and will never "need" or "desire" anything else again! In fact, I don't pray for her at all now because she is in a place which is, as they say, "as good as it gets!"

I can now dust her framed kindergarten picture on the bedside table in her bedroom and her bridal portraits hanging on the walls in our hallway and not cry. I actually smile now when I look at the pictures of her life. I'm thankful. "Thank you, Lord, for her life. I praise you for Jamie. Thank you that she is with you and I will see her again one day."

Jamie's life intersected with many and left an indelible impression. She left her footprints in many hearts. And because of her life, the world is a better place.

If Jamie could speak to us today, I think she would say this: "Don't just grow old in Jesus; grow up in Jesus. Be so full of His love and His Word that He just naturally overflows onto others—and seeds are planted."

From Jamie's graduate course writings (2009):

We must spread the Good News if we want the Lord to return. It is not our responsibility (nor are we capable) to save the world. But we are responsible to proclaim the Gospel to every nation. Only then will all have a chance to be saved, and only then will the end come. Abraham did his part by obeying and trusting God. Christ did His part by dying on the cross. Now the Church must do our part by spreading the Gospel of the Kingdom. "And this gospel of the kingdom will be preached in the whole world as a testimony to all nations, and then the end will come" (Mt. 24:14).

To fear God and yet continue in sin is a moral impossibility. "And he said to the human race, 'The fear of the Lord—that is wisdom, and to shun evil is understanding'" (Job 28:28). "Do not be wise in your own eyes; fear the Lord and shun evil" (Prov. 3:7). "The fear of the Lord is the beginning of wisdom, and knowledge of the Holy One is understanding" (Prov. 9:10).

Jamie's simple prayer at age four still works today for anyone of any age: "Dear Jesus, please forgive me of all my sins and come live in my heart. I love you, Jesus. Amen."

> But I want you to know that the Son of Man has
> authority on earth to forgive sins.
>
> —Mt. 9:6

So that Christ may dwell in your hearts through faith.

—Eph. 3:17

This life—today—now—is the only time we have to get it right. What will you do with your time today? "Seek the Lord while he may be found; call on him while he is near" (Isa. 55:6). Every life has a ripple effect. Outlive your life! Can God use your story for His glory?

## Psalm 145

1 I will exalt you, my God the King;
I will praise your name for ever and ever.
2 Every day I will praise you
and extol your name for ever and ever.
3 Great is the Lord and most worthy of praise;
his greatness no one can fathom.
4 One generation commends your works to another;
they tell of your mighty acts.
5 They speak of the glorious splendor of your majesty—
and I will meditate on your wonderful works.
6 They tell of the power of your awesome works—
and I will proclaim your great deeds.
7 They celebrate your abundant goodness
and joyfully sing of your righteousness.
8 The Lord is gracious and compassionate,
slow to anger and rich in love.
9 The Lord is good to all;
he has compassion on all he has made.
10 All your works praise you, Lord;
your faithful people extol you.
11 They tell of the glory of your kingdom
and speak of your might,
12 so that all people may know of your mighty acts
and the glorious splendor of your kingdom.
13 Your kingdom is an everlasting kingdom,
and your dominion endures through all generations.

The Lord is trustworthy in all he promises
and faithful in all he does.
14 The Lord upholds all who fall
and lifts up all who are bowed down.
15 The eyes of all look to you,
and you give them their food at the proper time.
16 You open your hand
and satisfy the desires of every living thing.
17 The Lord is righteous in all his ways
and faithful in all he does.
18 The Lord is near to all who call on him,
to all who call on him in truth.
19 He fulfills the desires of those who fear him;
he hears their cry and saves them.
20 The Lord watches over all who love him,
but all the wicked he will destroy.
21 My mouth will speak in praise of the Lord.
Let every creature praise his holy name
for ever and ever.

# Endnotes

1. Hospice in the Pines, 1504 W. Frank Avenue, Lufkin, TX 75904
2. GriefShare, P. O. Box 1739, Wake Forest, NC 27588

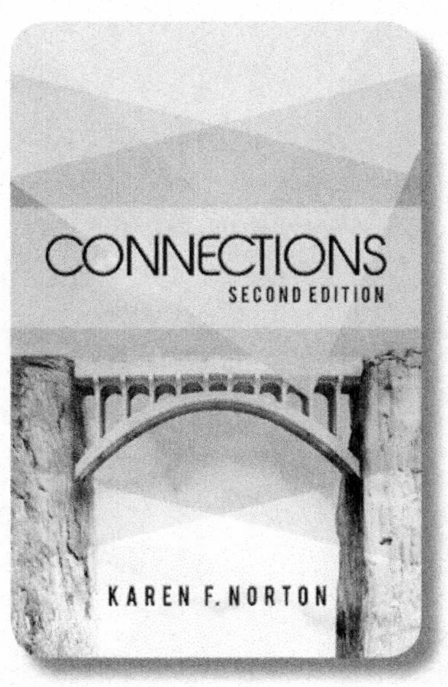


Another book by Karen F. Norton, *Connections Second Edition*, is a daily devotional that will help you read the Bible completely through in chronological order. Discover the major themes of the Bible and how the Old and New Testaments interlock. Take charge of your spiritual growth. Grow more in love with Jesus Christ and God's Word every day.

www.karennorton.com

CPSIA information can be obtained
at www.ICGtesting.com
Printed in the USA
LVOW03s0117061217
558800LV00001B/91/P